The Biblical Roots
of American
Constitutionalism

The Biblical Roots of American Constitutionalism

From "I Am the Lord" to "We the People"

Joseph Livni

LEXINGTON BOOKS
Lanham • Boulder • New York • London

Published by Lexington Books
An imprint of The Rowman & Littlefield Publishing Group, Inc.
4501 Forbes Boulevard, Suite 200, Lanham, Maryland 20706
www.rowman.com

6 Tinworth Street, London SE11 5AL, United Kingdom

Copyright © 2021 by The Rowman & Littlefield Publishing Group, Inc.

All rights reserved. No part of this book may be reproduced in any form or by any electronic or mechanical means, including information storage and retrieval systems, without written permission from the publisher, except by a reviewer who may quote passages in a review.

British Library Cataloguing in Publication Information Available

Library of Congress Control Number: 2021930742

ISBN 9781793637215 (cloth) | ISBN 9781793637239 (pbk)
ISBN 9781793637222 (epub)

Contents

Acknowledgments		vii
Introduction: Nice to Meet You . . .		1
1	Once Upon a Time . . .	13
2	The Difference between Political Concessions and Constitutional Liberties	23
3	The Covenant of Israel: Customary Law or Law	35
4	The Covenantal Society: Lex Rex	47
5	The Covenantal Society, Structure, Organization, and Power Flow	57
6	Justice Administration in Biblical Israel	73
7	Inventing a Covenantal Society Is Impossible	83
8	Covenantal Psychology	93
9	Evolution Tree	101
10	God Gave Moses the Law	115
11	The Supremacy of the Law	121
12	Evolution, Customs, and Law	127
Bibliography		139
Index		155
About the Author		161

Acknowledgments

On September 30, 2010, I retired from aerospace engineering and started a new career in a new cross-disciplinary field. Eight years later, Prof. Eugene Stanley of BU opined that the most appropriate designation of my new field is socio-physics. Not surprisingly, my education in socio-physics started in elementary school and therefore I first need to express my deep gratitude to my astonishing mathematics and physics teacher, the late Mrs. Viorica Davidovici.

In high school, I had the privilege to be a student of Mr. Boris Mălai who inspired his students by his rigorous treatment and straightforward dealing while handling mathematical expositions.

I am indebted to my higher education teachers of whom the most remarkable names are the late Professor Emeritus Arthur Shavit, the late Professor Emeritus Menahem Baruch, both from the Technion, Israel Institute of Technology, and Prof. Jacob Aboudi of the University of Tel-Aviv. I shall not close the list related to my higher education period without mentioning the memorable late Yehuda Thomas Radday, a Bible scholar who unlocked my interest in the complex problematics of critical perception of the biblical text.

My engineering experience gave me the tools to examine theories by mathematical modeling. I feel indebted to five notable engineers who encouraged me in carrying out such endeavors: Elazar Barak, Dov Raviv, Dave S. Steinberg, Tony Linsdell, and Dave Miles.

My new research period opened opportunities to contact several scholars in various fields. I will mention the names of a few who were essential to arrive at this monograph: the widely known archaeologists Avraham Faust and Amihai Mazar, the famous demographer Massimo Livi Bacci who answered my queries not only with patience but also in a surprisingly friendly tone, the mathematician Anatole Joffe who hit the nail on the head showing me why one of my articles was not understood, and four scholars who made my life easier by agreeing to coauthor articles with me: Lewi Stone, a well-known bio-mathematician, Karl Skorecki, a prominent population geneticist, Ilie Bădescu, the director of Sociology Department at the Romanian Academy of Science, and last but not least my brother Haim Livni.

Thank God I have a large family and many friends whom I should thank for graciously listening, debating, agreeing with me, and disagreeing with me. There is one person who more than anyone else had to put up with me and my bent priorities: Daniela, my wife. Thank you Dani!

Introduction
Nice to Meet You . . .

In a true democracy, everyone has the right to offer an opinion; however, only few win the privilege to be listened to. In the academic world, and even more in the one studying what democracy is about, lecturing about democracy takes more than a proven record attesting that one exhausted the subject, and rightly so. No one seeks to give an opinion about methods for calculating the pKa values,[1] binding constants of ligands,[2] and changes in protein stability unless he knows what those things are. But who doesn't have an opinion about the past, present, and mostly the future of our democracy? While you the reader prepared your seminar about the Equal Protection Clause of the Fourteenth Amendment, I struggled in a science lab applying Fourier series for signal processing. No wonder you the reader wonder what news I can bring to you. So let me get there.

The description of my last specialization is biophysicist and socio-physicist. Physicists love mathematics because mathematical expressions and models enhance the understanding of natural phenomena. Hypotheses are translated into quantitative expressions which allow accurate verification by algebraic manipulation and/or experimental confirmation. For the last two decades, I have applied this approach to testing competing theories in biology and social studies. Biophysics is an established field and my contribution to the field is far from being pioneering work. As far as socio-physics is concerned, I was surprised to meet many other scholars who also mathematically simulate the past,[3] the present,[4] and the brave ones even the future.[5] Nevertheless, the field is in its initial stages.

Throughout my career, I have built and utilized such models for various purposes. Mathematical models tell not necessarily the truth, rarely the whole truth; they tell only in exceptional cases nothing but the truth. Models accurately predict the behavior of the reality they represent. If that reality coincides with the phenomenon under study then the model's predictions are credible; in other words, if the model is sufficiently representative then so are its predictions. For example, this work stems from a model borrowed from biophysics used to predict the outcome of epidemics. In epidemics, there are three conflicting magnitudes that are fighting each other: contagion, healing, and immunity. The biophysical model that establishes the mathematical relations among these magnitudes has been established and accepted long time ago.[6] The adaptation of this model to combating crime would be adequate if crime were contagious and if enforcement of criminal sentences were correcting wrongdoers in the sense that some convicts become immune to temptation of crime for a while. As long as some individuals anticipate that crime pays, there will be individuals who are susceptible to the contagion effect of criminals. If the correction facilities didn't manage to convince some prisoners that crime doesn't pay then criminality would reach 100%. Thus, the analogy of infectious disease to crime holds a considerable amount of truth. Infection is not subject to conscientious decisions while crime is; this implies that the analogy may not comply with the "nothing but the truth" expectation. And even the old accepted model of epidemiology doesn't tell the whole truth because it involves simplifications, like the assumption that the rate of healing is proportional to the number of infected. *The truth, the whole truth, and nothing but the truth* is not a criterion for evaluating mathematical models. Physicists and engineers call a model "good enough" if within limits of a specific application the simplification is justified. For example, in the case of the rate of healing, the assumption of proportionality is adequate for a time period of a few years; however, it is not true over several generations.[7] Therefore, the model is "good enough" for studying the outbreak of an epidemic because its duration is sufficiently short. There are established practices on how to verify what good enough means in every application and their discussion is out of scope. This language of discussion touched the borderline of exact science lingo. At this point, I need to ask you not to lose appetite. I learned that communication across fields is easier if the presentation avoids mathematical equations, symbols, and jargon, and I promise to keep away from equations with a very few unavoidable exceptions. I published mathematical justifications in several articles and this work will only explain the common sense logic behind the mathematical expressions providing citations to references as usual.

Before I specify why the subject of this work captured me and why it should capture my reader, I need to clarify who my reader is. This work is intended for readers who specialized in the common area of two fields: constitutional law and political science. As any author, I imagine that there are other scholars interested in what this book introduces: historians, sociologists, anthropologists, biblical archaeologists, and with some hesitation I will include even scholars of religion.[8]

I promise to discuss a novel and stimulating view of how and when the constitution germinated and how it reached its current maturity. Currently, we witness a hot political debate around the constitution. Although this book is not about current constitutional disputes, it does contribute a more dynamic view of how the stipulations of the constitution came into the colonial American national conscience and from there into the constitution. This work opens the door to re-examining the constitutional process, this time with tools and conclusions of at least one more discipline. The book is not intended to shake your understanding of the constitution; however, it will answer questions you might have asked or even questions you never asked. This work is similar to an ancestry analysis of an individual. Finding out ancestral roots doesn't change one's view about oneself; however, the ancestry tree provides a better perception of why we are what we think we are. In this case, the evolution tree of the constitution clarifies not only where the idea of a supreme law came from but it also describes its embryonic version and the links of its evolution. This evolutionary approach provides a pedestal of confidence in detecting the fair-minded meaning of a constitutional article. For this work consistently shows that covenantal and constitutional ruling was not an expression of speculated justice but of practiced tradition of established fairness.

This work assembles wisdom from many fields. The common subject of all fields is a political model called the covenantal model. The most prolific scholar of the covenantal model is a political scientist: Daniel J. Elazar. This work will mention many other scholars who studied the societies of this model while not aware of how much their subjects overlap. In my view, one of the reasons of the dissociation is because these scholars came from different disciplines. For example, other important sources of this work are De Lagrèze, a law scholar who studied the societal network called *besiau* of the Pyrenees, the Romanian sociologists Henri Stahl and Ilie Bădescu who investigated a similar network in the Carpathians, and Pierrette Paravy and Emilio Comba, both historians of religion who will frequently be mentioned due to their ample account of the Waldensian network of the valleys of the Alps. None of the three groups of researchers was aware of how the three networks are alike. This book will reveal to the reader not only the common origin of these three networks but also their relationship with other similar better known covenantal organizations such as the English and American Puritans and others. The reader will find out why my research using methods of biophysics brought about discovering that these unconnected studies are in reality tightly related. Moreover, the book will make clear why mathematical modeling connected these studies to the evolution of the constitution.

In the academic world, we communicate knowledge by publishing articles, books, and conference papers. Nowadays, the easiest and fastest method of sharing knowledge is blogs. However, this knowledge I share with you is substantiated by rigorous research, some of it is mine and most of it I learned from others. Blogs offer an expressway for opinions; this work is substantiated knowledge and its communication channel should be the old slow road of published science. The following paragraphs expose what is the knowledge in your field offered in this book.

The conventional wisdom has it that the roots of American democracy and constitutionalism can be traced to Athens, Rome, and England.[9] The itinerary makes sense. England set up the first colonies, founded many institutions, and imparted the language and many other cultural, artistic, spiritual, legal, and political manifestations of the American civilization. We read:

> It was the constitutional character of those relatively early periods of development in the two rival systems of common law which still dominates the Western world; for in them were shaped those fundamental principles of both private and public law which constitute the true spirit of Roman and of English constitutionalism.[10]

As far as democracy is concerned, I have no reason to disagree with an Athenian birth place. However, constitutionalism is a different question. On this point, I beg to differ. My thesis is that the roots of modern constitutionalism germinated neither on the Tiber nor on the Thames, but on the hills of Judah and Samaria in the days when "there was no king in Israel."[11] I admit that one needs a significant chutzpah to disagree with Pauley and McIlwain. However, I will start my justification with the line of reasoning of Thomas Paine debated by McIlwain himself. McIlwain finds "remarkably accurate" Paine's following analysis about the American constitution:

- That there is a fundamental difference between a people's government and that people's constitution . . .
- That this constitution is "antecedent" to the government.
- That it defines the authority which the people commits to its government, and in so doing thereby it limits it.
- That any exercise of authority beyond these limits by any government is an exercise of "power without right."
- That in any state in which distinction is not actually observed between the constitution and the government there is in reality no constitution.[12]

Chapter 1 "Once Upon a Time . . ." deliberates that in ancient Rome and in post *Magna Charta* England, none of the five bullets were respected.

Consequently, either in ancient Rome or in medieval England there was "in reality no constitution."

Before I take you back in time and far away to ancient Levant, I need to answer McIlwain's questions related to Paine's five bullets listed earlier:

> Is it possible to incorporate in the framework of the state itself some provision or institution by which a governmental act or command ultra vires may be declared to be such, and subjects therefore exempted from its operation and released from any legal obligation to observe or obey it? In short, can government be limited legally and effectively by any method short of force?[13]

Naturally, McIlwain answers that "in every case there seems no recourse except to force of some kind."[14] This answer is so carefully crafted that one cannot disprove it. In its broad meaning, this question deserves special attention and I dedicated chapter 2 "The Difference between Political Concessions and Constitutional Liberties" to discuss the question without pretentions to exhaust it. However, in its restricted meaning, force of some kind consists of the various branches of justice administration and law enforcement. Therefore, I suggest addressing the following question: Is it practical to envisage a constitution that:

(a) is antecedent to government,
(b) limits the authority of government, and
(c) is protected against "power without right?"

This is the relevant question examining the first premise of my thesis, namely that the Covenant of *Israel of the Judges* was the first incarnation of the constitutional concept. Israel of the Judges (also known as *Proto-Israel*)[15] was a pre-state society; however, unlike the typical pre-state pattern[16] Proto-Israel did have a law, and unlike customary law it was enforceable and enforced (see more in chapter 3 "The Covenant of Israel: Customary Law or Law"). Point (a) above is answered in the chapter 2 "The Difference between Political Concessions and Constitutional Liberties."

It is relatively easy to examine point (b) above regarding limitation of government. Elazar's explanation of covenant is:

> An idea which defines political justice, shapes political behavior, and directs humans toward an appropriately civic synthesis of the two in their effort to manage political power.[17]

The evidence that Elazar meant among others the Covenant of Israel is easy to produce:

> The classic Jewish political tradition of the Bible makes it clear that sovereignty is God's but that day-to-day governance is in the hands of the people within the framework of the Divine constitution.[18]

Elazar was a political scientist and this description is not about spiritual beliefs, but about certain political structure, practical organization, and social control. He coined the term *covenantal model* for this societal solution (see more in chapter 5 "The Covenantal Society, Structure, Organization, and Power Flow").

This work uses the term *covenantal society*. I admit Elazar's term *model* is more rigorous. There is no society that is entirely *covenantal*, or *hierarchical*, or *oligarchical*. Societies are a mixture of the three; this monograph utilizes the term *covenantal society* to designate a society in which the dominant features of social structure, power flow, public psychology, and justice administration meet the description of the covenantal model. The description of these features is part and parcel of the chapters of this book.

To examine point (c) above, I studied together with Lewi Stone whether a community with no police can control deviations from lawful behavior. The fundamental premise of the study was that Proto-Israel consisted not of incorruptible righteous people, but of regular folks with variable tendencies to respect the law. We borrowed well-known methods of biophysics developed to investigate spread of infections.[19] The answer is yes, provided certain conditions are met (see details in chapter 6 "Justice Administration in Biblical Israel").

Chapter 7 "Inventing a Covenantal Society Is Impossible" explains why one cannot devise such a society from scratch. Other chapters explain why one can't design a covenantal network using recipes from the Scriptures. The book will show that a viable covenantal organization requires a continuous inheritance of traditions, values, customs, meeting-culture; if copied properly, these traditions and customs balance authority of office holders with the general assembly's power of control. Like the art of riding a bicycle, the covenantal model works if one possesses all the necessary skills; if one of the essential behavioral components is absent then the covenantal society fails fast (see more in chapter 5 "The Covenantal Society, Structure, Organization, and Power Flow").

Chapter 12 "Evolution, Customs, and Law" explains in terms of *cultural evolution* how a successful proto-type came into being.[20] *Cultural evolution* also explains subsequent incarnations of the primitive covenantal model of Proto-Israel by copying its covenantal traditions. Their survival entailed adopting in practice the essential functions and mindset (see chapter 9 "Evolution Tree"). This point is new in the study of the covenantal model; it became apparent only because of the biophysical methodology that shed light on the coincident conditions of survival. Elazar describes the sequence of covenantal incarnations as events separated in time implying that they developed their covenantal tradition based on the biblical blueprint. For example, describing the rise of Swiss Protestantism:

> The renewed interest in the Bible and in the post Biblical Jewish classics manifested by Christians and humanists generated what came to be known as Christian Hebraism which was most pronounced amongst those who founded the Reformed wing of Protestantism.[21]

My previous investigations taught me that unlike Elazar's previous inference, the Bible is not a cook-book of recipes for setting up the simultaneous conditions required for a successful run of a covenantal community (see conditions listed on page 85 in chapter 7). Biophysical simulation of the mathematical model revealed that the biblical prohibition of work on Sabbath is a necessary, but not a sufficient condition. A hypothetical founder of a covenantal system born in a hierarchical tradition carries the core principles and ideals upon which a hierarchical culture operates. For example, for the founder in question minding one's own business is a virtue. A covenantal community with no dedicated law enforcement will fall apart in a matter of a few weeks if the congregants will keep minding their own business.[22] Chapter 8 "Covenantal Psychology" discusses the necessary psychological ingredients for a successful operation of a covenantal way of life. Chapter 10 "God Gave Moses the Law" illustrates why studying the Bible is not sufficient to grasp those ingredients and why only vertical transmission from one generation to the next assures the successful continuity of a covenantal practice.

This work is about the evolution of American constitutional democracy. I already touched on the perils of lecturing about democracy; evolution is less dangerous; however, it is still slippery. For example, scholars of performance studies debated the evolution of tragedy from Ancient Greece:

> The nature of the evolution in the shape and function of the theatre from that early period has generated much speculation, and not a little controversy.[23]

Even top scholars of Darwin's theory are justly blackballed by this debate. And what has evolution to do with algebra? The good news is that evolution has everything to do with algebra. Ronald Fisher explained evolution in terms that even mathematicians understand.[24] This allowed the proliferation of mathematical analysis of evolution.[25] I will spare you the equations. Suffice to say that for the purpose of this work, the evolution of a sociopolitical concept like the constitution consists of a succession of value-added incarnations. The sequence of versions of a manuscript from conception to publication stands for the evolution chain of a book.

Equations may be boring and nuisance; however, the mathematical analysis sometimes sheds light on a process that otherwise is unnoticed. For example, earlier I mentioned that this thesis argues that the concept that the constitution, as supreme law of the country is the source of government legitimacy came from the Proto-Israelite covenant of the beginning of Iron Age.

This proposition is not unheard-of. If the sermon of Bishop Joseph Hall[26] convinces the reader that the concept of "constitution" and the nation of Israel germinated simultaneously then I rest my case. I mentioned earlier Elazar implying that for Jews the Hebrew Bible is a divine constitution (page 6). Many others claimed that the American covenantal faith has biblical roots.[27] This work stipulates that the association is not due to intellectual propagation of spiritual conviction but it is by a chain of covenantal links tangibly contacting each other in time and space. In other words, each link of the chain (chapter 9 "Evolution Tree") copied essential ingredients of the practice from a living example. Reasonably, there are some readers out there who would want to see some additional substance to this claim. And that is what we bring here.

Chapter 1 "Once Upon a Time . . ." on page 13 explains why the mainstream English legal approach was opposed to covenantal philosophy and therefore it didn't spawn the American constitutional persuasion. Moreover, the chapter will stipulate that the covenantal practice was indeed imported from England on the Mayflower; however, Plymouth, the first covenantal manifestation on American soil, was not a produce of English legal tradition but its audacious opponent.

The chapter will then turn to the Southern Levant. The sifting of the archaeological evidence will illustrate that, as the Bible claims, Proto-Israel had no king; however, they had a law and some mechanism that enforce the law. Chapter "The Covenant of Israel: Customary Law or Law" proves this statement.

Chapter 4 "The Covenantal Society: Lex Rex" compares the stratified realm with the covenantal legal system shedding light on the similarity and the distinction.

Please allow me to close this introduction by reiterating the three concepts of the *thesis of this work*:

(a) The roots of American constitutionalism are in biblical Israel; this concept has been debated by scholars of constitutional history.
(b) Proto-Israel also known as Israel of the Judges had no king as the Book of Judges claims; however, it had a covenant which it enforced. Naturally, this belief is as old as the Bible; however, its proof is new.

(c) American constitutionalism did not stem from studying and applying biblical recipes. It rather evolved through a sequence of embodiments each passing on the torch of essential traditions to its heir. This concept is new.

NOTES

1. The pKa value indicates the strength of an acid.

2. Ratio is associated with the binding and unbinding reaction of receptor (R) and ligand (L) molecules.

3. A survey of several works of this specialization is found in Juan A Barceló and Florencia Del Castillo, "Simulating the Past for Understanding the Present. A Critical Review," in *Simulating Prehistoric and Ancient Worlds*, eds. Juan A Barceló and Florencia Del Castillo (Cham, Switzerland: Springer, 2016).

4. For example, A Georges L Romme, "Unanimity rule and organizational decision making: A simulation model," *Organization Science* 15, no. 6 (2004): 704–718.

5. For example, Luca D'Acci, "Simulating future societies in Isobenefit Cities: Social isobenefit scenarios," *Futures* 54 (2013): 3–18.

6. William O Kermack and Anderson G McKendrick, "A contribution to the mathematical theory of epidemics" (paper presented at the Proceedings of the Royal Society of London A: mathematical, physical and engineering sciences, 1927).

7. A rigorous derivation of the proportionality assumes a constant probability of infection in case of a meeting between a susceptible and an infected individual. In reality, this probability varies over long terms, that is, generations; the same derivation applies for criminal contagion.

8. This work neglects faith discrepancies in favor of manifestation of social ethos; for example, the thesis presented here lumps together Jews and Calvinists because both practice equality in the eyes of the Lord; at the same time I separate Calvinists from Lutherans because Lutherans practice is hierarchical.

9. For example, Mathew A. Pauley, *Athens, Rome, and England: America's Constitutional Heritage* (New York: Intercollegiate Studies Institute (ORD), 2014).

10. Charles Howard McIlwain, *Constitutionalism: Ancient and Modern* (Clark, NJ: Lawbook Exchange, 2005), 53.

11. Judges 21:25

12. McIlwain, *Constitutionalism: Ancient and Modern*, 9.

13. Ibid.

14. Ibid.

15. William G. Dever, *What Did the Biblical Writers Know and When Did They Know It?: What Archeology Can Tell Us About the Reality of Ancient Israel*, Kindle ed. (Grand Rapids, MI: Eerdmans Publishing Company, 2002).

16. To avoid confusion, one should not call *law* the *law-like phenomena* of pre-sate societies" Sally Falk Moore, *Law as Process: An Anthropological Approach* (Hamburg: Lit Verlag, 2000), 18.

17. Daniel J. Elazar, *The Covenant Tradition in Politics*, vol. 1 (New Brunswick, NJ: Transaction Publishers, 1995), Introduction.

18. Daniel J Elazar, "Judaism and Democracy: The Reality," *Jerusalem Letter*, no. 48 (1986): 1–5.

19. Joseph Livni and Lewi Stone, "The stabilizing role of the Sabbath in pre-monarchic Israel: A mathematical model," *Journal of biological physics* 41 (2015): 203–221.

20. The prototype started with egalitarian pastoralist tribes settling on the hills of Judah and Samaria. Customary law containing the required habits became in short time enforced law by applying peer pressure on transgressors see more in Joseph Livni, "The cultural evolution of an institution: the Sabbath," *Cliodynamics* 8 (2017): 59–74.

21. Daniel J. Elazar, *Covenant & Commonwealth: From Christian Separation through the Protestant Reformation* (New Brunswick, NJ: Transaction Publishers, 1995). Elazar calls the Swiss Reformation the Reformed wing of Protestantism and noting that its leaders "leaned heavily on the Hebrew Bible" "Switzerland as a Model in the Commonwealth Tradition," in *Commonwealth: The Other Road to Democracy—the Swiss Model of Democratic Self-government*, ed. D.J. Elazar, et al. (Lanham, MD: Lexington Books, 2001), 247.

22. See, for example, Figure 3 of the investigation about the evolution of the institution of Sabbath Livni, "The cultural evolution of an institution."

23. Rush Rehm, *Greek Tragic Theatre* (London: Routledge, 2003).

24. Ronald A. Fisher, *The Genetical Theory of Natural Selection* (Oxford, UK: Oxford University Press, 1999); "The Wave of Advance of Advantageous Genes," *Annals of Eugenics* 7 (1937): 355–369.

25. For example, Christopher A. Edmonds, Anita S. Lillie, and L Luca Cavalli-Sforza, "Mutations arising in the wave front of an expanding population," *Proceedings of the National Academy of Sciences* 101, no. 4 (2004): 975–979; K.P. Hadeler and F. Rothe, "Travelling fronts in nonlinear diffusion equations," *Journal of Mathematical Biology* 2, no. 3 (1975): 251–263 etc.

26. "The first instance given in the Oxford dictionary of the use of the word 'constitution' for the whole legal framework of a state is a phrase of Bishop Halls in 1610, 'The constitution of the Commonwealth of Israel'" McIlwain, *Constitutionalism: Ancient and Modern*, 25.

27. For example, G.A. Moots, *Politics Reformed: The Anglo-American Legacy of Covenant Theology* (Columbia, MO: University of Missouri Press, 2010), 112; Eric Nelson, *The Hebrew Republic* (Cambridge, MA: Harvard University Press, 2010); Ismael Kurun, *The Theological Origins of Liberalism* (Lanham, MD: Lexington Books, 2016); Shaun A De Freitas, "*Samuel Rutherford on Law and Covenant: The Impact Of Theologico-Political Federalism On Constitutional Theory*" (Bloemfontein: University of the Free State, 2003); Daniel J. Elazar, *Covenant and Polity in Biblical Israel* (New Brunswick, NJ: Transaction Publishers, 1998); *Covenant & Constitutionalism: The Great Frontier and the Matrix of Federal Democracy* (New Brunswick, NJ: Transaction Publishers, 1997); Donald S. Lutz, *The Origins of American Constitutionalism* (Baton Rouge, Louisiana: Louisiana

State University Press, 1988); Steven Alan Samson, "Theological Sources of American Constitutionalism," *Faculty Publications and Presentations. 54.* Liberty University (1991); "Covenant Origins of the American Polity," *Faculty Publications and Presentations. 5.* Liberty University (1994).; see also "parallels between the American system and the biblical system" Alan M. Dershowitz, *The Genesis of Justice* (New York: Warner Books, 2000); Sanford Levinson, *Constitutional Faith* (Princeton, NJ: Princeton University Press, 2011), 11.

Chapter 1

Once Upon a Time . . .

Once upon a time, there was a vast kingdom. People called it England. The king ruled over it because:

> From the beginning of time kings have assumed the right to rule; but in the wilderness of the Western world the exiles from Scrooby and Austerfield take the sceptre into their own hands, and inaugurate a new era in human affairs.[1]

The exiles from Scrooby and Austerfield were the pilgrims. This account validates an ancient piece of wisdom: "What has been will be again, what has been done will be done again."[2] In other words, the beginning of this story is almost a replica of another beginning. With your permission, I will replace "the wilderness of the Western world" with "the hills of Judah and Ephraim" and "Scrooby and Austerfield" with the "wilderness of the desert" and I needn't worry about a sharper introduction to my thesis.

A good storyteller doesn't start his story all over again. That is because his story expresses true occurrences combined with ancient wisdom wrapped in imagined events and heroic figures beautifully crafted by many other storytellers that transmitted that wisdom from time immemorial. However, my audience is made of adults who graduated law school, political science, with occasional scholars of history, sociology, archaeology, anthropology, and perhaps even divinity schools. Consequently, my story needs to stick to actual events, to tell the truth and nothing but the truth, with no ambition to bore the audience with the whole truth. Therefore, I beg you to allow me to restart my story; I promise that I will come back to Scrooby and Austerfield when the story as it unfolds leads me there. So with your permission here it is:

Once upon a time, there was a nation who had no king. A powerful king in the neighborhood, Pharaoh Merneptah annihilated that nation and with the occasion of this great victory the mighty Pharaoh left an inscription about the glorious event. Therefore, we know that the defeated nation of our story was called Israel. The inscription survived and was discovered by Flinders Petrie in 1896 at Thebes, and now it is found in the Egyptian Museum in Cairo. However, in spite of the sensational victory, the people of Israel also survived! Not only did they survive but they established permanent towns and villages for cultivation of wheat, barley, grapes, and olives.[3] Consequently, we know that they owned land and stored their products. They encountered neighboring people which whom we know they traded because archaeologists tell us so.[4] We also believe that sometimes they encountered their neighboring nations in skirmishes because the Bible tells us so.[5] Most archaeological scholars don't accept the biblical message as evidence of historicity. Nevertheless, those stories about skirmishes are credible. After all, the era of the Judges or of Proto-Israel took place at a time when Bronze Age gave way to the Iron Age, that is, about three thousand years ago; in those days, skirmishes were the rule, beating swords into ploughshares was the exception. In spite of all these scuffles with next-door Canaanites and Philistines, "there was no king in Israel."[6] All the neighboring people had kings who "assumed the right to rule"[7] as kings do; however, the Israelite settlers were kingless; archaeologists who developed means to detect rankless societies even say they had no ranks.[8] Nowadays, there are many nations that get along pretty well without a king. As a matter of fact, the most powerful nation on Earth has never had a king. However, the United States has had a constitution.

Notwithstanding Bishop Hall's contention,[9] Ancient Israel had no constitution. Proto-Israel consisted of nomadic pastoralists who settled down on the highlands of the Land of Canaan. They carried from the desert habits of deeply rooted freedoms typically enjoyed by nomads such as freedom of speech, freedom of association, and the right to carry arms; they imported a nomadic persuasion of equality in the eyes of the Lord; they overruled pretentions to nobility[10] and they conserved clan traditions of government.[11] Among the last of their worries were democratic elections, taxation authority, separation of powers, and extradition procedures. They had to learn how to grow barley, wheat, olives, and grapes, how to inhabit a town, how to protect one's property, how to buy and sell crops and tools. The natives of that land, their Canaanite neighbors offered perfect examples of living in cities, farming, fishing, and trading.

As they settled, the Proto-Israelites discovered civilized living in city states where rulers set rules intended to preserve the two essential purposes of civilized existence: peace and justice.[12] Had Proto-Israel copied everything from their Canaanite neighbors, they would have been swallowed by the Canaanites. Proto-Israel learned many Canaanite lessons; however, they rejected the idea of rulers decreeing and enforcing rules. Reasonably, their pastoralist ancestors followed rules, customs, and traditions inherited one generation after the other as do many other nomadic populations. In general, this type of rules is known as tradition or in legal terminology *customary law*. This tradition became later a covenant. At this point, it is worthwhile emphasizing that this covenant was not necessarily what currently is known as either the "Ten Commandments" or the more elaborate set of rules known by biblical scholars as Covenant Code which is found in Exodus 19:1–24:18. One cannot rule out that the covenant was only in the hearts and minds of the settlers and the actual appearance of a written covenant and its ark took place a few generations later if at all. The thesis of this book doesn't stem from the historicity of the ark or the content of the covenant. The covenant persisted in the awareness and took root in the memory of those Proto-Israelite settlers; it consisted of customary rules daily practiced inherited from earlier traditions. They needed to obey those rules to reconcile their egalitarian ethos with their new existence of settled farmers. Not only each one needed to obey the customs but each one felt the need to make sure that the others obey the same customs (see chapter 8 "Covenantal Psychology"). It was helpful to rely on the concept that these rules represent a covenant with the divinity.

Nevertheless, a society ruled not by a ruler but by a covenant is a problematic arrangement; consequently, I dedicated an important chapter to discuss it (see chapter 6 "Justice Administration in Biblical Israel"). At this point, I am ready to postulate that the covenant of Proto-Israel was the prototype of the concept that rules of behavior are not necessarily decrees of a ruler but they are commandments derived from a body of fundamental laws. In this context, the term *fundamental law* designates a rule that ordinary laws must comply with. In other words, this book will substantiate that the covenant of Proto-Israel set off a process ending with the U.S. Constitution.

What about democratic Athens? Didn't Aristotle write the "Constitution of Athens?"[13] While this chapter recognizes that the term *constitution* circulated in ancient Greece and Rome, it stipulates that the term didn't mean what the modern world understands by *constitution*. This book will substantiate that the *constitution's* meaning of *supreme law* grew from the primitive *covenant* in spite of its Roman name borrowed from ancient Roman legal lexicon.

> By means of words contracts are created, statutes are enacted, and constitutions come into existence. Yet, in spite of all good intentions, the meanings of the words found in documents are not always clear and unequivocal.[14]

The word *constitution* is ambiguous. Aristotle's "The Athenian Constitution" is an important account of how the Athenian democracy was governed. The work describes the *constitution* of Draco as well.[15] The draconian "constitution" legislated that some debtors who can't pay their debts are to become slaves.[16] No doubt, for Aristotle constitution (πολιτεία) is makeup of government.[17]

For others, *constitution* may mean written law or recognized tradition,[18] "above all the state as actually is."[19] If Aristotle understands that *constitution* is makeup of government then reasonably, the Athenian political philosophy entailed none of the five bullets of Paine listed in the introdoction "Nice to Meet You . . ." Athens was the cradle of democracy; however, constitutionalism stems from somewhere else.

Neither is Ancient Rome a good example of limiting the authority of government. "Legum servi sumus," wrote Cicero[20]; the prevalent interpretation is that one obeys both: just and unjust laws.[21] In American practice, unjust laws are termed *unconstitutional*.[22] And Cicero was a republican[23] in the Roman sense of the word. One shouldn't arrive at any conclusion about Roman constitutionalism without revisiting Cicero's famous words: *Cum potestas in populo, auctoritas in senatu.*[24] In the Roman Republic, the Senate was the government.[25] McIlwain uses the quote to explain that "observance of the Senate decrees always depended on a 'convention of constitution' rather than a law."[26] This explanation is as concise as Cicero's line; more exploration is needed to find out to what extent the people ran the show in the ancient Roman Republic. Let me take a shot at it. Cicero's words are usually used to distinguish between two abilities to achieve compliance with rules put in place for the public. Cicero calls one authority and the other power; I believe the two are sufficiently similar to impose a search for definitions in another relevant field. Sociology distinguishes between the two:

> "*Power* refers to the ability to have one's will carried out despite the resistance of others . . .
>
> *Legitimate authority* (sometimes just called *authority*), Weber said, is power whose use is considered just and appropriate by those over whom the power is exercised."[27]

Before we put to test the applicability of sociologists' definition of *power* and *authority* to Cicero's idiom, please allow me to dissect McIlwain's expression "convention of a constitution." Aristotle meant by constitution makeup of government. This makeup functions because of a public consent to it:

> Even the most powerful and the most despotic government cannot hold a society together by sheer force; to that extent there was a limited truth to the old belief that governments are produced by consent.[28]

Even if one disagrees with Sabine, one realizes that merely a few governments function thanks to sheer force only; needless to say, those governments are not relevant to our debate. I will therefore borrow McIlwain's expression "convention of constitution" to designate the almost omnipresent consent of the ruled. An examination of the specific case of Roman Republic reveals that indeed the *convention of constitution* gave people power. The *magistrates*[29] were elected by the popular assemblies. And at first sight, the legislative branch was in the hands of the people; however, one observes that the popular assemblies only produced bills, a bill required ratification by patrician senators to become *law*. This provision is mentioned as *autorictas patrum*. After 287 BCE, this provision was replaced by another means of senatorial control, that is, "no one but a magistrate could bring a bill before one of the popular assemblies for action and the Senate found means of maintaining control over magistrates."[30] One of Paine's tests of constitution is "that it defines the authority which the people commits to its government, and in so doing thereby it limits it" (page 4). So far, this *convention of constitution* does exactly the opposite: its provisions are rules of the government limiting the power of the people.

On the other hand, the Senate did not pass laws; it pronounced senatorial advices.[31] This does sound like limiting the authority of government. A senatorial advice was not equal to a law. It could not annul or contradict a law.[32] However, the senatorial government had no need to annul laws; it could veto bills before becoming laws. Moreover, senatorial advices were directives equivalent to laws in issues not yet covered by laws.[33] These advices were obeyed in virtue of Senate's authority see (Weber's interpretation above). Senators were not elected; they served for life lessening senators' accountability before the people. Not all senators were equal; they were ranked and their order of participating in the debate was according to their rank; the chairman could stop the debate before the lower ranks had the occasion to express their views. Senators were not paid. Therefore, as in other typical oligarchies, only those who were rich enough to live without work could serve as senators. This reminds us of Aristotle's note that only people who enjoy sufficient leisure participate in government.[34]

This examination of Cicero's power of the people and Senate's authority indicates that the Roman Republican *convention of constitution* did indeed afford power to the people; however, instead of containing provisions limiting the authority of government it contained provisions of limiting the power of the people. Needless to say, the Roman Empire had less inclination to limit government.[35] Constitutionalism as framed by Paine did not originate in Rome.

On the other hand, one cannot claim disconnect between the ideas of Thomas Paine and the British Isles. Chapter 2 "The Difference between Political Concessions and Constitutional Liberties" discusses the contribution of English royal compromises like Magna Carta to the enactment of the constitution. The chapter will show that these royal guarantees of liberties served as advocacy tools for defending the case for an American Constitution before the English Crown and Parliament rather than guided the framers of the constitution.

England's contribution to the American Constitution is central not necessarily because Paine was born in Thetford, Norfolk, England. The British Isles played an important role because England shipped to America aboard the Mayflower the idea "to covenant and combine ourselves together into a civil body politic, for our better ordering and preservation, and furtherance of the ends aforesaid."[36] Rumors regarding British origin of limiting government's authority reached even the king's ears:

> King George III reportedly denounced the American Revolution as "a Presbyterian rebellion." The sentiment was correct. It was the Presbyterian ideas of Lex Rex, which were brought into America by the preachers, and which legitimated, and even mandated, revolution as a Christian duty against tyrants.[37]

Lex Rex[38] appeared in 1644 in Scotland. However, the first presentation of idea that "it was possible for kings to be subject to the law"[39] took place at the inaugural lecture of Dorislaus at Cambridge University in 1627.[40] The lecture "caused a sensation"[41] in England. Rutherford equates the English *jus regis* to tyranny and oppression.[42] Lex Rex was deemed dangerous and ordered to be burned.[43] Dorislaus was assassinated in 1649.[44] It is safe to conclude that English legal tradition was in direct opposition to Lex Rex.

Consequently, Paine's challenging government's unlimited authority was not because of the mainstream English legal tradition but in spite of it. The English origins of limiting government were not in Norfolk but in Plymouth, UK, the port where the Mayflower set sail. The passengers carried with them the principles of Lex Rex that Paine reiterated decades later. As soon as they spotted American Land, they crafted the Mayflower Compact.

> The world never before has seen such a paper. That writing given in the green meadows of Runnymede by John Lackland was a compact between two parties—the king and the barons ;barons; but here is only one party—the people. The paper is a constitution. It is fundamental—a new beginning the founding of a state on a written law, emanating not from the king, but from themselves.[45]

The Pilgrims landed. "New World Israelites, they had, with God's help, finally found their Canaan."[46]

The thesis of this book is that not only the landing on their promised land associated the Pilgrims to Israelites but also the proclamation that the Mayflower Compact is "the only legitimate source of government."[47] This

Mayflower Compact belongs to a long conceptual lineage established by a similar founder treaty: the Covenant of Israel. At first sight, this argument contradicts another opinion claiming that the appeal to "written words" that allowed anyone to read exactly what a government had the power to do grew from "Charter Constitutionalism."[48] This seeming conflict of Bowie's proposition with the thesis of this work is reconciled remembering that both the Mayflower Contract and the Charter Constitutionalism have their origins in the Puritan covenantal philosophy, as testified by one of the Framers of the Constitution describing the Puritan beginnings as follows:

> Their greatest concern seems to have been to establish a government of the church more consistent with the Scriptures, and a government of the state more agreeable to the dignity of human nature, than any they had seen in Europe, and to transmit such a government down to their posterity, with the means of securing and preserving it forever.[49]

It is noteworthy that the Mayflower Compact inaugurates a civil government in spite of being authored by devoted Calvinists. Nevertheless, the structure of that civil government, its direction of power flow from town to state and from state to federation (see chapter 5 "The Covenantal Society, Structure, Organization, and Power Flow") follows the blueprint of the typical Calvinist Church administration.

The chapter 12 "Evolution, Customs, and Law" explains in terms of cultural evolution how the ancient Covenant of Proto-Israel developed into the modern American constitution.

NOTES

1. Charles Carleton Coffin, *The Story of Liberty* (New York: Harper & brothers, 1879), 404.
2. Ecclesiastes 1:9
3. For example, Israel Finkelstein and N. A. Silberman, *The Bible Unearthed: Archaeology's New Vision of Ancient Israel and the Origin of Sacred Texts* (Simon & Shuster, 2002), 115.
4. For example, Ibid.
5. For example, 1 Samuel 4:1
6. Judges 21:25
7. Coffin, *The Story of Liberty*, 404.
8. Finkelstein and Silberman, *The Bible Unearthed*, 110.
9. Charles Howard McIlwain, *Constitutionalism: Ancient and Modern* (Clark, NJ: Lawbook Exchange, 2005), 25.

10. see Hackett's interpretation of Gideon's refusal to be king Jo Ann Hackett, "There was no King in Israel," in *The Oxford History of the Biblical World*, edited by Michael David Coogan (New York: Oxford University Press, 1998).

11. Previous customs of periodic tribal meetings evolved into compulsory meetings of town assemblies, Joseph Livni, "The cultural evolution of an institution: The Sabbath," *Cliodynamics* 8 (2017): 59–74; these assemblies are the archetype of covenantal community government.

12. "Peace and justice are the two things that make the crown says Braxton," McIlwain, *Constitutionalism*, 84.

13. Aristotle, *The Athenian Constitution* (Start Publishing LLC, 2013).

14. Sanford Schane, "Ambiguity and Misunderstanding in the Law," *T. Jefferson L. Rev.* 25 (2002).

15. Aristotle, *The Athenian Constitution*, Part 4.

16. Morris Silver, *Economic Structures of Antiquity* (Westport CT, London: Greenwood Press, 1995), 117.

17. Aristotle, Benjamin Jowett, and Henry William Carless Davis, *Politics*, Kindle edition ed. (Mineola, NY: Dover Publications, 2000), Kindle locations: 169, 70, 89, 217, 31, 716, 885, 931, 33, 39, 53, 69, 1090, 122, 128, and so on.

18. Michael Gagarin, *Early Greek Law* (Berkley—Los Angeles—London: University of California Press, 1989).

19. McIlwain, *Constitutionalism*, 28.

20. John R. Stone, *The Routledge Dictionary of Latin Quotations: The Illiterati"'s Guide to Latin Maxims, Mottoes, Proverbs, and Sayings* (New York and London: Taylor & Francis, 2013), 272.

21. For example, Conyers Middleton, *The Life and Letters of Marcus Tullius Cicero* (London: Henry G. Bohn, 1848), 96.

22. For example, *Arizona v. United States*, 567 U.S. 387 (2012) and Illinois's wiretapping law (720 Illinois Compiled Statutes 5/Criminal Code of 2012, Article 14) were ruled unconstitutional.

23. For example, Robert T. Radford, *Cicero: A Study in the Origins of Republican Philosophy* (Amsterdam: Rodopi, 2002), 75.

24. The people hold the power, the senate owns the authority, (my translation); cited often to distinguish between power and authority, for example, Jeannette Money and George Tsebelis, "Cicero's puzzle: Upper House power in comparative perspective," *International Political Science Review* 13, no. 1 (1992): 25–43; Stephen R. Latham, "Medical professionalism," *Mount Sinai Journal of Medicine* 69 (2002): 363–69; McIlwain, *Constitutionalism*, 45.

25. Frank F. Abbott, *A History and Description of Roman Political Institutions* (Boston and London: Ginn, 1901), 68–69.

26. McIlwain, *Constitutionalism*, 45.

27. Steven E. Barkan, "Sociology Comprehensive Edition v. 1.0," Retrieved from h ttp://2012books.lardbucket.org/pdfs/sociology-comprehensiveedition.pdf on October 24 (2012).

28. George H. Sabine and Thomas L. Thorson, *A History of Political Theory* (Oxford: Oxford and IBH Publishing, 2018), 731. cited by Bas Dianda, *A History*

of the Seventies: The Political, Cultural, Social and Economic Developments that Shaped the Modern World (Wilmington, DE: Vernon Press, 2019), 347.

29. Office holders in the Roman administration: for example, *consul*—limited term to one year—presided over the Senate, the popular assemblies, commander in chief, Abbott, *A History and Description of Roman Political Institutions*, 175–81; *praetor*—term limit one year—judge, governor of province, and administrative officer (e.g., substitute for consul) ibid., 186–90; *censor*—limited term to one year and a half—*assess property* of citizens, and arranging them in tribes, classes and centuries (these were comparable to current electoral districts and constituencies and the arrangement in tribes, classes, and centuries was an ancient equivalent to modern American gerrymandering); the censor *collected revenue,* and was responsible for *public expenses*; the censor was in charge for a while to *appoint senators* when vacancies required; ibid., 190–95.

30. Ibid., 53.

31. Momigliano Arnaldo and Cornell Tim, *Senatus Consultum* (Oxford: Oxford University Press).

32. Abbott, *A History and Description of Roman Political Institutions*, 233.

33. Ibid.

34. Aristotle, Jowett, and Davis, *Politics*, 81.

35. McIlwain cites Gibbon's description of the Principate: "an absolute monarchy disguised by the forms of a commonwealth" McIlwain, *Constitutionalism*, 55.

36. Mayflower Compact Nathanel Philbrick, *Mayflower: A Story of Courage, Community, and War*, Kindle Edition ed. (New York: Penguin Publishing Group, 2006), Kindle location 697–99.

37. David B. Kopel, "The Scottish and English religious roots of the American right to arms: Buchanan, Rutherford, Locke, Sidney, and the Duty to Overthrow Tyranny," *Bridges* 12 (2005): 299.

38. Samuel Rutherford, *Lex, Rex, Or, The Law and the Prince* (Penn Laird, VA: Sprinkle Publications, 1982).

39. Charles Spencer, *Killers of the King: The Men Who Dared to Execute Charles I* (New York: Bloomsbury Publishing, 2015). Chapter 2, A King on Trial.

40. The date of his inaugural lecture is from "Dorislaus (Doreslawe), Isaac (DRSS631I)". A Cambridge Alumni Database. University of Cambridge.

41. Spencer, *Killers of the King*. Chapter 2, A King on Trial.

42. Question XVIII, Rutherford, *Lex, Rex, Or, The Law and the Prince*, 78

43. Shaun A De Freitas, "*Samuel Rutherford on Law and Covenant: The Impact Of Theologico-Political Federalism On Constitutional Theory*" (Bloemfontein: University of the Free State, 2003), 192.

44. From "Dorislaus (Doreslawe), Isaac (DRSS631I)." A Cambridge Alumni Database. University of Cambridge. Noteworthy coincidence: Dorislaus was the first to teach on English soil that the king is not above the law. King Charles I was the unfortunate victim of this suggestion. As a result of Dorislaus's lecture, both paid with their life, both in the same year: 1649.

45. Coffin, *The Story of Liberty*, 390–91.

46. Philbrick, *Mayflower*, Kindle loc. 1153.

47. John Quincy Adams, "Oration at Plymouth—Delivered at Plymouth Mass. December 22, 1802 in Commemoration of the Landing of the Pilgrims," *The Daily Republican*, Dec 22, 2002, 1802.

48. Nikolas Bowie, "Why the Constitution Was Written Down," *Stan. L. Rev.* 71 (2019).

49. John Adams, "A Dissertation on the Canon and Feudal Law," in *The Works of John Adams*, ed. Charles Francis Adams (Boston: Little, Brown, 1851).

Chapter 2

The Difference between Political Concessions and Constitutional Liberties

This chapter disputes the theory that constitutional liberties started as Roman or English concessions extracted from the respective governments.

Law enforcement is one of the three essential functions of a state defined by Adam Smith: defense, justice administration, and public works.[1] In a typical society where the rules are decreed by a ruler, the efficiency of law enforcement is a variable that plays a role in the *sustainability* and *resilience* of the state.[2] The ruler steers its strength according to needs and possibilities set by other state variables. Chapter 1 "Once upon a time . . ." mentioned that typically a government doesn't achieve the consent of the governed by sheer force only. Consequently, another important variable related to adjustments of law enforcement is the ruler's legitimacy. Valentinian's law allowing police to detain senators and Gratian's law repealing it[3] are examples of how rulers maneuvered the balance between the size of police force and their own legitimacy. No one should confuse such gubernatorial tightrope walking with acts of constitution.

More relevant to the American Constitution is the English legal tradition. Article III, Section 2 of the constitution guarantees a jury trial in all criminal trials and Article 1, Section 9 prevents the suspension of habeas corpus, unless when in cases of rebellion or invasion the public safety may require it. In regular circumstances, Section 9 requires legal cause to hold or imprison someone. The connection of these liberties to the English Magna Carta is well rooted in the tradition of the American Revolution (figure 2.1). Not only general media link Thomas Jefferson to the Magna Carta but also legal scholars subscribe to the association of the constitution with the Magna Carta:

> Thus, for example, it provides for taxation by the legislature only, for the privilege of the writ of habeas corpus, for trial by jury in criminal cases, for the

Figure 2.1 "By the sword we seek peace, but peace only under liberty"—sword in the right hand and Magna Carta in the left hand.

prohibition of bills of attainder, ex-post facto laws, laws impairing the obligation of contracts, and laws imposing religious tests. These and other provisions, derived in large measure from English and colonial precedents, constitute a body of constitutional guaranties of the highest value.[4]

The association stems from an important document related to the drafting of the constitution. The first Continental Congress drafted a Declaration of Rights and Grievances against King George III. The document establishes the rights and liberties of the people of the colonies:

That the inhabitants of the English Colonies in North America, by the immutable laws of nature, the principles of the English constitution, and the several charters or compacts, have the following Rights:

Among others, the document lists the right to "life, liberty, and property," the right to "a free and exclusive power of legislation in their several provincial legislatures," the "privilege of being tried by their peers of the vicinage," and it ends with declaring that the exercise of legislation in the colonies by an appointed council is *unconstitutional*. We are told that the *Magna Carta* is mentioned on an image on the title page.

We mentioned in chapter 1 "Once Upon a Time . . ." that in spite of the carefully crafted declaration, the king considered the American Revolution as a Presbyterian rebellion and his government acted accordingly. Perhaps, the "Declaration of Rights and Grievances" attempted to avoid bloodshed; my readers are better qualified to judge whether the use of terms such as "English constitution" or unconstitutional appointments was wise. In any case, the reference to earlier concessions of the Crown was intended to make the case for acquiring the mentioned rights building upon a body of English legal precedents.

Associating taxation with representation follows from their local practices since the landing of the Mayflower. "Local legislatures and towns in each of the colonies"[5] levied taxes. A body of taxes imposed by one's representative is bad news; additional taxes imposed by legislators with no accountability naturally worsen the message."

As far as the writ of habeas corpus is concerned, this was indeed an English procedure used by courts to verify unjustified captivity of alleged offenders:

> By the reign of Charles I, in the 17th century, the writ was fully established as the appropriate process for checking the illegal imprisonment of people by inferior courts or public officials.[6]

The colonial practice of North America extended the writ as a right of colonists.

> In the British colonies in North America, by the time of the American Revolution, the rights to habeas corpus were popularly regarded as among the basic protections of individual liberty.[7]

Article 1, Section 9 proclaims that "the Privilege of the Writ of Habeas Corpus shall not be suspended." This indicates that the practice existed before the legislation. The innovation of this legal procedure is indeed English. However, its incorporation in the constitution is the news here. Enforcing a law indeed requires "force of some kind."[8] Enforcing a constitution implies boosting the legitimacy of its statutes rather than policing infringements. This is consistent with McIlwain's critical observation:

> A constitutional state was one that had preserved an inheritance of free institutions. . . . It was the retention of "ancient" liberties for which liberals were fighting, not the creation of new ones a priori.[9]

The memorable act of the framers is incorporating the writ of the habeas corpus and prohibition of "ex-post facto laws" in the will of "We the people" and not the invention of the practices. The notions of immutable law and unconstitutional law were not an English tradition, but a covenantal one; they have been established on American soil by the Mayflower Compact. This example is consistent with the widely accepted view that structural social processes are ultimately more important than conscious ideas or ideologies. The rationale of the three concepts of the thesis of this book (see end of chapter "Nice to meet you . . .") as well as several lines of reasoning in this book rest on this proposition.

Therefore, the enforceability of these rights and liberties flowed from the colonial practice from its inception; the common consciousness grounded in covenantal practice of preserving these rights and liberties is the secret of the exceptional vitality of the American constitutional principles.

The "Declaration of Rights and Grievances" expressed the public criticism of the British rule comparing it against the Magna Carta, an *idealized English benchmark"* unpracticed, but not unforgotten."[10] However, the spirit of the constitution is not only the rupture from English sovereignty but also the protection of the sovereignty of the people. The earlier discussion of Cicero's contention regarding the power of the people in the Roman Republic is only one of many examples confirming the following wisdom of Tocqueville.

> "The will of the nation" is one of those expressions which have been most profusely abused by the wily and the despotic of every age.[11]

Tocqueville however describes with enthusiasm how the sovereignty of the people is established in the every-day lives of the Americans; it "is recognized by the customs and proclaimed by the laws."[12] Not surprisingly, this has nothing to do with the Magna Carta. It was established not because of the English rule but in spite of it. The English law regime bred antagonism between government and local communities; "[the sovereignty of the people] was therefore obliged to spread secretly, and to gain ground in the provincial assemblies, and especially in the townships."[13]

This outcome is the essence of articles 1, 2, and 3 of the constitution. Protecting the established power of the state governments and the local communities and maintaining both the existing structure of the institutions and the prevailing direction of power flow. One of the fundamental supports of my thesis is that this structure of institutions was inherited from the first Puritan settlements of New England (figure 5.2). The chapter "The Covenantal society, Structure, Organization, and Power Flow" discusses that this structure has been inherited from Proto-Israel and its origin pre-dates even Proto-Israel and most likely will be found in the beginning of pastoralist nomadism which historians place at the dawn of the agriculture. As far as the more important power flow is concerned, its direction comes from the assembly of each community.

To preserve this structure and its power flow, the constitution stipulates that:

1. The Senate composed of two Senators from each State (article 1). The number of Representatives in the House is according to the size of the population in each state (article 1). Equal representation of the states in the Senate intended to protect the states and their existing local governments from reversal of the power flow direction. For example, in chapter "The Supremacy of the Law," the discussion after endnote 14 shows how an unchecked House could lead to a sovereignty of the central legislature or a power flow from central to local governments; however, not the central government but the local practices and local laws have protected the rights of individuals in communities since the Mayflower landed in Plymouth.
2. The President shall be elected by the Electoral College; the number of electors the number of representatives in the House + two (the number of senators); the states decide the process of electing the electors (article 2). This provision intended to protect local customs and authority in the electoral procedure.
3. "The judicial Power of the United States shall be vested in one supreme Court, and in such inferior Courts as the Congress may from time to time ordain and establish." Judges of the Supreme Court are nominated by the President in consultation with the Senate (article 2 sec 2). Since judges serve for life, their election requires the approval of the Senators who are accountable to the people for periodic re-elections every six years. Each state has the same share in the senate thus balancing local against central power.

The purpose of this brush up of articles 1–3 of the constitution is not to teach the reader what he already knows, but it is to illustrate that the core principles of the constitution protect the people's sovereignty, equality, and freedom that have been established on ground since the signing of the Mayflower Compact.

The chapters "Evolution tree" and "Evolution, Customs, and Law" explain how the covenant of the Pilgrims evolved by direct cultural transmission from their first-known ancestor: the covenant of Proto-Israel.

Therefore, neither the Charter of Liberties of Henry I (1100) nor the Magna Charta (1215) qualifies as precursor of a constitutional concept. The liberties promised by these statutes were practiced neither before nor after the said statutes were decreed, signed, and sealed. Similarly, the Provisions of Oxford (1258) were annulled by the Dictum of Kenilworth (1264).

On the other hand, the concept of Covenant of Proto-Israel does answer the criteria. To substantiate this statement, I need to start with the semi-nomadic pastoralist past of Proto-Israel. I admit the nomadic beginning of Proto-Israel is controversial. One reads claims that the settlers were not pastoralist nomads[14] but Canaanite peasants or "lower classes oppressed by the Egyptian crown . . . welded together in the cult of Yahweh."[15] I examined various theories of the origins of Proto-Israel using mathematical tools and concluded that the pastoralist origin makes more sense than its rival hypotheses.[16] In a demographic analysis, I found inconsistencies in published figures related to the size of the Israelite population along the centuries.[17] The conflicts may be reconciled if one accounts for the existence of an invisible population in the eleventh-century BCE. Invisible population is characteristic for nomads because they rarely tend to leave traces to be unearthed by later archaeologists.

Numerous volumes shed light on many meanings of "cult of Yahweh." For the purpose of this thesis, I will borrow Max Weber's take on it: "In this manner Yahweh became not only the God of the confederacy but also the contractual partner of its law established by berith, above all the socio-legal orders."[18] A confederacy of nomads is not unusual in the early Old World:

> Still, another evident alternative to the state seems to be represented by the supercomplex chiefdoms created by some nomads of Eurasia—the number of the structural levels within such chiefdoms appear to be equal, or even to exceed those within the average state, but they have an entirely different type of political organization and political leadership; such type of political entities do not appear to have been ever created by the agriculturists.[19]

I mentioned earlier Weber's connection between the military confederacy and the covenant (*berith*) which adequately is termed law. After all, the principal test of law is "legitimate physical enforceability."[20] The covenant was not only enforceable but also enforced. Chapter "The Covenant of Israel: Customary Law or Law" examines zoo-archaeological evidence with statistical tools and proves that Proto-Israel had no king; however, it possessed enforcement capabilities.

Pastoralist nomads settled and kept their customs. However, settled existence adds a new dimension to their sociopolitical needs. Land and stored surplus implied protection from predators both from outside and inside. Peace and justice made monarchy tolerable.[21] The pastoralists who settled on the Central Hill of the Land of Israel tried an alternative. They formed a confederacy to protect the peace and agreed to a covenant to enforce justice. This combination survives only if every member not only obeys the covenanted customs but also makes sure that his neighbor obeys them as well.

Customary law evolves into law as it becomes enforced.[22] The covenantal arrangement came into being by an evolutionary mutation that consisted of mutual enforcement of previously existing customs.

Covenants existed in Israel's ancient world.[23] However, in Proto-Israel, the covenant transferred the pastoralist past into a new socioeconomic reality. A confederation of tribes consisting of men and women free-willingly covenanting to maintain not only a military alliance but also old customs and traditions of freedom and equality under law. We know that not only from the book of judges claiming that "there was no king in Israel."[24] We also know that from the archaeological evidence: "No monumental or 'elite' structures of any kind have been found in any of these Iron I villages, only clusters of courtyard houses, up to a half dozen or so."[25]

Equality under law was not a trivial concept as it sounds nowadays: "If a man has destroyed the eye of a member of the aristocracy, they shall destroy his eye . . . If he has destroyed the eye of a commoner . . . he shall pay one mina of silver."[26]

In the reality of the ancient justice administration headed by kings and priests, the Hammurabi formula seemed unavoidable. As a pastoralist workaround, the Hebrew Bible prescribes *"an eye for an eye."*[27] The punishment for destroying the eye of a notable is the same as for destroying the eye of a commoner. No doubt, the literal interpretation sounds cruel and it has been condemned as unforgiving[28]; however, it unequivocally expresses what equality before the law stands for.

To achieve that, they attributed sovereignty not to a mortal prince but to the Lord. There is good reason to believe that the preamble of this covenant started with "I am the Lord." This pre-state arrangement was "the retention of 'ancient' liberties"[12] as McIlwain would asses it. It was not yet a constitutional state but no doubt it was a precursor of it: the covenantal society.

> Equality under the general rules of law and conduct, however, is the only kind of equality conductive to liberty, and the only equality which we can secure without destroying liberty.[29]

Did the pastoralists know this rule? Reasonably, they didn't. The sociopolitical model of Proto-Israel is fragile and yet it survived. It survived only when a set of coincidental requirements (see chapter "Inventing a Covenantal Society is Impossible") were satisfied.

Naturally, the first conflict of covenantal Proto-Israel meet was the establishment of monarchy. Scholars detected evidence that the covenantal spirit did not vanish in spite of its conflict with centralist elitist pressure applied by Royal Court and Temple:

1. The archaeological evidence, that is, the size and shape of dwellings, food processing installations, storage facilities, traces of public works revealed a contrast between urban and rural settlements[30]:
   a. In the rural settlements, the pre-monarchic organization was maintained.
   b. The findings point at cooperation equality and no social stratification.
   c. In the rural settlements, elders maintained their position and judicial authority.
2. Biblical scholars detected two opposite priestly attitudes: the earlier Priestly Torah (PT) and the later Holiness School, (HS).
   a. PT does not forbid labor on Sabbath while HS does.[31]
   b. PT does not decree the Sabbath to be a holy convocation while HS does.[32]
   c. "The earlier school—PT—has a purer Priestly cultic conception . . . while . . . the Holiness School displays a priestly-popular orientation."[33]

The forbidden labor and holy convocation are significant because the holy convocation served as town meeting and the forbidden labor assured participation of all. HS started editing during the First Temple.[34] This analysis concludes that at the beginning of the monarchy, the priests wanted to centralize rituals to the Temple and at the same time they attempted to discontinue covenantal Sabbath meetings. The later priestly addition of HS sanctioned the Sabbath convocations and forbade work as the custom demanded. Rabbinical texts are ambiguous regarding monarchy as Christian Hebraists testify:

1. Milton on one hand entreats rabbinical texts explaining that God became angry with the Israelites when they requested a king in 1 Samuel 8.[35]
2. Reverend William Smith of Philadelphia argues that other rabbis interpret that Deuteronomy 17 declares monarchy "an affirmative commandment."[36]

The rabbinical writings are equivocal about the monarchy. This is consistent with the archaeological evidence showing that during the monarchy, in rural areas the covenantal system stubbornly struggled against extinction. The covenantal-elitist conflict resurfaced during the Second Temple between the priestly Sadducees and populist Pharisees. The destruction of the Temple virtually ended elitist practices in Jewish life.

The analogy of the resistance to absolute monarchy in ancient Israel with the debate about protecting the people's sovereignty, equality, and freedom in the American Constitution is striking. In both cases, the attempt to cancel acquired rights was rejected; abolishing such rights is not wise because it involves forced coercion of the governed. Neither Proto-Israel nor its successors secured their liberties enacting laws copied from a book. Their success proves that they adopted the covenantal way of life of their parent organization, accustoming the liberties, the obligations, and incorporating them in their own statutes (see chapter "Evolution tree"). From Proto-Israel to Pilgrims, the essential concepts of liberty and equality and their practical preservation have been replicated up to what was destined to become the United States. "[T]he early settler bequeathed to their descendants those customs, manners, and opinions which contribute most to the success of a republican form of government."[37]

The Puritans brought the covenantal concept to the New World. This concept encompassed "the only kind of equality conductive to liberty"[38] acknowledged by Hayek. Hayek was awarded a Nobel Prize for "pioneering work in the . . . penetrating analysis of the interdependence of economic, social and institutional phenomena." In my view, Hayek's remarkable understanding of the American experience is one of many examples what Hayek's penetrating analysis stands for.

The covenant and not the Magna Charta point at "the destiny of America embodied in the first Puritan who landed on those shores, just as the human race was represented by the first man."[39]

The political concessions of Roman emperors and English kings did not herald the American constitution; however, the covenant of Proto-Israel did.

NOTES

1. Philip A. Klein, *Beyond Dissent: Essays in Institutional Economics* (Armonk, NY: M.E. Sharpe, 1994), 22. Elsewhere one also finds that "Peace and justice are the two things that make the crown says Braxton" Charles Howard McIlwain, *Constitutionalism: Ancient and Modern* (Clark, NJ: Lawbook Exchange, 2005), 84.

2. An explanation of the terms *sustainability* (equilibrium) and *resilience* (stability) is found in Joseph Livni, "Investigation of collapse of complex socio-political systems using classical stability theory," *Physica A: Statistical Mechanics and its Applications* 524 (2019): 553–562. The paper shows that pre-industrial states grow in complexity because they need to deal with more variables protection of the law being only one of them. This growth of complexity reduces the resilience and at a point causes collapse. The terms are also explained in Joseph A. Tainter, *The Collapse of Complex Societies* (Cambridge: Cambridge University Press, 1990).

3. Richard Ira Frank, "Ammianus on Roman taxation," *The American Journal of Philology* 93, no. 1 (1972): 76.

4. Harold Dexter Hazeltine, "The influence of Magna Carta on American constitutional development," *Columbia Law Review* 17, no. 1 (1917): 1–33.

5. Alvin Rabushka, *Taxation in Colonial America* (Princeton: Princeton University Press, 2015), xviii.

6. The Editors of Encyclopaedia Britannica, "Habeas corpus," in *Encyclopaedia Britannica* (Chicago: Encyclopaedia Britannica, inc., 2019).

7. Ibid.

8. McIlwain, *Constitutionalism*, 9.

9. Ibid., 13.

10. Emilio Comba, *History of the Waldenses of Italy: From Their Origin to the Reformation*, trans. Teofilo Comba (London: Truslove & Shirley, 1889), 9. Here I deliberately quote Comba out of context; he referred to a *tradition* not a *written concession*; to my defense I argue that Comba's inspiring characterization of "not practiced, but not unforgotten" is proper for the Magna Carta yet not credible for a tradition.

11. Alexis de Tocqueville, *Democracy in America*, Kindle ed., vol. 1 (Chicago: The University of Chicago Press, 2000), 33.

12. Ibid.

13. Ibid.

14. Norman Gottwald, *Tribes of Yahweh: A Sociology of the Religion of Liberated Israel, 1250-1050 BCE* (Sheffield: Bloomsbury Publishing, 1999), 437.

15. Ibid., 455.

16. Joseph Livni, "Testing competing archaeological theories of Israel's origins using computation techniques," *Archeologia e Calcolatori* 28, no. 1 (2017): 108–128.

17. Joseph Livni, "Investigation of population growth of ancient Israel," *Ugarit Forschungen*, no. 46 (2015): 214–234.

18. Max Weber, *Ancient Judaism* (New York & London: Free Press, 2010), 131.

19. Dmitri M. Bondarenko, Leonid E. Grinin, and Andrey V. Korotayev, "Alternatives of social evolution," *The Early State, Its Alternatives and Analogues* (2004): 12.

20. Sally Falk Moore, *Law as Process: An Anthropological Approach* (Hamburg: Lit Verlag, 2000), 18.

21. "Peace and justice are the two things that make the crown says Braxton" McIlwain, *Constitutionalism*, 84.

22. Moore, *Law as Process*, 18.

23. For example, the Hittite covenant in George E. Mendenhall, *Law and Covenant in Israel and the Ancient Near East* (Pittsburgh: Biblical Colloquium, 1955), 29

24. Judges 21:25.

25. William .G. Dever, *What Did the Biblical Writers Know and When Did They Know It?: What Archeology Can Tell Us About the Reality of Ancient Israel*, Kindle ed. (Grand Rapids, Michigan: Eerdmans Publishing Company, 2002), Kindle Locations 1342–43.

26. Code of Hammurabi.

27. [Leviticus 20:20].

28. See of course Matthew 5:38,39 in Sermon on the Mount; also Talmud Bavli Bava Kamma 84a–b interprets paying compensations to the victim; the paragraph discusses "equal justice".

29. Fridrich A. Hayek, *The Constitution of Liberty* (University of Chicago Press, 1978), 85.

30. Avraham Faust, "The Rural Community in Ancient Israel During Iron Age II," *Bulletin of the American Schools of Oriental Research* 317 (2000): 32

31. Israel Knohl, "The priestly Torah versus the Holiness School: Sabbath and the festivals," *Hebrew Union College Annual* (1987): 76.

32. Ibid., 77.

33. Ibid., 102.

34. *The Sanctuary of Silence: The Priestly Torah and the Holiness School* (Winona Lake, IN: Eisenbrauns, 2007), 220.

35. Eric Nelson, "'Talmudical Commonwealthsmen'and the rise of republican exclusivism, " *The Historical Journal* 50, no. 4 (2007): 784.

36. Ibid., 798.

37. Alexis de Tocqueville, *Democracy in America*, trans. Henry Reeve, Kindle Edition ed., vol. 1 (Project Gutenberg, 2006), 233.

38. Hayek, *The Constitution of Liberty*.

39. Tocqueville, *Democracy in America*, 1, 233.

Chapter 3

The Covenant of Israel
Customary Law or Law

This chapter substantiates that the Covenant of Proto-Israel was enforced, hence it was law. Anyone who accepts the biblical text as evidence will find this chapter not necessary. However, even these readers would find interest in supporting the claim that Israel of the Judges enforced its covenant. I have not found any extra-biblical proof that Proto-Israel enforced its laws. Nevertheless, such a proof is essential to the defense of my thesis (closing of chapter "Nice to meet you . . .") and I believe it is also important to the reader, because after all it is about law and its enforcement in a chiefdom-like pre-state deprived of the institution of chief.

The proof will sift through archaeological evidence and post-process it by statistical analysis. The analysis consists of very elementary and well-established probabilistic methods; therefore, it is not worthy of publication in statistical journals. However, the results of the analysis are of interest to the audience of this book because it makes a difference between intuition and proven knowledge regarding the information that Israel obeyed its covenant during the period of the Judges.

The raw archaeological evidence reveals several customs that are indicative of lawful behavior. Reasonably, chiefdoms had customs; however, that proves neither laws nor law enforcement. The chapter will explain that of all customs, only one can be used to prove the existence of law enforcement, namely prohibition of pork consumption.

The Highland settlements represent not only a geographic designation but also a distinct socioeconomic sociographic pattern:

[they were a] non-urban sedentary society, living in small communities of farmers and herders, without a central political authority, though probably with central cultic centers like the one at Shiloh. The archaeological evidence appears to indicate that this was an egalitarian society that was striving for subsistence in the harsh environmental conditions of the forested mountains and semiarid regions of Israel.[1]

Scholars concluded that the Highland (i.e., Proto-Israel) was egalitarian from analyzing archaeological material such as burial sites,[2] lack of Temples,[3] absence of decorated and imported pottery,[4] and the typically Israelite four-room house.[5]

All these cultural traits are customs that functioned as leveling mechanism maintaining a "politically correct" posturing of equality. For example, a household showing off decorated pottery would raise indignation of the neighbors rather than their respect. Therefore, these cultural traits indicate ideological solidarity rather than law enforcement.

The only custom that provides no leveling mechanism is pork-avoidance. Table 3.1 compiles raw data of the percentage of pig remains in various sites some on the *Highland* and some in the *Lowland* of the Land of Israel of Iron Age I.

The column "Highland" of table 3.1 lists widely accepted continuous Highland sites. However, one notes the following exceptions:

Table 3.1 Raw Data of Pork Consumption in Non-Philistine Sites of the Land of Israel of Iron Age; Highland stands for Proto-Israel and Lowland stands for Canaan

Lowland			Highland		
Location	%Pig	Reference	Location	%Pig	Reference
Tel Kinrot	1.13%	6	Dan	0.00%	7
Tel Yoqneam	1.56%	8	Mount Ebal	0.00%	9
Dor	1.62%	10	Izbet-Sarta III	0.40%	11
Megiddo	7.80%	12	Shiloh	0.08%	13
Tel-Rehov	0.84%	14	Ai	0.00%	15
Beth-Shemesh	0.13%	16	Hirbet Qeyafa	0.00%	17
Tel Qiri	1.40%	18	Hirbet Raddana	0.00%	19
Tel Michal	0.70%	20	Tel Masos III	0.00%	21
Wawiyat	4%	22	Tell-es-Seba	0.00%	23

1. Dan belongs to the Highland in spite of geographic discontinuity[24] because its material culture follows the pattern of the Proto-Israelite settlements.[25]
2. Tel Masos and Tel-es-Seba belong to the Highland settlements in view of evidence of expansion of inhabitants of the Judean Hills into the Valley of Beer-Sheba. This evidence is not deducted from pork remains but from other identifiers like the period of the settlement and the four-room house.[26]

The *Highland* column of table 3.1 indicates that Proto-Israelites consumed practically no pork. The data of table 3.1 generated two opposed theories:

1. Some archaeologists concluded that Israel practiced a taboo on pigs already in Iron Age I.[27]
2. Others noted that "pigs do not appear (or appear in small numbers) in Lowland sites that cannot be identified with the Highland population or with highland rule."[28] The same publication[29] postpones Judah's biblical legislation against pork to Iron Age II; the increased pig husbandry in Samaria evidenced by the pig remains of Iron Age II better known as Monarchic Israel indicates that Judah-Samaria rivalry caused the pork prohibition[30]:

One may wonder why the biblical author promoted the obvious—pig avoidance—which was the reality in the highlands in the Iron Age I and in the Judahite lowlands and highlands throughout the Iron Age II.[31]

If both the Highland (Israel) and Lowland (Canaan) avoided pork consumption then the findings of table 3.1 indicate a custom that either Israel copied from Canaan or the other way around. Custom is very often a source of law[32]; however, it is not law. Often customary law is observed as law.[33] Therefore, for the purpose of avoiding ambiguity, I will borrow the term *custom* to designate "a set of practices of social coordination that arise from informal agreements without being imposed by enacted law."[34]

This definition is consistent with the notion that custom can be source of law and it is observed as law where there is no applicable law.[35] Even a King "neither wishes nor dares to go against customs" when custom is old and just[36] and as a consequence rulers frequently decreed law from custom.

Monarchic Israel was no exception. Archaeology scholars observed that the biblical text "may be distilled from long oral traditions."[37] Biblical researchers also noted that a great part of the Hebrew Bible converted existing popular practice into law.[38] This clarification also answers the previous

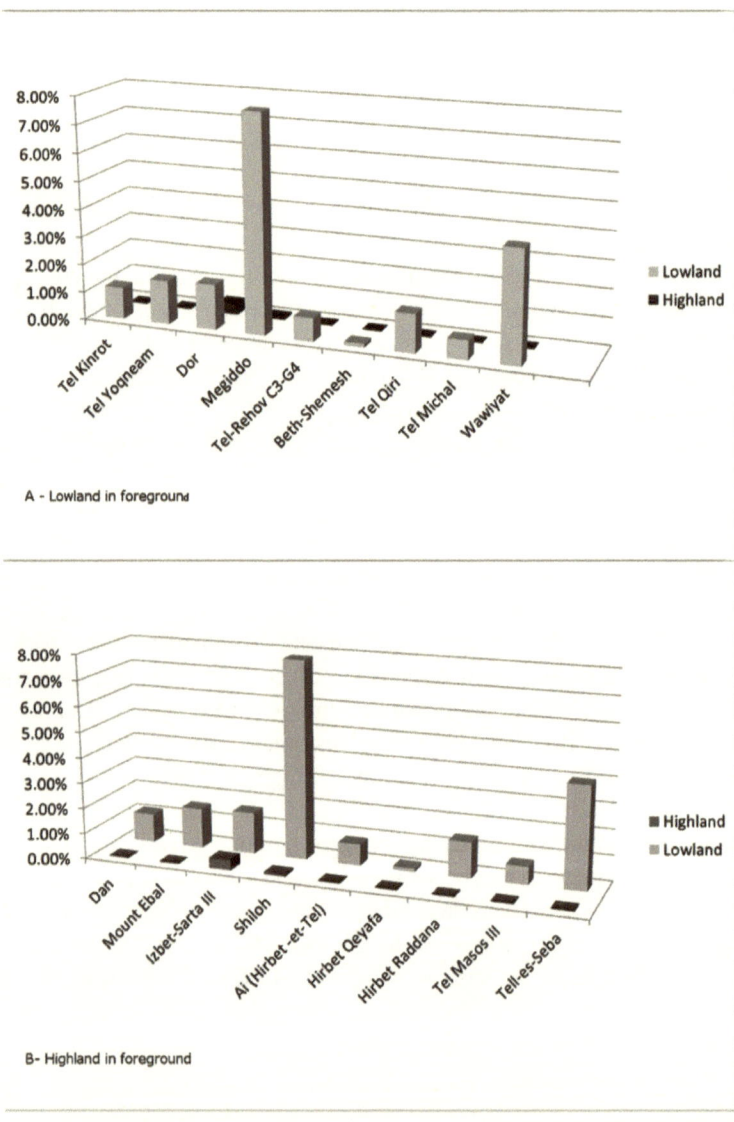

Figure 3.1 **Graphical Representation of the Data of Table 1; A-column "Lowland" in foreground, B-column "Highland" in background.** Created by the author.

question of Sapir-Hen et al. namely "why the biblical author promoted the obvious?"

All of the above, however, doesn't answer the question whether pork prohibition was custom or law during the period of the Judges. The archaeological research reveals a massive interest in the reason for pork avoidance. Many scholars associate the reason for the Proto-Israelite pork ban with resistance to Philistines[39]; others dispute the theory of anti-Philistine sentiments.[40] As mentioned earlier, the pork taboo is also associated with a later Judah-Israel rivalry during the monarchic period. As far as why Israelites and Canaanites refrained from consuming pork is concerned, the raw archaeological data (table 3.1) is mute. Nevertheless, the figures of table 3.1 may be interrogated whether the two columns designate one or two distinct populations. Figure 3.1 graphically replicates the information of table 3.1. The graphical representation intuitively indicates that the Lowland data describe a distinct population as far as pork avoidance is concerned. Nevertheless, the question whether we see two distinct customs is decisively answered by dedicated statistical tools such as Analysis of Variance (ANOVA) for two groups.[41] Introducing the two columns of table 3.1 into an ANOVA procedure available in Excel one obtains the output of table 3.2.

Three numerals of the result of table 3.2 answer the question whether the Highland and Lowland column describe the same level of pork avoidance. If the value *F* exceeds *F crit* and the *P-value* is less than .05 then the assumption that the Highland data and Lowland data represent the same population must be rejected.[42] The threshold of .05 for the *p-value* is not arbitrary; it signifies that the probability of error of this decision is less than 5%.[43]

The dissimilarity between the two columns of table 3.1 consists of the variance of pig scarcity. The variance is a measure of how different the nine sites of each column are from the average of each column. For example, the average of two students on three mid-term exams can be equal to 90%. However, one student obtained it by a sequence of 89%, 90%, and 91% and the other by a sequence of 81%, 90%, and 99%. The variance of the first student is significantly lower than that of the second student; in other words, the first student consistently obtains about 90%. Figure 3.1 indicates that both columns of table 3.1 consumed little pork. However, the uniformity of the Highland points at a low *variance* of the Israelite column while the Lowland shows inconsistency of the nine findings, or a high *variance*. A reduced *variance* in random variables is obtained by controlling the process. This is known:

(a) in technology[44]
(b) in nature[45]
(c) in society.[46]

Table 3.2   ANOVA of the Data of the Two Columns of Table 3.1

SUMMARY

Groups	Count	Sum	Average	Variance
Highland	9	0.0048	0.000533	1.76E-06
Lowland	9	0.1918	0.021311	0.000568

ANOVA

Source of Variation	SS	df	MS	F	P-value	F crit
Between Groups	0.001943	1	0.001943	6.814553	0.018934	4.493998
Within Groups	0.004561	16	0.000285			
Total	0.006504	17				

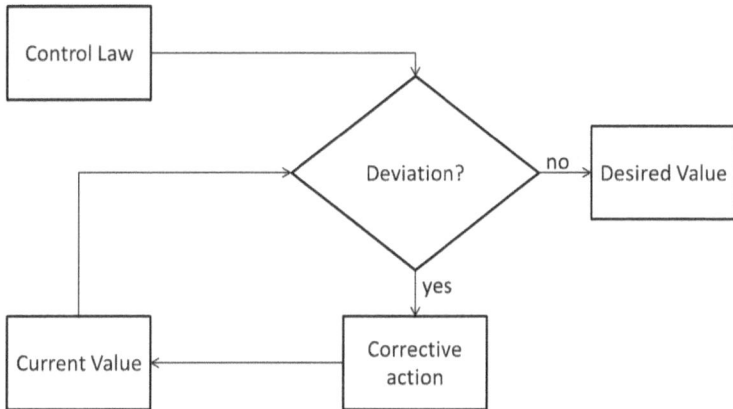

Figure 3.2 Generic Control Loop Model; it represents quality control, temperature control, crime control, and so on. Created by the author.

The essential components of control are *control law*, *detection of deviations*, and *corrective action*. In our case, the extremely low variance of the *Highland* column indicates the existence of *all three components* (figure 3.2). Chapter "Justice Administration in Biblical Israel" details how this system worked. However, for the time being one concludes that the results show that in the Highland not only a custom of pork avoidance "followed more strictly than before,"[47] but also the presence of a social mechanism detecting deviations and subsequent corrective actions. This control system was required to keep transgressions within tight boundaries.

I would suggest distinguishing between the Highland and Lowland pork consumption habits by calling the Lowland situation *pork avoidance* which is a custom while the Highland pig remains point at *pork prohibition*. Prohibition is indicative of a law enforced by a control mechanism (figure 3.2).

The message of the pig remains of Proto-Israel is that Israel of the Judges had a law and it enforced it. According to conventional wisdom, that law was called covenant. I could rest my case at this point; however, archaeologists still have a point that was not addressed. In Beth-Shemesh, the archaeological evidence shows that the town was not part of Proto-Israel, yet the pig remains also indicate zero pork consumption. Was there a prohibition in effect in Canaanite Beth-Shemesh? The answer is that in Beth-Shemesh there is no evidence of law prohibiting pork consumption and the explanation follows.

The insignificant percentage of pig remains of Canaanite Beth-Shemesh (table 3.1 and figure 3.1) prompted the hypothesis that "the pig taboo could have spread eastward into the hill country."[48] The theory that resistance to

Philistines was the main motive of pork avoidance is better aligned with the theory of eastward propagation of this cultural trait. Let us test however an opposing theory according to which the custom of pork avoidance propagated westward from *Highland* to *Lowland*. After all, in nature solutes spread from high to low concentration.[49] This law is also true for the propagation cultural traits.[50]

How did pork avoidance decrees of Highlanders infiltrate into a custom of Beth-Shemesh? Cultural traits spread by migration.[51]

Let us assume a migrant from Kiryat-Yearim, Judah settled in Beth-Shemesh, Canaan. The proportion of pork avoidance increased. However, one migrant hardly makes a significant change.[52] Even if the number of migrants was more than one, let's say a small proportion of the population size of Beth-Shemesh, even then the impact of migration was not significant. The immigrants established new families. Let us assume *random mating*,[53]—that is, the immigrants did not prefer fellow Highlanders for spouses.

Reasonably, the probability of an offspring of mixed marriage to adopt his/her mother's pork consumption habits is the same as the chance to follow the father's example. In some places, this was less than 50% in some places it was more than 50%. One can justify more than 50% applying the research of Boyd and Richerson.[54] According to it one adopts such *marker traits* in early childhood and the chances of its adoption are proportional to a weighted average of the behavior of the people around the child (*socializers*). In other words, if most people around the child were *PA* (pork avoider) then the child had a more than 50% chance of becoming *PA*. In Beth-Shemesh, this requirement was reasonably met because already in the Late Bronze Age, Beth-Shemesh showed low pig consumption.[55]

One can safely assume a low chance that two pork consumer (*PC*) parents will produce a *PA* offspring (e.g., about 1%). It has been calculated that these assumption lead to an initial growth of pork avoidance until the proportion of pig avoiders doesn't grow anymore and settles at a constant value p_e.[56] This value is calculated by an algebraic expression in which one inserts the probabilities discussed earlier (equation 2.2.8 of Cavalli-Sforza).[57]

Figure 3.3 plots the results of the expected proportion of pork avoidance at equilibrium for various probabilities using that equation. If the probability PA offspring is 60% from a mixed *PA-PC* family, 95% from a *PA-PA* family, and 1% from a *PC-PC* family then after a few years the proportion of pig avoidance settles at close to 90%.

The same equation also explains pork consumption habits of the other sites of table 3.1. The pork consumption of Megiddo implies lower probabilities of a *PA-PC* mixed family to become parents of a *PA*. Boyd and Richerson envisage that this probability depends on the demographic composition of

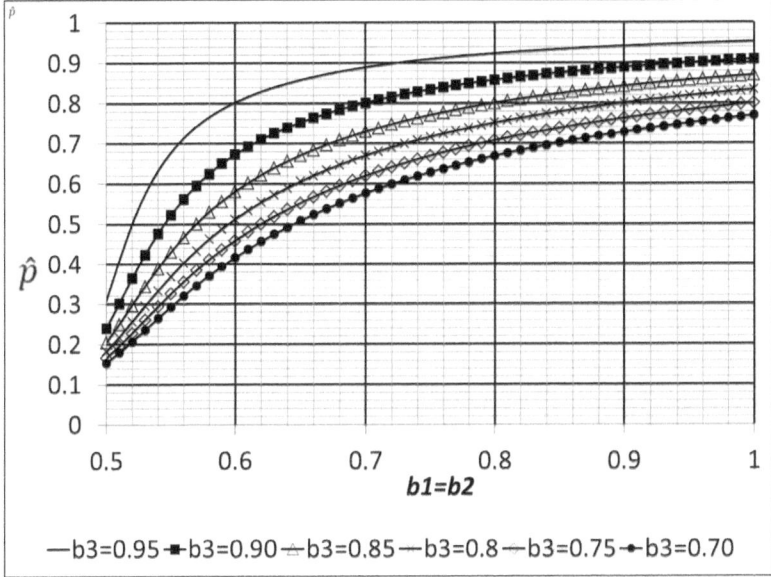

Figure 3.3 Plots Results of p_e using Equation 2.2.8 of Cavalli-Sforza. The chart indicates that an insignificant immigration of PA Highlanders will start a snowball of PA and after a few generations the town will settle at 80% PA for a probability of b_1 = b_2 = 60% of a PA offspring in a PA-PC mixed family (reasonable in Beth-Shemesh); the curve assumes that the probability of a PA offspring of a PC-PC family is b_0 = 1%; the probability of a PA offspring of a PA-PA is variable between 70% and 95% and it is the parameter b_3 of the chart. Created by the author.

the site population.[58] Consequently, children of *PA-PC* families saw a higher proportion of *PA socializers* in Beth-Shemesh than in Megiddo. This predicts higher probabilities of an offspring of a *PA-PC* mixed family to become *PA*. The curves of figure 3.3 were obtained assuming random mating. Another equation[59] proves that the pork avoidance will not grow in the case of purely assortative mating.

In other words, if the population had practiced assortative mating then pork avoidance would not have taken off. Therefore, the pig remains of Beth-Shemesh hint that in Beth-Shemesh of Iron Age I, there was more random than assortative mating.

The analysis of the Beth-Shemesh pig remains shows that pork avoidance in this particular location was a strongly observed custom. It is represented by one datum of table 3.1. One datum yields neither an average nor a variance. Consequently, one cannot conclude from it that it was a result of an enforced prohibition.

The message of the pig remains of Proto-Israel is unequivocal: during the period of the Judges, there was a covenant and the covenant was imposed by an effective enforcement mechanism detecting deviations and applying corrective measures.

NOTES

1. Amihai Mazar, "The Israelite Settlement," in *The Quest for the Historical Israel: Debating Archaeology and the History of Early Israel*, eds. Israel Finkelstein and Amihai Mazar (Atlanta, GA: Society of Biblical Lit., 2007), 92.
2. Burial sites reveal the social status of the buried individual; Proto-Israel left very little burial sites leading to the conclusion that "it is probable that all individuals during this period were buried in simple inhumations Avraham Faust, *Israel's Ethnogenesis: Settlement, Interaction, Expansion and Resistance"* (London: Equinox Pub., 2006), 93.
3. Ibid.
4. A reasonable explanation of this absence is "an ideology of egalitarianism and simplicity" ibid., 59.
5. It has been rationalized that this layout is related to an egalitarian ideology ibid., 79.
6. Lidar Sapir-Hen et al., "Pig husbandry in iron age Israel and Judah," Zeitschrift des Deutschen Palästina-Vereins (1953-) H 1 (2013).
7. Ibid.
8. Ibid.
9. Ibid.
10. Ibid.
11. Brian Hesse, "Pig lovers and pig haters: Patterns of Palestinian pork production," *Journal of Ethnobiology* 10, no. 2 (1990): 195–225.
12. Sapir-Hen et al., "Pig husbandry in iron age Israel and Judah.".
13. Ibid.
14. Ibid.
15. Ibid.
16. Ibid.
17. Ibid.
18. Hesse, "Pig lovers and pig haters."
19. Bunimovitz and Lederman, "A Border Case".
20. Hesse, "Pig lovers and pig haters."
21. Sapir-Hen et al., "Pig husbandry in iron age Israel and Judah."
22. Hesse, "Pig lovers and pig haters."
23. Sapir-Hen et al., "Pig husbandry in iron age Israel and Judah."
24. To avoid circular logic, this work doesn't consider pig-bone scarcity at Dan as a factor identifying Dan with the Highland.
25. Mazar, "The Israelite Settlement," 92.
26. See more in Aharon Kempinski, "Tel Masos," *Expedition* 20, no. 4 (1978).

27. For example, Israel Finkelstein, "Pots and People Revisited: Ethnic Boundaries in the Iron Age I," in *The Archaeology of Israel: Constructing the Past, Interpreting the Present*, ed. N.A. Silberman and D.B. Small (Sheffield, UK: Bloomsbury Publishing, 1997), 230–231; Avraham Faust and Justin Lev-Tov, "The constitution of Philistine identity: Ethnic dynamics in twelfth to tenth century Philistia," *Oxford Journal of Archaeology* 30, no. 1 (2011): 18; Anson F. Rainey, "Whence came the Israelites and their language?," *Israel Exploration Journal* (2007): 48; Lawrence E. Stager, "Forging an Identity, The Emergence of Ancient Israel," in *The Oxford History of the Biblical World* (New York: Oxford University Press, 1998), 150.

28. For example, Lidar Sapir-Hen et al., "Pig husbandry in iron age Israel and Judah," *Zeitschrift des Deutschen Palästina-Vereins (1953-)* H 1 (2013), 10.

29. Ibid.

30. Ibid.

31. Ibid., 13.

32. James Bernard Murphy, *The Philosophy of Customary Law* (Oxford New York: Oxford University Press, 2014), x.

33. "*Inveterata pro lege non immerito custidotur*: Inveterate custom is not undeservedly observed as law" Alexander Mansfield Burrill, *A New Law Dictionary and Glossary* (New York: J. S. Voorhies, 1859), 361.

34. James Bernard Murphy, *Habit and Convention at the Foundation of Custom*, ed. Amanda Perreau-Saussine and James Bernard Murphy (Cambridge: Cambridge University Press, 2007), 54.

35. "consuetudo pro lege servatur" [custom serves as law] where there are no specific laws, the issue should be decided by custom Jon R. Stone, *More Latin for the Illiterati: A Guide to Medical, Legal and Religious Latin* (London and New York: Taylor & Francis, 2003).

36. Charles Howard McIlwain, *Constitutionalism: Ancient and Modern* (Clark, NJ: Lawbook Exchange, 2005), 65.

37. William G. Dever, *What Did the Biblical Writers Know and When Did They Know It?: What Archeology Can Tell Us About the Reality of Ancient Israel*, Kindle ed. (Grand Rapids, MI: Eerdmans Publishing Company, 2002), Kindle location 1197.

38. For example, Israel Knohl, "The priestly Torah versus the Holiness School: Sabbath and the festivals," *Hebrew Union College Annual* (1987): 102.

39. Philip J. King and Lawrence E Stager, *Life in Biblical Israel* (Louisville, KY: Westminster John Knox Press, 2001), 119; Lidar Sapir-Hen, Meirav Meiri, and Israel Finkelstein, "Iron Age pigs: New evidence on their origin and role in forming identity boundaries," *Radiocarbon* 57, no. 2 (2015): 313; Faust and Lev-Tov, "The constitution of Philistine identity," 17; Faust, *Israel's Ethnogenesis*, 35–40; Brian Hesse and Paula Wapnish, "Can pig remains be used for ethnic diagnosis in the ancient Near East?," *Journal for the Study of the Old Testament Supplement Series* (1997): 263; Stager, "Forging an Identity, The Emergence of Ancient Israel," 165; Israel Finkelstein and N.A. Silberman, *The Bible Unearthed: Archaeology's New Vision of Ancient Israel and the Origin of Sacred Texts* (Simon & Shuster, 2002), 120; Avraham Faust, "Pigs in space (and time): Pork consumption and identity negotiations in the

Late Bronze and Iron Ages of ancient Israel," *Near Eastern Archaeology* 81, no. 4 (2018): 276–299.

40. For example, Aren M. Maeir and Louise A. Hitchcock, ""And the Canaanite Was Then in the Land"? A Critical View on the "Canaanite Enclave" in Iron Age I Southern Canaan," in *Alphabets, Texts and Artifacts in the Ancient Near East: Studies Presented to Benjamin Sass*, ed. Israel Finkelstein, Christian Robin, and Thomas Römer (Paris: Van Dieren, 2016); additional reasons for the pork avoidance are listed in Richard A. Lobban, "Pigs and their prohibition," *International Journal of Middle East Studies* 26, no. 1 (1994): 57–75.

41. Timothy C. Urdan, *Statistics in Plain English* (Mahwah, NJ and London: Lawrence Erlbaum Associates, 2005), 101.

42. See a similar example in Clive.R. Ireland, *Experimental Statistics for Agriculture and Horticulture* (Cambridge: CABI, 2010), 107.

43. The same technique is used to distinguish between the effects of two treatments: one with a drug and one with a placebo; if the measured results show that they belong to two distinct populations then the drug effectivity is considered statistically significant Andy Field, Jeremy Miles, and Zoë Field, *Discovering Statistics Using R* (Los Angeles, London: SAGE Publications, 2012), 412, 53.

44. For example, Krishna B. Misra, *Handbook of Performability Engineering* (London: Springer 2008), 209., in manufacturing quality control.

45. For example, Sharon L. Hanks, *Ecology and the Biosphere: Principles and Problems* (Boca Raton, FL: Taylor & Francis, 1996), 59; Vito Volterra, "Variations and fluctuations of the number of individuals in animal species living together," *ICES Journal of Marine Science* 3, no. 1 (1928): 3–51—controlling the size of prey and predator populations.

46. For example, Carla Rossi, "The role of dynamic modelling in drug abuse epidemiology," *Bulletin on Narcotics* LIV, no. 1 and 2 (2002).- controlling drug addiction.

47. Faust, "Pigs in space (and time)."

48. Shlomo Bunimovitz and Zvi Lederman, "A Border Case: Beth-Shemesh and the rise of ancient Israel," *Israel in Transition: From the Late Bronze II to Iron IIa (c. 1250–850 bce)* 1 (2008): 48

49. For example, Roger Thies et al., *Physiology* (New York: Springer 1995), 1.

50. Luigi Luca Cavalli-Sforza and Marcus W. Feldman, *Cultural Transmission and Evolution* (Princeton, NJ: Princeton University Press, 1981), 40.

51. Ibid., 40, 68, 158.

52. Just as one swallow doesn't make a summer.

53. Cavalli-Sforza and Feldman, *Cultural Transmission and Evolution*, 79.

54. Robert Boyd and Peter J. Richerson, "The evolution of ethnic markers," *Cultural Anthropology* 2, no. 1 (1987).

55. Table 1 of Sapir-Hen et al., "Pig husbandry in iron age Israel and Judah."

56. Cavalli-Sforza and Feldman, *Cultural Transmission and Evolution*, 79.

57. Ibid.

58. Boyd and Richerson, "The evolution of ethnic markers."

59. Cavalli-Sforza and Feldman, *Cultural Transmission and Evolution*, 97.

Chapter 4

The Covenantal Society
Lex Rex

Sometimes analogies of phenomena of one discipline are useful to discuss another discipline. For example, the analogy between control systems[1] in technology and justice administration is relevant to the thesis of this book. Therefore, models of control in technological applications are useful to study the control of social deviations and vice versa.

Figure 3.2 illustrates the analogy between a typical technical control system and the specific application of control of social deviation. In the eyes of a control specialist, a typical model of justice administration requires setting normative rules which are analogous to control laws of figure 3.2. The two remaining functions namely detecting deviations and applying corrective actions are well-known tasks of justice administration.

Civilized life requires minimizing these deviations; consequently, citizens are interested in proper functioning of the model. Typically, the citizens of early civilizations accorded full legitimacy to a *sovereign* overseeing all three components of justice administration: "the king acts as the embodiment of law."[2] The process started before even states were formed. For example, in the Gouroun chiefdom "the political authority is based in the *kwara* a protective spirit with a material fetish that only the *pio* can access."[3] Naturally, as the *kwara* became the politically correct wisdom, equality exited the Gouroun stage.

The complexity of the society increased; military, priestly, and administrative circles grew around the chief. Most often a pyramidal structure emerged with the ruler on top. The fetish developed into godly sovereigns as, for example, in Mesopotamia,[4] Pharaonic Egypt,[5] Hellenistic Greece,[6] and Maya.[7]

Catholic and Protestant Christian monarchs ruled claiming sacred authority.[8] Not surprisingly, so did the Russian czars.[9]

Athens was democratic; however, it featured social classes and inequality.[10] In other societies, the ancient Roman Republic, the Venetian Republic, the Florentine Republic prominent statesmen presided over an aristocratic council such as the Roman Senate, Great Council of Venice, and the Signoria of Florence. These examples had a ruling class with authority to legislate privileges for themselves. Elazar calls this political arrangement *organic model*.[11] This work shall stick with the Aristotelian name *oligarchy*. Chapter "The Difference between Political Concessions and Constitutional Liberties" offers a discussion of how oligarchies reconcile the need for support of the many with legislation maintaining privileges for the few.

As mentioned earlier, the Roman Republic was such an oligarchy. Even after it transitioned to hierarchy during the Empire, the old oligarchic values were kept in the Western Roman Empire. For example:

> The clarissimate was hereditary for men born after their father's promotion, the sons and grandsons sons of an original nonsenatorial office holder would be absorbed into the ranks of the senatorial class.[12]

There have been atypical societies opting for equality. Most frequently they maintained ancestral customary rules; however, deviations were not treated by determining culpability and punishment. For example, the Longhouse Justice System solved grievance by mediation between perpetrator and victim, through an arbitration "and resolution of the harm caused by an offence rather than determining guilt and punishing an offender."[13]

Proto-Israel arrived at another way of maintaining equality before law. Reasonably, before the pastoralist nomads put down roots in the Land of Israel they, as many other nomads, behaved according to customary rules. Somehow they figured out that if the customary rules were legislated by an omnipotent, immortal, and unseen Sovereign then all mortals would be practically equal. Since equality rules out kings, one deduces that they possessed no dedicated police force either. Reasonably, if they had a police force and no king then the chief of the police force would have performed the role of king. As a consequence, the detection of lawlessness and execution of punishment was the responsibility of an assembly of all individuals. Chapter "Justice Administration in Biblical Israel" details the mode of operation of such a society with no dedicated police.

Chapter "Inventing a Covenantal Society is Impossible" rules out the feasibility of inventing such a society from scratch. However, a culture with customary traditions including a periodic assembly and habits of watching each other could evolve into a society that obeys the *covenant* of an immortal Sovereign.[14]

If later they form an alliance with similar groups and if after all the alliance agrees to a king then what will distinguish them from the rest of the world? The answer is that in such a monarchy, the king is limited by the covenant. Such a society fits Rutherford's concise title: Lex Rex (figure 4.1).

The descendants of Proto-Israel adopted such a formula beginning with monarchic Israel. In other words, in the kingdoms of Judah and Israel central authority managed essential state functions (e.g., national defense and public works). Nevertheless, local *elders* and local assemblies kept their prestige and authority.[15]

Since then covenantal societies adopted a capability to coexist autonomously within hierarchies and oligarchies. The coexistence was expressed by mutual agreement; sometimes these agreements were written contracts. Naturally, the particular formula *Lex Rex* was never subject to agreement. The hierarchic monarch understood that order infers the Rex Lex model (figure 4.1); he viewed the covenantal communities as a black box module bound to him by an agreement that he signed or inherited. The monarch did not care about the internal power flow of the covenantal black box as long as the egalitarian ethos didn't spread to populations that were bound to him by natural hierarchic obedient ties. The following examples illustrate how the contradiction in power flow didn't disturb cohabitation.

A pointed analysis of the biblical text related to the social structure of the Jewish Babylonian exile concludes that

> the presence of elders suggests that the Jewish settlements governed themselves similarly to the pre-exilic urban existence, even to the point of maintaining gatherings for decisions and the hearing of prophets.[16]

Reasonably, Jewish self-government was tolerated by Babylonian victors. The biblical text conveys that the communities made an effort to "seek the peace of the city [of Babylon]."[17]

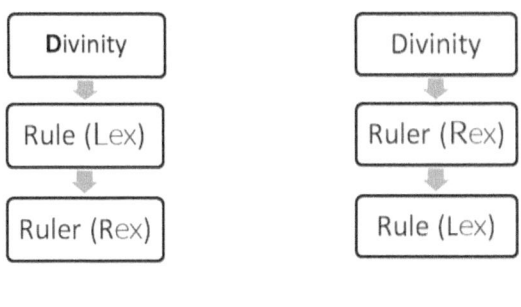

Lex Rex Model *Rex-Lex Model*

Figure 4.1 Flow of Authority. Created by the author.

Cyrus defeated Babylon and not only allowed Jewish self-government but also authorized the Jews to return to their ancestral land and rebuild the Temple.[18] As a consequence, in Jewish tradition, Cyrus won the title of Messiah.[19] After the fall of the Second Temple, the Jewish Diaspora continued the tradition of self-governing communities in numerous kingdoms of the world.[20] In Spain of the twelfth-century Judah Halevi taught that "[t]he law is the true king of Israel."[21] As in the first exile the covenant was the supreme law; however, the communities also obeyed the rule of the land.[22]

The autonomous reality of Jewish communities proves that their self-rule was agreed by local princes. In many cases, like in Aragon of thirteenth and fourteenth century, "the royal power considers the Jewish minority as an ally for economic and political reasons."[23] Some monarchs were more tolerant than others. The tradition remembers the remarkable ones. Seventh-century Count of Nîmes is remembered for taking the Jews under his protection.[24] According to Jewish rabbinical tradition, Charlemagne invited Rabbi Kalonymos of Lucca to establish a school in Mayence.[25] "Ottoman Sultan Mohammed II was endowed with the title of 'Divine Messiah of Israel'."[26] The *millet* system of the Ottoman Empire fostered the autonomy of Jewish communities particularly because "among the Jews, ethnicity, religion and community coincided."[27] Eliahu Morpurgo praised the Hapsburg Emperor Josef II for his Edict of Tolerance and Y. L. Gordon, honored Tsar Alexander II in a poem.[28]

Early Christians also managed their internal disputes discouraging litigations "in front of unbelievers."[29] Nevertheless, in exceptional cases, Christian communities did "seek intervention" of the pagan Empire's justice administration.[30]

In the county of Bigorre, in the valleys of the Pyrenees, the Counts were obliged to take an oath of faithfulness to ancient customs, practices, and institutions and occasionally were reminded to keep their oath.[31] The lingo of the document compellingly reminds of an old covenant:

> In nomine Domini, amen! As it is clear, certain, widely known and obvious that in the country of Azun, there are forums and customs formerly conceded by his lordship and by his heirs (*autreyats ab antich per lo senhor et per los autres qui sun venguts après*) that these forums and customs have been confirmed by the people of Azun (*per lo pople Azun*), kept and preserved by all and that they regulate the administration of justice according to the practice in the court of Azun.[32]

The communities named *vesiau* or *besiau*[33] are "an assembly of individuals entitled to privileges and to the exercise of their community's lawful jurisdiction."[34] Similar to the Carpathians[35] and opposed to the Alps, there is no rupture from the hierarchical Church either. The synergetic relationship between local assemblies and the feudal rulers arrived in the Pyrenees at unprecedented level to the extent that the assemblies were often consulted "as a power" in the country's major affairs.[36] As prescribed by the customs of the land, these affairs included major judicial debates as in the case of a severe dispute between the Crown prosecutor and two members of the community (*vesiau* a.k.a. *besiau*).[37] At the same time, there is evidence of malfunction in this symbiotic duality resulting in friction because of dual jurisdiction.[38] "The religious inclinations of the land founded on a traditional faith were kept in spite of contact with outsiders."[39] The Lex Rex model was assured by a system of laws called *Fors*, "a disparate collection of legal regulations in various states of evolution through customary practice, detailed decisions and judgments, decrees by the Viscount and the Court of Béarn and charters issued, all covering a long period, 11th-14th centuries."[40] Surprisingly, Bidot-Germa uses the term *pactist organization*[41] for the Pyrenean incarnation of the Lex Rex model. For some reason, the priests in these valleys were recruited among locals explaining how unnecessary conflicts with Rome were avoided.[42] Therefore, they remained Catholics. The written understanding with the local lords (*the Fors*) contained privileges and obligations to the members of the *vesiau* (neighbors). The fact that they were not a sectarian community raised the question who is a neighbor? The tradition allowed an incomer to apply for the status of neighbor if he lived in the community at least for one year and one day. The neighbors accepted or rejected such applications. Another difficulty was to define where the limits of the neighborhood were. The neighborhoods were within walls. Researchers found that the walls served *"defining a social space free from the encroachments of aristocratic power, a space that was produced by the collective mustering of a watch, a police just as much as a military force."*[43] Thus, the wall circumscribed an area around the neighborhood defining a "very particular jurisdiction"[44] and within which the inhabitants owned or could apply for a status comparable to citizenship.

A similar pattern took place in Romania. Dimitrie Cantemir, a Moldavian historian who happened to also be *boier* (noble landlord) and even ruler of the principality of Moldova (1693, 1710–1711), testifies to an agreed special status of Romanian autonomous regions. Cantemir mentions three *republics* living according to local customs and autonomous justice administration; they paid taxes set by agreements between the ruler and the *republic*.[45] The description and the names of the *republics* leave no doubt that these are the networks of communities called *obște* studied by Stahl and Bădescu.[46]

The tenth–eleventh centuries saw the appearance of many European village communities acting "as corporate bodies."[47] The *vesiau* or *vicinal system*[48] and its *voisins* (neighbors) are listed among them.[49] However, for the purpose of this thesis, the *obște* and the *vesiau* differed from the others because the *neighbors* of the vicinal system managed not only the husbandry of their community but also their own justice administration. The neighbor as mentioned earlier had the privilege to exercise his/her community's lawful jurisdiction. "The fundamental principle of justice in Bigorre is that the count never judges."[50] Similarly, the Romanian aristocrat "owned the houses on his the estate, the tithe of the seeds, the pond, the forest, the mill and the pub, but never the right to judge and punish."[51] Opposed to that, the inhabitants of all the other medieval communities were under the jurisdiction of feudal landlords and their courts of justice.[52]

Perhaps, the Pilgrims better exemplify the equivocal attitude toward the king. William Brewster and Edward Winslow overtly criticized the king in 1618 revealing their covenantal *Lex Rex* persuasion.[53] However, the source of authority of the Mayflower Compact (1620) is not only the "glory of God," but also "honor of our King."

Needless to say, the puritans of England and Scottish Presbyterians had similar patterns of coexistence of the covenantal community and the king. The community's persuasion regarding the supremacy of their covenants conflicted with the king's pretention to divine right of ruler; nevertheless, the conflict was mostly avoided.[54]

The Lex Rex model is well and alive. In 1776, Founding Father Thomas Paine paved the way to irreversibly engrave it in the hearts and minds of modern democracies: "For as in absolute governments the King is Law, so in free countries the Law is King."[55]

The important role of the Founding Fathers notwithstanding, the Mayflower Compact, the Fundamental Orders of Connecticut, the Rhode Island Charter of 1663, the first state constitutions, the Declaration of Independence, and the Articles of Confederation served as rough draft constitution in form and in content. More importantly, the indispensability of such a covenantal statute started not in Philadelphia as some scholars prefer, but in Plymouth, regardless whether the framers were conscientiously aware of it:

> In their understandable obsession with the Philadelphia Convention (1787) and the subsequent ratification of the second American Constitution (1789) political scientist have often overlooked this aspect of American constitutional development and have accordingly underestimated the practical realities of the colonial experience in contributing an indigenous aspect to American federalism.[56]

This work stipulates that the evolution of the American constitution consists of a lineage of many descendants of an archetype. The Christian covenantal societies described in this chapter cohabited with stratified host states. The peculiar details of these egalitarian networks living semi-autonomously within principalities and kingdoms have been noticed and recorded thanks to a few perceptive scholars such as Dimitrie Cantemir, Gustave Bascle de Lagrèze, Frédéric Le Pay, Hélène Couderc-Barraud, her advisor Benoît Cursente, Dimitrie Gusti, Henri Stahl, and Ilie Bădescu. This chapter complements their contribution observing that all these Christian covenantal societies inherited common strings of organizational DNA from their most recent common ancestor: apostolic Christianity.

NOTES

1. Control systems keep desired variables such as temperature, pressure, speed, and quality within desired limits; examples are the temperature control in the office, quality control in production, and cruise control in a car.

2. Aristotle, Benjamin Jowett, and Henry William Carless Davis, *Politics*, Kindle edition ed. (Mineola, NY: Dover Publications, 2000), Kindle location 206.

3. Stephen A. Dueppen, *Reinventing Equality: The Archaeology of Kirikongo, Burkina Faso* (Ann Arbor: University of Michigan, 2008), 284.

4. Irene Winter, "Touched by the gods: Visual evidence for the divine status of rulers in the ancient Near East" (paper presented at the Oriental Institute Seminars 4, Chicago, 2008).

5. HF Lutz, "Kingship in Babylonia, Assyria, and Egypt," *American Anthropologist* 26, no. 4 (1924): 448.

6. Angelos Chaniotis, "The divinity of Hellenistic rulers," *A Companion to the Hellenistic World* (2003).

7. Stephen Houston and David Stuart, "Of gods, glyphs and kings: Divinity and rulership among the Classic Maya," *Antiquity* 70, no. 268 (1996): 289–312.

8. Melvyn Bragg et al., "The Divine Right of Kings," in *In Our Time*, ed. Melvyn Bragg (London: BBC Radio 4, 2007).

9. "The Emperor of All the Russias possesses Supreme Sovereign Power." Obedience to His authority, not only out of fear, but in good conscience, is ordained by God Himself. (Fundamental State Laws—Chapter one, http://www.imperialhouse.ru/en/dynastyhistory/dinzak1/441.html).

10. Nigel Guy Wilson, *Encyclopedia of Ancient Greece* (New York: Routledge, 2006), 511.

11. Daniel J. Elazar, *The Covenant Tradition in Politics*, vol. 1 (Transaction Publishers, 1995), Introduction.

12. Michele Renee Salzman, *The Making of a Christian Aristocracy: Social and Religious Change in the Western Roman Empire*, Kindle Edition ed. (Cambridge, MA: Harvard University Press, 2002), Kindle Location 367–68.

13. Elizabeth Jane Dickson-Gilmore, "Resurrecting the peace: Separate justice and the invention of legal tradition in the Kahnawake Mohawk Nation" (London School of Economics and Political Science (United Kingdom), 1996), 169.

14. Joseph Livni, "The cultural evolution of an institution: The Sabbath," *Cliodynamics* 8 (2017).

15. The evidence regarding elders consist of analysis of the archaeological findings Avraham Faust, "The rural community in ancient Israel during Iron Age I," *Bulletin of the American Schools of Oriental Research* 317 (2000): 17–39.

16. Daniel L. Smith-Christopher and Katherine Southwood, *The Religion of the Landless: The Social Context of the Babylonian Exile* (Eugene, OR: Wipf and Stock, 2015), 97.

17. (Jeremiah 29:7)

18. Elias Bickerman, "The Edict of Cyrus In Ezra," in *Studies in Jewish and Christian History, Volume 1*, ed. Amram Troper (Leiden Boston: Brill, 2007), 88.

19. (Isaiah 45:1).

20. Instead of reference to any particular work, I invite the reader to visit to the Museum of the Jewish People: https://www.bh.org.il/; from one kingdom to the other from one century to the next the same organization of 3.3; titles may change however structure, institutions, and power flow doesn't.

21. Rémi Brague, *The Law of God: The Philosophical History of an Idea* (Chicago: University of Chicago Press, 2007).

22. *dina de-malkhuta dina* (*Aramaic*—the statute of the kingdom is law) is a rabbinic rule commanding to obey the law of the host state.

23. Claire Soussen Max, ""Iudei Nostri," pouvoir royal, communautés juives et société chrétienne dans les territoires de la Couronne d''Aragon au XIIIe et première moitié du XIVe siècle" (St Quentin en Yvelines, 2005).

24. Elizabeth C. Hirschman and Donald N. Yates, *When Scotland Was Jewish: DNA Evidence, Archeology, Analysis of Migrations, and Public and Family Records Show Twelfth Century Semitic Roots* (Jefferson, NC and London: McFarland, Incorporated, Publishers, 2015), 84.

25. Chaim Schloss, *2000 Years of Jewish History: From the Destruction of the Second Bais Hamikdash Until the Twentieth Century* (Jerusalem: Feldheim Publishers, 2002), 88; Yaakov Bar Yosef, *Netzari Emunah Rashi* (Raleigh, NC: Lulu .com), 22. this is an understatement; two independent population genetic studies concluded that all Ashkenazi Jews descend from 300 people living around Mainz XE "Mainz" (Mayence), Speyer, Worms, Trier and Metz Shai Carmi et al., "Sequencing an Ashkenazi reference panel supports population-targeted personal genomics and illuminates Jewish and European origins," *Nature Communications* 5 (2014): 1–9; Haim Livni and Joseph Livni, "Interpretation of findings of founder population genetics studies applying lineage extinction theory," *Physica A: Statistical Mechanics and its Applications* 462 (2016): 641–653; consequently that school of Kalonymos and the congregations it served were the beginning of many communities from which descend about ¾ of the current Jewish population.

26. Yaacov Shavit and Barbara Harshav, "Cyrus King of Persia and the return to Zion: A case of neglected memory," *History and Memory* 2, no. 1 (1990): 50; William Thomas Gidney, *The Jews and their Evangelization* (London: Student Volunteer Missionary Union, 1899).

27. Gary J. Jacobsohn, *Apple of Gold: Constitutionalism in Israel and the United States* (Princeton, NJ: Princeton University Press, 2017), 26.

28. Shavit and Harshav, "Cyrus King of Persia and the return to Zion."

29. 1 Corinthians 6:6

30. note 25 of Lesson VI; Edwin Hatch, *The Organization of the Early Christian Churches* (London: Rivingtons, 1882), 152.

31. Gustave Bascle de Lagrèze, *Histoire du droit dans les Pyrénées - comté de Bigorre* (Paris, Imprimerie Impériale, 1867), 34.

32. my translation of ibid., 60.

33. Hélène Couderc-Barraud, *La violence, l'"ordre et la paix: résoudre les conflits en Gascogne du XIe au début du XIIIe siècle* (Toulouse: Presses universitaires du Mirail, 2008), 176; de Lagrèze, *Histoire du droit dans les Pyrénées*, 42, 126, 472, 74; Unknown, *Revue de Gascogne: Bulletin Bimestrial de la Société Historique de Gascogne* (AUCH: Imprimerie et Litographie Foix, 1901), 86. The name should be vesiau, in modern French it became voisinage; the local prononciation sounded more like besiau; they belong to people about which it was said *Beati populi quibus bibere est bibere*—Lucky people for whom to drink is to live - ibid., 83.

34. My translation of Couderc-Barraud, *La violence, l'"ordre et la paix*, 41

35. For a very thorough description of the social dynamics of the dual system see Ilie Bădescu, "Communal society and the "dual system" equality and inequality in the Carpathian Valleys," *Revista română de sociologie* anul XXX, no. 3–4 (2019): 1–43.

36. de Lagrèze, *Histoire du droit dans les Pyrénées*, 60.

37. Ibid., 126.

38. Ibid., 129.

39. My translation of Frédéric Le Play, *L'"organisation de la famille selon le vrai modèle signalé par l'"histoire de toutes les races et de tous les temps* (Mame, 1895).

40. Footnote 4 of Dominique Bidot-Germa, "The specific features of medieval notaries north and south of the Pyrenees: The example of Béarn," *Imago temporis: medium Aevum* (2011): 176

41. In French, the term *covenant* is *pacte*, a relative of the English *compact*; therefore, the link to Israel's Covenant and to the Mayflower Compact is plausible.

42. Frédéric Le Pay, *La Réforme sociale en France déduite de l'observation comparée des peuples européens*, 3 vols. (Paris: Tours, 1874), 127.

43. Mireille Mousnier, Roland Viader, and Guilhem Ferrand, "Le rempart de la coutume," *Archéologie du Midi médiéval* 25, no. 1 (2007): 123–133.

44. My translation of ibid.

45. Dimitrie Cantemir, *Descrierea Moldovei* (Bucharest: Grup Editorial Litera, 2016), 79.

46. For example, Henri H. Stahl, *Traditional Romanian Village Communities* (Cambridge: Cambridge University Press, 1980); Ilie Bădescu, Ozana Cucu-Oancea, and Gheorghe Șișește, *Dicționar de sociologie rurală* (Bucharest: Editura Mica Valahie, 2005).

47. Jerome Blum, "The European village as community: Origins and functions," *Agricultural History* 45, no. 3 (1971): 161.

48. Augustine Robert Whiteway, "The Pyrenean neighbour; or, the vicinal system in the western Pyrenees," *Archaeological Journal* 58, no. 1 (1901): 182–198.

49. see footnote 28 in Blum, "The European village as community," 162.

50. My translation of Couderc-Barraud, *La violence, l'"ordre et la paix*, 29.

51. My translation of Nicolae Iorga, "Scrisori de Boieri Scrisori de Domni," in *Din publicațiile casei școalelor*, ed. Casa școalelor (Vălenii de Munte, Romania: Editura casei școalelor; Datina Românească, 1925).

52. Francis Robin Houssemayne Du Boulay, "Law enforcement in medieval Germany," *History* 63, no. 209 (1978): 386–387; Marc Bloch, *Feudal Society* (London, New York: Routledge, 2014).

53. Nathanel Philbrick, *Mayflower: A Story of Courage, Community, and War*, Kindle Edition ed. (New York: Penguin Publishing Group, 2006), Kindle location 344.

54. Mostly, but always; Lex, Rex was burnt and King Charles I was beheaded on January 30, 1649

55. Tomas Paine and Gordon S. Wood, *Common Sense and Other Writings* (New York: Modern Library, 2003), 31.

56. Michael Burgess, *Comparative Federalism: Theory and Practice* (London and New York: Taylor & Francis, 2006), 52.

Chapter 5

The Covenantal Society, Structure, Organization, and Power Flow

This chapter describes the political structure of all covenantal societies (table 5.2). Following the advice of Romanian sociologist Ilie Bădescu, who thoroughly studied the Romanian communities of this type, I defined the covenantal society as an egalitarian or communalist societal type with a vigorously[1] enforced law.[2] I still believe that the definition is valid. However, it doesn't really help in deciding whether a society is covenantal.

The notion of covenantal model was introduced by Elazar, a political scientist. He distinguished three fundamental political models: hierarchic, oligarchic, and covenantal.[3] He was right to call them models because no society behaves according to one single model. In this work, a covenantal society is a societal type organized according to the pattern and power flow described in this chapter. Table 5.2 lists examples of covenantal societies.

The fundamental political unit in a covenantal society is the *congregation*. I used the term congregation not because of its religious implication but because it is the term used by scholars of Pilgrims.[4] For Pilgrims and Puritans have a major role in defending the thesis of this work: the evolution from "*I am the Lord . . .*" to "*We the people . . .*" The biblical source hints at the term *town* as the earliest designation of what later meant congregation.[5] Archaeological scholarship concurs; the evidence indicates subsistence production at the town level, and "corporate unit"[6] configuration. The *town* (רֵיע) sounds similar to the English word *ear*) or *mishpachah* are the biblical names for the fundamental societal group greater than the extended family. The word *mishpachah* (*family* in Modern Hebrew) implies actual kinship while the word *town* refers to geographical locality; it is not unusual that members of covenantal communities claimed common ancestry to enhance their cohesion.[7] Figure 5.1 describes the sociographic structure of premonarchic Israel also known as *Israel of the Period of Judges* by biblical scholars or *Proto-Israel* and *Israel of Iron Age I* by archaeologists.

57

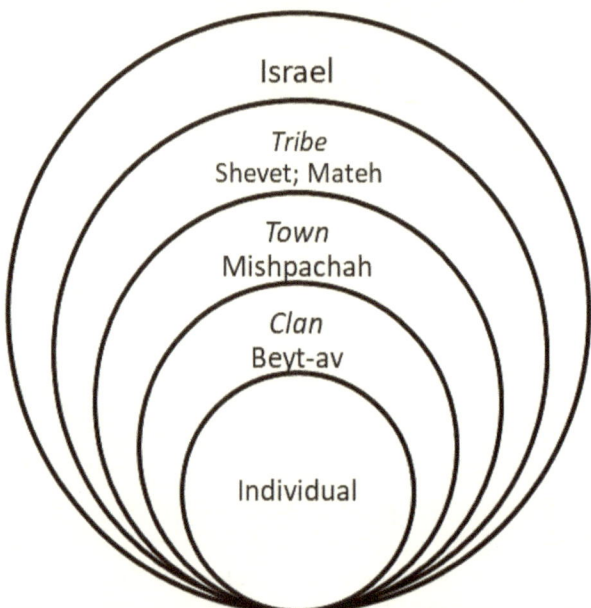

Figure 5.1 Ancient Israel Sociographic Model. Very common in nomadic societies[8]; anthropologists call it "horizontal lineage organization"[9]; Wilson[10] endorses the historicity of this structure taking into account the ideological bias and the unreliable dating of the biblical source[11]; Created by the author.

The *clan* was probably a true biological kinship and it vanished along the evolutionary process. Its function was replaced by the nuclear family for kinsfolk's matters and by the town for public concerns as it happened in the history of many cultures.[12]

The remaining organization of three levels has been inherited by all incarnations of the covenantal organisms. For example, figure 5.2 shows the modern Presbyterian version[13]; Jewish communities follow the same pattern of Kehilah (*congregation*); Va'ad (regional confederation) and Medinah (national confederation).[14]. Romanian sociologists of the Romanian covenantal model[15] describe the same three-level networks in Romania: *village* (sat), *inter-village confederation* (ocol), and *land* (țara).[16]

No doubt many cultures show similar administrative organigrams. For example, the administrative divisions of modern France follow a similar pattern: national, department, administrative region, and the commune. The pattern is covenantal, only if the power flows from the local to the national level and not the other way as in modern France.[17] In every covenantal organization, "the only biblically sanctioned organizational unit was the individual congregation."[18] The second concept of my thesis is that the Pilgrims did not pick up this principle from a biblical decree. The biblical text can be taken to mean the opposite. For example, a distinguished law professor interprets the

Book of Judges teaching "that confederacy is not viable as a form of national government over the long term"[19] and rightly so.

The covenantal system is opposed to hierarchy. Justice administration is the responsibility of the entire community. Therefore, each community enforces the covenant internally. Figure 5.2 illustrates that the communities are tightly connected with neighboring communities and loosely bound to a network of such tightly knit communities. The common feature of the justice administration of the whole organization is not a shared ruler decreeing laws, commanding the police, and heading the courts. Neighboring and far communities are united by a common covenant and a shared respect for its commandments.

Perhaps, one can trace the organigram of figure 5.3 reading the Bible. However, biblical insight cannot generate a power flow from the assembly to the office holder in a culture where leaders command and people obey.[20] Only a society that has preserved its *"reverse dominance hierarchy"*[21] from time immemorial will subordinate office holders to the assembly. In their investigation of the Cairo Geniza manuscripts, Goitein and Lassner observe:

> There was a feeling that next to God as revealed in his Law, it was the people who wielded the highest authority.[22]

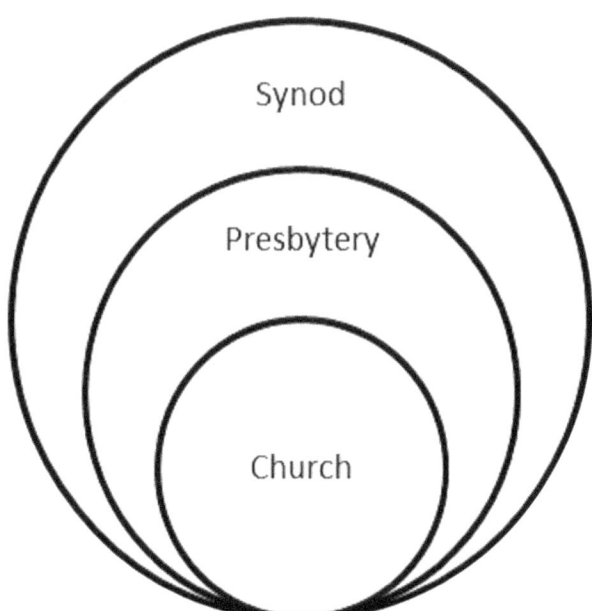

Figure 5.2 The Presbyterian Organization. It preserved the model of figure 5.1 not only in shape but also in its power flow from the fundamental autonomous body (the church = congregation) to the regional network of congregations (presbytery) and the network of presbyteries (synod.). Created by the author.

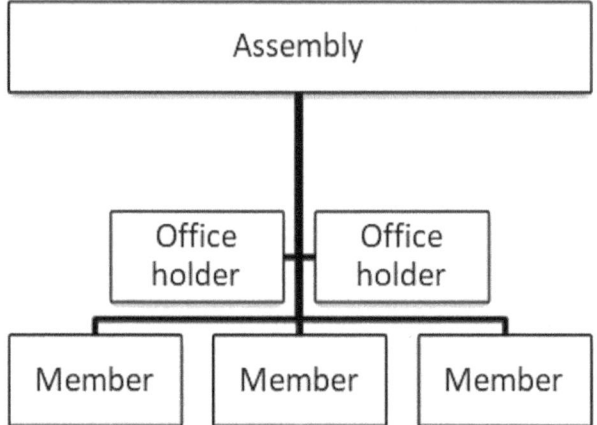

Figure 5.3 Covenantal Assembly Oversees Administrators (Office Holders). Office holders have no ranks; their authority is revocable and not inheritable. Created by the author.

This power of the people in covenantal societies is not a brain-washing slogan like the "people's democracy" of Communist Eastern Europe.[23] Traces of "reverse dominance" are found in modern states:

> The New Englander is attached to his township, not only because he was born in it, but because it constitutes a social body of which he is a member, and whose government claims and deserves the exercise of his sagacity.[24]

An American sees nothing peculiar about his empowerment. It is no coincidence that Tocqueville, a European sage and not an American found it remarkable. For Tocqueville understood that a similar empowering of municipal bodies in Europe may endanger the unity and peace.[25] The direction of power flow is not a result of the constitution, but rather the constitution reflects the actual power flow. Tocqueville links the feasibility of this power structure to education that "was complete when the people first set foot upon the soil."[26] No doubt, he meant Pilgrims and Puritans.

Pilgrims imported the principle of community control over office holders to America. One minister entered a confrontation with his flock "by claiming that he and his elders, or church officers, could dictate policy to their congregation."[27] Even the military were subordinated to the congregation. They fired a strong competent officer if he had the tendency to rule.[28]

The Puritans were not a democracy; however, the power belonged to the congregation and office holders had the choice to conform or leave:

> Cotton's illustrious father allowed that he was free to leave his Boston parish if the Lord called him elsewhere, if his pay proved insufficient, or if he suffered "persecution" by his congregation.[29]

Table 5.1 Comparison of Covenantal Features between Early Christians and Waldensians

Feature		Early Christians (reference)	Waldensians (reference)
1 No ranks		See list[30]	See list[31]
2 Assembly government		See list[32]	Comba[33]
3 Office holders	-not inheritable	See list[34]	Léger[35]
4	-elected or venerated	See list[36]	See list[37]
	-controlled by assembly	See list[38]	See list[39]
5 Supremacy of a covenant/decree of council/discipline		See list[40]	See list[41]
6 Community cohesion		Trebilco[42]	Alexis[43]
7 Public repentance		Alling & Schlafer[44]	Léger[45]
8 Prohibition of work on Sundays		Llewelyn & Nobbs[46]	Léger[47]
9 Minding other people's business		See list[48]	Léger[49]
10 Federation of neighboring communities		Elazar[50]	See list[51]
11 Larger federation of the regional federations		Heffele & Clark[52]	See list[53]

Puritans were Calvinists and they learned this practice from Calvin who himself was dismissed from his ministry in 1537[54] by local authorities. Calvin the minister couldn't learn such a practice from his Bible Studies. However, Calvin the lawyer had the opportunity to observe the covenantal practice of the Waldensians. "Calvin himself was led to his great work by Olivetan, a Waldensian."[55] The conventional wisdom teaches that Pierre Valdès founded the heretic Waldensian sect in Lyon at about 1170[56] or in 1173.[57] According to the opposed hypothesis, the Waldensians are descendants of Christian communities "forming religious congregations, free of the yoke of Rome"[58] these communities have kept one generation after the other the organization of apostolic congregations. This hypothesis claims that after Constantin, "the Roman patricians gradually invaded the bishopric . . . and laid the groundwork of the Catholic hierarchy."[59] From this point of view, the Church of Rome is the deviant, while the Waldensians continued the legacy of the apostles.[60]

Table 5.1 examines the structural and organizational features of the Waldensians. The table deliberately ignores divergent theological doctrines[61] like salvation,[62] prayers for the dead,[63] and Purgatory.[64] Could "ignorant and illiterate people"[65] reconstruct so faithfully the apostolic Christian organization? The proper functioning of this organization wins the praise of one of the most ardent proponents of the hypothesis that Pierre Valdès is the founder of the Waldensians: Pierrette Paravy. She realizes that this organization of the Waldensians proved to be the vital tool for the "communities to take charge of their own destiny."[66] Another advocate of the theory that Valdès is the founder of the Waldensians, Gabriel Audisio rightly notices that Paravy's analysis not only sheds light on the "maturity of their organization" but also Paravy's "use of plural ('communities') points at the decentralized and multinuclear aspect of the Waldensian dissidence."[67] Paravy observes that "communities and families constituted the center of gravity of the Waldensian practice"[68] leaving no doubt that this decentralized multinuclear set of communities is the network of figure 5.2 which is the organization scheme shared by all covenantal formations of table 5.2. Intriguingly, Paravy notes that studying this organization "one detects one of the most vigorous roots of the discipline of protestant Churches."[69] This observation strongly supports my thesis confirming that Calvinism adopted Waldensian principles of organization. Nevertheless, Paravy refuses to admit that the same logic leads to the conclusion that the Waldensian network organization also has deep roots and that they are established in apostolic Christianity. The good news is that this refusal left a worthy objective for this book, namely to prove that Early Christianity is the ancestor of the Waldensian practice. Therefore, let me return to this point.

Chapter 7 "Inventing a Covenantal Society is Impossible" demonstrates that even if Valdès were a farsighted innovator he couldn't guess so many things right. The same chapter also shows how a biophysical model predicts failure unless continuity of practice from previous generations is assured. This doesn't mean that the Waldensian sect existed in apostolic

Table 5.2 Covenantal Societies and Their Institutions

When/Where	Office Holders		Body of officers	Congregation
	Native language	English		
Roman Palestine	Tuvey h'yr[70] Parnasim[72]	Good men of the town Shepherds[73]	Sinedria[71]	Synagogue
Israel Iron Age	Zekenim[74]	Elders[75]	City gate[76]	Town
Early Christians	Presbiteroi[77] Episkopoi	Elders Overseers, Bishops[79]	Ordo[78]	Ecclesia
Waldensians	Elder[80] Barbes[81]			églises communauté
Romania	Oameni buni și bătrâni	Good and old men		
Pyrenees	Boni homines[82]	Good men		Vesiau[83]
Swiss Calvinists	Anciens[84]	Elder	Consistory	City
Puritans	Pastors[85] Teachers[86] Deacons[87]		Presbytery[88] Senate of elders[89] Consistory[90]	

times. The term *Waldensian* was coined by the Inquisition[91] which was created precisely to fight the Waldensians[92] in the last quarter of the twelfth century; consequently, no earlier document could mention the term *Waldensian*. Table 5.1 only indicates that the organizational practice of Early Christians has been left unchanged by these "*montagnards* rather than heretics."[93] More importantly for the discussion of this chapter, the Waldensians preserved the same flow of authority, that is, from community to office holders. For example, in Metz of about 1200, the community terminated the ministry of preachers "whose lives did not conform to the apostolic model."[94]

In other mountain societies (table 5.2), a similar covenantal network existed within the feudal system. In Gascony and Romania, the feudal contract was not between a lord and his vassal but between the landlord and the community.[95] In Bigorre, Gascony, the assembly administered community matters notwithstanding the feudal system.[96] Despite the Catholic faith clergy is local, grown in the spirit of local traditions and accepting the judgment of local leadership.[97] I reiterate that the Bible is not an instruction manual for erecting covenantal societies. Maybe some scholars did discover hints to community empowerment in the Bible:

> 1 Jn [i.e. 1 John] suggests that the community did not conceive of authority in any individuals who functioned at times as leaders, but rather in the group as a whole.[98]

Nevertheless, the Roman Catholic doctrine legitimizes the church hierarchy or the concept of *apostolic succession*[99] by reference to the Bible as well. The doctrine of *apostolic succession* is postulated on the premise that Christ authorized Peter to build his church.[100]

Early Christians adopted the spirit of Jewish organizations.[101] As the Jews of their time, Early Christians also saw "the locus of authority as the community,"[102] I submit that most Early Christian ecclesiae[103] adopted the Jewish pattern of authority with modifications that varied in place and time.

This Jewish model contemporary with apostolic Christianity is well investigated. "In Roman Palestine the administration of justice and of local affairs was in the hands of elders of towns, who formed a 'synedrion' or local court."[104] Seven elders were called in Hebrew *tuvey ha-ir* (pronounced too-vey ha-ear), which translates to *good men of the town*: three elders were called archon and one of the archons was the mayor.[105] More importantly, the power flew from the general assembly to the elders:

These institutions derived their mandate from the local town assembly which served as the legal organ of the men of the town (anshey ha-'yr). The town assembly was an active participant in municipal affairs and voted not only on matters of great importance, but occasionally on more mundane affairs.[106]

So far we established that the Waldensians inherited their organization from apostolic Christianity and that Calvinism adopted Waldensian patterns. The link between Calvinism and Pilgrims and Puritans is not disputed. How much did the framers of the constitution know about past covenantal organizations? The thesis presented here doesn't rest on the proposition that the framers of the constitution were familiar with the particular histories and sociopolitical organizations of the societies of table 5.2. Even the study of the social structure and of the inverted hierarchy that characterized the first Puritan settlements of New England was not a pre-requisite for the framers. The model of Plymouth has been preserved in New England with quasi-autonomous towns managing their justice administration and with quasi-sovereign rights the colonies possessed in matters of justice.

> The early seventeenth century colonies were permitted to form and operate their own governments provided that the laws passed by them in their local legislatures did not conflict with the laws made by The English Parliament.[107]

This is the reality the framers knew; the fact that they knew about the ideology of seventeenth-century Plymouth, Salem, and Andover is irrelevant. The reason for that is not news:

> Though ignored by most historians of the Constitution, there is a tradition of federalism that pervaded the entire colonial era, developed in distinctive way apart from European thinkers, and formed the background of experience upon which the leaders of the Revolution and new nation relied as they shaped the institutions of what became the United States of America.[108]

This work provides no proof that Madison, or Hamilton, or Jefferson or any other framer knew the history of seventeenth-century America. The colonies however adopted the political framework of Plymouth, Salem, and other towns.[109] Instead of functioning as centrally administered consolidated political entities,[110] they operated as "a collection of towns and counties":[111]

> In their understandable obsession with the Philadelphia Convention (1787) and the subsequent ratification of the second American Constitution (1789) political scientist have often overlooked this aspect of American constitutional

development and have accordingly underestimated the practical realities of the colonial experience in contributing an indigenous aspect to American federalism.[112]

It is worthwhile to follow the itinerary of the designation *boni homines* held by some office holders in Roman Palestine, Gascony[113] and Romania (table 5.2). This term is not a biblical term. The proper biblical term is *zekenim* (elder) which was translated into presbyter (old in Greek), *bătrân* (old in Romanian) or elder. The origin of the term *boni homines* is in republican Rome. The term *boni viri* is mentioned by Cicero to designate good citizens, for example, *boni viri* often served on juries.[114] Thus, the term started in the Roman republic; reasonably, it entered the lingo of Roman Palestine as a paraphrase of the older term zekenim (*elder*). Most Early Christians used the Greek biblical term *presbyter* which became *prete*, *prêtre*, or *priest* in Italian, French, and English, respectively; however, some preferred the *boni homines* alternative.[115] The Romanians combined both.

I mentioned this itinerary because the concept of covenant followed a similar path and that is consistent with the thesis of this work.

NOTES

1. The term *vigorous* is borrowed from another sociologist of the same school Iancu Filipescu, "Din contribuțiile profesorului Henri H. Stahl la dezvoltarea sociologiei istoriei," [Contributions of Professor Henti Stahl to the development of history's sociology.] *Sociologie Romanească* IV, no. 3 (2006): 27–33.

2. Joseph Livni, "Christianity and the Romanian communities named obște," *Romanian Journal of Sociological Studies*, 1 (2016): 61–71.

3. For example, Daniel J. Elazar, *Covenant & Constitutionalism: The Great Frontier and the Matrix of Federal Democracy* (New Brunswick, NJ: Transaction Publishers, 1997).

4. Nathanel Philbrick, *Mayflower: A Story of Courage, Community, and War*, Kindle Edition ed. (New York: Penguin Publishing Group, 2006), Kindle Loc. 257.

5. [Deut. 21:19, 21:20, 25:8, NIV].

6. William G. Dever, *What Did the Biblical Writers Know and When Did They Know It?: What Archeology Can Tell Us About the Reality of Ancient Israel*, Kindle ed. (Grand Rapids, MI: Eerdmans Publishing Company, 2002), Kindle location 1343; Avraham Faust, "The rural community in ancient Israel during Iron Age I," *Bulletin of the American Schools of Oriental Research* 317 (2000): 17–39.

7. Robert R. Wilson, "Israel's judicial system in the preexilic period," *The Jewish Quarterly Review* 74, no. 2 (1983): 233; Ilie Bădescu, Ozana Cucu-Oancea, and Gheorghe Șișește, *Dicționar de sociologie rurală* (Editura Mica Valahie, 2005), 539.

8. Sergey Gavrilets, David G. Anderson, and Peter Turchin, "Cycling in the complexity of early societies," *Issue: Cliodynamics* 1, no. 1 (2010): 168.

9. Wilson, "Israel's Judicial System in the Preexilic Period," 234–35.

10. Ibid.

11. E.g. Numbers 1:20; 1 Samuel 10:21.

12. See, for example, Maurice Godelier, "Systèmes de parenté, formes de famille Quelques problèmes contemporains qui se posent en Europe occidentale et en Euro-Amérique," *La revue lacanienne*, no. 3 (2010): 37–48.

13. I had a conference lunch-break discussion with a scholar who happened to be Presbyterian. It took place about the time I started to follow the covenantal structure; I laid out to my Presbyterian peer that the Presbyterian organization reminds of Israel of the Judges; the peer asked "how so?"; I started with the Presbyterian *congregation—presbytery—synod* and continued with the analogous structure: *town*; the colleague interrupted me saying the rest: *tribe* and *Israel*. Then I turned to discuss the power flow: the assembly is Sovereign. The Presbyterian scholar vigorously objected: "No, the assembly is government the Sovereign is . . ." pointing upwards; I learned a lesson. Some call it the assembly of the people and some call it the Lord. No wonder years later I entitled my book: From *I am the Lord* to *We the people*.

14. Daniel J. Elazar and Stewart Cohen, *The Jewish Polity: Jewish Political Organization from Biblical Times to the Present* (Bloomington, IN: Indiana University Press, 1985), 186, 87.

15. In the Carpathian valleys have existed covenantal communities called *obște* Livni, "Christianity and the Romanian communities named obște."

16. Filipescu, "Din contribuțiile profesorului Henri H. Stahl"; Ilie Bădescu and Darie Cristea, *Elemente pentru un Dicționar de sociologie rurala: Concepte—Teme—Teorii* (Bucharest: Editura Mica Valahie, 2011), 80; Bădescu, Cucu-Oancea, and Șișește, *Dicționar de sociologie rurală*, 616.

17. In France, an attempt giving the people the source of local authority failed; in 1800, the central authority returned to nominate prefects Adolphe Chéruel, *Dictionnaire historique des institutions, moeurs et coutumes de la France, 1* (Paris: Libr. de L. Hachette, 1865), 270.

18. Philbrick, *Mayflower*, Kindle Loc. 257.

19. Geoffrey P. Miller, "Monarchy in the Hebrew Bible," *NYU School of Law, Public Law Research Paper*, no. 10–76 (2010).

20. See note 12 above.

21. Christopher Boehm et al., "Egalitarian behavior and reverse dominance hierarchy [and comments and reply]," *Current anthropology* 34, no. 3 (1993): 227–254.

22. Shlomo Dov Goitein and Jacob Lassner, *A Mediterranean Society: An Abridgment in One Volume* (Berkley: University of California Press., 1999), 93; the Cairo Geniza describes Egyptian Jewish communities of the tenth to thirteenth centuries.

23. The use of expressions like "constitution" and "people's democracy" was not only allowed but also obligatory in that world that practiced neither constitution nor democracy, for example, Richard Felix Staar, *Communist Regimes in Eastern Europe* (Stanford: Hoover Press, 1971), 63.

24. Alexis de Tocqueville, *Democracy in America*, trans. Henry Reeve, Kindle Edition ed., vol. 1 (Project Gutenberg, 2006), 42; Kindle Location 1210.

25. Ibid.; Kindle Location 1210; see also note 12 of this chapter.

26. Ibid., 42.

27. Philbrick, *Mayflower*, Kindle Loc. 317.

28. Ibid., Kindle loc. 923.

29. Stacy Schiff, *The Witches: Suspicion, Betrayal and Histeria in 1692 Salem*, Kindle Edition ed. (New York Boston London: Little Brown, 2015), 33.

30. Karl Olav Sandnes, "Equality Within Patriarchal Structures," in *Constructing Early Christian Families: Family as Social Reality and Metaphor*, ed. Halvor Moxnes (London: Taylor & Francis, 2002), 150, 53, 62.

31. Monastier, *Histoire de l'Eglise vaudoise—Tome I*, 140; Audisio, "The Waldensian Dissent, 21.

32. John Laurence Mosheim and Archibald Maclaine, *An Ecclesiastical History Antient and Modern from the Birth of Christ to the Beginning of the Eighteenth Century, in Which the Rise, Progress, and Variations of Church Power are Considered in Their Connexion with the State of Learning and Philosophy and the Political History of Europe During that Period* (London: Strahan and Preston, 1811), 99; Hatch, *The Organization of the Early Christian Churches*, 39; Elazar, *Covenant & Commonwealth*, 41, 42.

33. Gilly, *Waldensian Researches*, 383; Emilio Comba, History of the Waldenses of Italy: From Their Origin to the Reformation, trans. Teofilo Comba (London: Truslove & Shirley, 1889), 251.

34. Mosheim and Maclaine, *An Ecclesiastical History Antient and Modern from the Birth of Christ*, 177; Charles A. Frazee, "The origins of clerical celibacy in the Western church," *Church History* 41, no. 2 (1972): 151.

35. Chap XXXII, Jean Léger, *Histoire generale des eglises evangeliques des Vallees de Piemont ou Vaudoises* (Leiden: Jean le Carpentier, 1669), 199.

36. Mosheim and Maclaine, *An Ecclesiastical History Antient and Modern from the Birth of Christ*, 101; Frazee, "The origins of clerical celibacy in the Western church," 151.

37. Comba, *History of the Waldenses of Italy*, 147; Chap XXXI Léger, *Histoire generale des eglises evangeliques des Vallees de Piemont ou Vaudoises*, 190, 91.

38. Mosheim and Maclaine, *An Ecclesiastical History Antient and Modern from the Birth of Christ*, 99; Frazee, "The origins of clerical celibacy in the Western church," 151; Hatch, *The Organization of the Early Christian Churches*, 119.

39. Chap XXXII, Léger, *Histoire generale des eglises evangeliques des Vallees de Piemont ou Vaudoises*, 199.

40. Hatch, *The Organization of the Early Christian Churches*, 7.

41. Muston Alexis, *L'Israël des Alpes: première histoire complète des Vaudois du Piémont et de leurs colonies*, vol. I (Paris: Libr. de Marc Ducloux, 1851), 11; Jean Rodolphe Peyran and Thomas Sims, *An Historical Defence of the Waldenses Or Vaudois: Inhabitants of the Valleys of Piedmont* (London: C. & J. Rivington, 1826), 130, 31; Chap XXXI, Léger, *Histoire generale des eglises evangeliques des Vallees de Piemont ou Vaudoises*, 190–199; Audisio, *The Waldensian Dissent*, 27.

42. Trebilco, *The Early Christians in Ephesus*, 415.

43. Alexis, *L'Israël des Alpes*, vol. I, 11.

44. Roger Alling and David.J. Schlafer, *Preaching as Pastoral Caring* (Harrisburg, PA: Morehouse Pub., 2005), 130.

45. Léger, *Histoire generale des eglises evangeliques des Vallees de Piemont ou Vaudoises*, 193.

46. Stephen R. Llewelyn and Alana M. Nobbs, "The Earliest Dated Reference to Sunday on Papyri," in *New Documents Illustrating Early Christianity, 9: A Review of the Greek Inscriptions and Papyri Published in 1986-87*, ed. Stephen .R. Llewelyn (Grand Rapids, MI: Eerdmans Publishing Company, 2002), 110.

47. Léger, *Histoire generale des eglises evangeliques des Vallees de Piemont ou Vaudoises*, 96, 209.

48. Eduard Schweizer, *The Good News According to Matthew* (Atlanta: John Knox Press, 1975), 373; Edward Gibbon, *The History of the Decline and Fall of the Roman Empire* (Boston: Little, Brown, 1854), 190; Hatch, *The Organization of the Early Christian Churches*, 119.

49. Léger, *Histoire generale des eglises evangeliques des Vallees de Piemont ou Vaudoises*, 193.

50. Elazar, *Covenant & Commonwealth*, 41.

51. Léger, *Histoire generale des eglises evangeliques des Vallees de Piemont ou Vaudoises*, 183; Paravy, *De la chrétienté romaine à la Réforme en Dauphiné*, 911.

52. C.J. Hefele and W.R. Clark, *A History of the Councils of the Church: From the Original Documents, to the close of the Second Council of Nicaea A.D. 787* (Wipf & Stock Publishers, 2007), 87.

53. Paravy, *De la chrétienté romaine à la Réforme en Dauphiné*, 1, 911; Audisio, *The Waldensian Dissent*, 20.

54. William E. Moller and Gustav Kawerau, *History of the Christian Church ...: A. D. 1517–1648, Reformation and Counter-Reformation*; ed. Dr. G. Kawerau ... trans. JH Freese (New York: S. Sonnenschein & Company, limited, 1900), 180; William C. Innes, *Social Concern in Calvin's Geneva* (Eugene, OR: Pickwick Publications, 1983), 121.

55. Benjamin G. Wilkinson, *Our Authorized Bible Vindicated* (Fort Oglethorpe, GA Teach Services, 2014). Ch. "Waldensian Bibles"; Reinhard Bodenmann, "Les Vaudois et la production du livre évangélique français (1525-1550)," *Revue Littératures| Université McGill* 24, no. 24 (1) (2017): 25–30.

56. Philippe Pouzet, "Les origines lyonnaises de la secte des Vaudois," *Revue d'histoire de l'Église de France* 22, no. 94 (1936): 11; Olivier Legendre and Michel Rubellin, "Valdès: un «exemple» à Clairvaux? Le plus ancien texte sur les débuts du Pauvre de Lyon," *Revue Mabillon* 11 (2000): 189.

57. anonymous chronicler cited by Pouzet, "Les origines lyonnaises de la secte des Vaudois," 8; Henry C Vedder, "Origin and Early Teachings of the Waldenses, according to Roman Catholic Writers of the Thirteenth Century," *The American Journal of Theology* 4, no. 3 (1900): 475; Legendre and Rubellin, "Valdès: un «exemple» à Clairvaux?," 191; Dennis McCallum, "The Waldensian Movement

From Waldo to the Reformation" (American Waldesian Society, History: Founded in the Middle Ages, Waldenses, Global Anabaptist Mennonite Encyclopedia, 2014).

58. (Monastier 1847, 20)

59. (Monastier 1847, 12)

60. (e. g. Gilly 1831, 6)

61. Opposite interpretations of Scripture defend opposite doctrines; the interpretation of Apostolic Christians is unknown.

62. McCallum, "The Waldensian Movement From Waldo to the Reformation."

63. Vedder, "Origin and Early Teachings of the Waldenses," 482; William Stephen Gilly, *Waldensian Researches During a Second Visit to the Vaudois of Piemont* (London: Rivington, 1831), 140.

64. Antoine Monastier, *Histoire de l'Eglise vaudoise—Tome I*, vol. 1 (Geneva: Kessmann, 1847), 14, 19; Pierrette Paravy, *De la chrétienté romaine à la Réforme en Dauphiné. Évêques, fidèles et déviants (vers 1340-vers 1350)*, vol. 1, COLLECTION DE L'ÉCOLE FRANÇAISE DE ROME (Rome: École française de Rome, 1993), 939, 44, 1158; Gabriel Audisio, "Des Pauvres de Lyon aux vaudois réformés," *Revue de l'histoire des religions* (2000): 49, 50; Adam Blair, *History of the Waldenses: With an Introductory Sketch of the History of the Christian Churches in the South of France and North of Italy, Till These Churches Submitted to the Pope, When the Waldenses Continued as Formerly Independent of the Papal See* (Edinborough: Λ. & C. Black, 1832), 161.

65. This is the description of Valdés and his people in the notes of the Inquisitor Bernard Gui. McCallum, "The Waldensian Movement From Waldo to the Reformation."

66. My translation of the original French text in Paravy, *De la chrétienté romaine à la Réforme en Dauphiné*, 1, 1182.

67. Gabriel Audisio, *The Waldensian Dissent: Persecution and Survival c. 1170-c. 1570*, trans. Claire Davison (Cambridge, 1999): 159.

68. My translation of the original French text in Paravy, *De la chrétienté romaine à la Réforme en Dauphiné*, 1, 1026.

69. Ibid., 1182–1183.

70. Safrai, *The Economy of Roman Palestine*.

71. Hatch, *The Organization of the Early Christian Churches*, 39.

72. Safrai, *The Economy of Roman Palestine*, 26.

73. For the translation see Edward H. Plumptre, *The Bible Educator*, ed. E.H. Plumptre, vol. 1 (London Paris New York: Cassell, Petter & Galpin, 1877), 268.

74. António Augusto Tavares, "Quelques termes bibliques relatifs à des institutions anciennes: problèmes de traduction et d'histoire," (1985): 349; Daniel J. Elazar, Covenant and Polity in Biblical Israel (New Brunswick, NJ: Transaction Publishers, 1998): 349.

75. Faust, "The rural community in ancient Israel during Iron Age I."

76. Mayer Sulzberger, *The Polity of the Ancient Hebrews* (Philadelphia: J.H. Greenstone, 1912), 3; Elazar, *Covenant and Polity in Biblical Israel*, 349.

77. Hatch, *The Organization of the Early Christian Churches*, 39.

78. Ibid.

79. Ibid.

80. Pierre Allix, *Some Remarks Upon the Ecclesiastical History of the Ancient Churches of Piedmont* (Clarendon, 1821), 242; Alexis Muston, *L'Israel des Alpes: Première histoire complète des Vaudois du Piémont et de leurs colonies*, vol. II (Paris: Marc Ducloux, 1851), 66.

81. Audisio, *The Waldensian Dissent*, 125; Gilly, *Waldensian Researches*, 140, 228, 35.

82. Couderc-Barraud, *La violence, l'ordre et la paix*, 96; Le Play, *L'organisation de la famille selon le vrai modèle signalé par*, 132, describes their function without the title; de Lagrèze, *Histoire du droit dans les Pyrénées - comté de Bigorre*, 100 translates the title to French *bon homme*

83. Couderc-Barraud, *La violence, l'ordre et la paix*, 173; de Lagrèze, *Histoire du droit dans les Pyrénées - comté de Bigorre*, 55, 56.

84. Isabella M. Watt et al., *Registres du Consistoire de Genève au temps de Calvin. Tome I, 1542–1544* (Geneva: Librairie Droz, 1996), viii.

85. Daniel Neal, Joshua Toulmin, and John Overton Choules, *The History of the Puritans* (New York: Harper & Brothers, 1844), Appendix; xii.

86. Ibid.

87. Ibid.

88. Ibid.

89. Ibid.

90. Ibid.

91. Audisio, *The Waldensian Dissent*, 3.

92. Yves Dossat and Marcelin Defourneaux, "Les dossiers de l'Universalis, L'Inquisition," in *Encyclopedia Universalis* (Boulogne-Billancourt2015), ii.

93. This observation of Michael Mullett, "Reviews: Euan Cameron, The Reformation of the Heretics. The Waldenses of the Alps 1480-1580, Oxford, Clarendon Press, xviii + 291pp; £22.50," *European History Quarterly* 16, no. 2 (1986): 219–221 is exceptionally pointed because other societies preserving similar Early Christion traditions are also *montagnards* living in the Pyrenees based on descriptions of Hélène Couderc-Barraud, *La violence, l'ordre et la paix: résoudre les conflits en Gascogne du XIe au début du XIIIe siècle* (Presses universitaires du Mirail, 2008); Gustave Bascle de Lagrèze, *La féodalité dans les Pyrénées, comté de Bigorre*, mémoire lu à l'Académie des sciences morales et politiques (Paris: A. Durand, 1864). Also in the Carpathians as described in Henri H. Stahl, *Traditional Romanian Village Communities* (Cambridge: Cambridge University Press, 1980); Bădescu, Cucu-Oancea, and Şişeşte, *Dicționar de sociologie rurală*; Livni, "Christianity and The Romanian communities named obşte." Bădescu, Cucu-Oancea, and Şişeşte, *Dicționar de sociologie rurală*.

94. Audisio, *The Waldensian Dissent*, 18.

95. In the Pyrenees Couderc-Barraud, *La violence, l'ordre et la paix*, 20; in the Carpathians Joseph Livni and Ilie Bădescu, "The Battle of the Covenantal Society against Elitism—An Overlooked Chapter in The History of Social Inequality," *Romanian Journal of Sociological Studies, New Series* (2020): 3–36.

96. Gustave Bascle de Lagrèze, *Histoire du droit dans les Pyrénées—comté de Bigorre* (1867), 56.

97. Frédéric Le Play, *L'organisation de la famille selon le vrai modèle signalé par l'histoire de toutes les races et de tous les temps* (A. Mame et fils, 1895), 127.

98. Paul Trebilco, *The Early Christians in Ephesus from Paul to Ignatius* (Grand Rapids, MI: Eerdmans Publishing Company, 2007), 489.

99. James M. Sawyer, *The Survivor's Guide to Theology* (Eugene, OR: Wipf & Stock Publishers, 2016), 38; Arnold Ehrhardt, *The Apostolic Succession: In the First Two Centuries of the Church* (Eugene, OR: Wipf & Stock Publishers, 2009).

100. [Mathew 16:18].

101. Edwin Hatch, *The Organization of the Early Christian Churches* (London: Rivingtons, 1882), 60, 61, 66, 84.

102. Trebilco, *The Early Christians in Ephesus*, 489.

103. Ecclesia is the Early Christian term for *congregation*. It is a Greek word for assembly.

104. Hatch, *The Organization of the Early Christian Churches*.

105. Zeev Safrai, *The Economy of Roman Palestine* (London—New York: Taylor & Francis, 2003), 25.

106. Ibid.

107. Michael Burgess, *Comparative Federalism: Theory and Practice* (London and New York: Taylor & Francis, 2006), 52.

108. Charles S. McCoy and Wayne J. Baker, *Fountainhead of Federalism: Heinrich Bullinger and the Covenantal Tradition* (Louisville, KY: Westminster John Knox Press, 1991), 88.

109. For example, Boston, Charlestown, Dorchester, Cambridge, Wenham, Roxbury, Woburn, Chelmsford, Springfield, Dedham, Haverhill, Marblehead, Andover, Medford, Lynn, and Malden in Massachusetts, Windsor Hartford, Guilford and Milford in Connecticut and Dover, Portsmouth, Exeter, and Hampton in New Hampshire.

110. Such as seventeenth-century New France, see Jacques Mathieu, *La Nouvelle-France: les Français en Amérique du Nord, XVIe-XVIIIe siècle* (Saint-Nicolas, Quebec, Canada: Presses de l'Université Laval, 2001), 105.

111. Burgess, *Comparative Federalism*, 52.

112. Ibid.

113. In the other side of the Pyrenees Catalan sources use the term *boni homines villae*, see Monique Bourin, "Historiographie des communautés de la France méridionale," in *La formation des communautés d'habitants au Moyen Âge. Perspectives historiographiques*, ed. Ludolf Kuchenbuch, Dieter Scheler, and Joseph Morsel (Xanten, Germany2003). *Boni homines villae* is an exact translation of the term *tuvey ha'ir* used in Roman Palestine, see Safrai, *The Economy of Roman Palestine*, 25.

114. Francesca Santoro L'Hoir, *The Rhetoric of Gender Terms: "Man", "Woman", and the Portrayal of Character in Latin Prose* (Leiden: Brill, 1992); Michele Renee Salzman, *The Making of a Christian Aristocracy: Social and Religious Change in the Western Roman Empire*, Kindle Edition ed. (Cambridge, MA: Harvard

University Press, 2002). note 217; they both quote Guy Achard, "L'emploi de boni, boni viri, boni cives, et leurs formes superlatives dans l'action politique de Cicéron," *Les Études Classiques* 41 (1973): 207–221.

115. The term returned to Italy in a somewhat similar interpretation, for example, to Pistoia Ludovico Zoekauer, "Sui framenti i piu antichi del constituto di Pistoia," in *Rivista italiana per le scienze giuridiche* ed. G. Fusinato and F. Schupfer (Roma: E. Loescher & Company, 1892), 75.

Chapter 6

Justice Administration in Biblical Israel

This chapter discusses the mode of operation of biblical justice administration shedding light on how the covenant has been enforced. Needless to say, understanding the justice administration of Proto-Israel is essential to the thesis of this work. Moreover, this aspect was practically left so far in the shade by all relevant disciplines: archaeology, biblical studies, law, anthropology, history, and sociology. The biblical text stating that "there was no king in Israel"[1] is problematic regarding justice administration. By definition, pre-state tribes and chiefdoms had no king. However, these chiefdoms controlled misbehavior because they were stratified and as a consequence they enforced justice.[2] Proto-Israel was also a pre-state society[3]; however, the archaeological evidence proves that Proto-Israel was not stratified. The consensus among archaeologists is that Proto-Israel consisted of settlements with no ranks[4] appearing on the hills of Judea and Samaria in about the thirteenth century BCE.[5]

The interpretation of Judges 21:25 could vary from political monarchist campaigning[6] to a spiritual claim that in Israel the Law is King.[7] However, the archaeological evidence indicates a literal interpretation of Judges 21:25.

On the other hand, the archaeological evidence indicates not only that Proto-Israel had laws but it strictly obeyed laws, (see chapter 3 "The Covenant of Israel: Customary Law or Law" on page 35) In other words, there was no king; yet there was law and the law was enforced. In a hierarchy, law enforcement is in the hands of dedicated institutions: police, prosecutors, jails, and so on. However, as noted earlier, the archaeological evidence concurs with Judges 21:25 proving that there were no ranks in Israel and consequently no king.[8] On the other hand, if "there was no king in Israel"[9] then there was no police. That is because if no one else were king, then the police chief would act as king leaving archaeological traces of a ranked society.

The archaeological evidence therefore supports that there was no dedicated police force.

In spite of a massive research of the Bible and its interpretation, we find "very little evidence to indicate how the system operated."[10] For example, as far as pre-exilic Israel is concerned, "outside the Book of Deuteronomy, the laws themselves say almost nothing about the covenant's enforcement mechanism."[11] The literature survey yielded a reference noting that in pre-exilic Israel the law was "enforced regardless of rank"[12] because "all were equal under the law"[13]; nevertheless, the reference doesn't stipulate how the law was enforced. Oddly enough, the Bible does bring up episodes related to shortcomings of biblical justice administration.[14] The Book's silence about what constrained the Israelites to obey the covenant brought to the speculation that prophets' proclamation of "divine judgment"[15] was effective. Reasonably, pre-exilic Israelites were not different from any other population; they also featured various degrees of criminal inclination when crime payed. Therefore, this work shall first discuss the evidence that the covenant was enforced and subsequently explain how.

Chapter "The Covenantal society, Structure, Organization, and Power Flow" stated that the assembly of the *town* was the government (figure 6.1). The biblical text[16] indicates that the covenant sanctioned the critical body of town assembly. The Bible proclaims the institution of "sacred assembly."

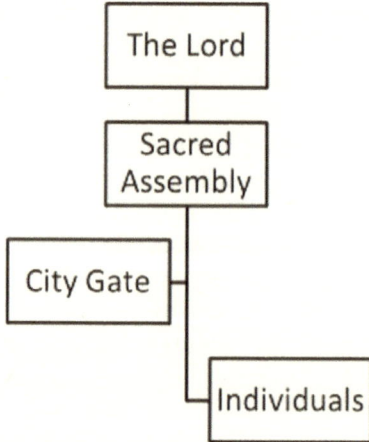

Figure 6.1 Government Institutions of Ancient Israel. The Lord is the Sovereign; Weekly Sacred Assembly is the government[17]; City Gate served as board of elders[18], court of justice[19], and so on. Created by the author.

There are six days when you may work, but the seventh day is a Sabbath of rest, a day of sacred assembly. You are not to do any work; wherever you live, it is a Sabbath to the LORD.[20]

However biblical scholars refer to Exodus 19:1–24:18 as the Covenant Code. In this limited portion of the Bible, we find the following:

Remember the Sabbath day, to keep it holy. Six days you shall labor and do all your work, but the seventh day is a Sabbath of the LORD your God; in it you shall not do any work, you or your son or your daughter, your male or your female servant or your cattle or your sojourner who stays with you.[21]

Why didn't the earlier Covenant Code[22] announce the "sacred assembly?" The answer is that there was no need for it. I substantiated in an earlier work that similar assemblies were a custom in the nomadic past.[23] Farming has a disrupting effect on attendance at the assembly. The Covenant Code only needed to prohibit work for each individual, his household, servants, cattle, and sojourner; the prohibition boosted turnout.

In my opinion, as many other *great ideas*, the day of Sabbath was not an invention of a great thinker of the stature of Aristotle. It was a result of cultural evolution. Evolution is a process of copied inheritance with eventual faulty duplication called *unintentional random mutation*. It was a random cultural mutation in the form of an unintentional habit of the pastoralist tribes to meet periodically and discuss community matters.[24] Pastoralists are not short of leisure time and reasonably all tribes had many encounters of intra-community chit-chat. If such encounters involved decisions regarding public affairs and the nomadic tribe happened to embrace an egalitarian ethos[25] then they convened an assembly of the community. Reasonably, in some of the many of egalitarian "supercomplex chiefdoms created by some nomads of Eurasia,"[26] the habit of ad-hoc general assemblies turned into a pattern of periodical assemblies.

Typically, when such nomadic people settled down, the periodic assemblies were not practical because of precedence of farming work. The new lifestyle overruled the egalitarian ethos, and decisions were taken by those who enjoyed *leisure* giving way to oligarchy.

In Proto-Israel, the archaeological evidence shows that the egalitarian ethos prevailed. If the general assembly of the nomadic ancestors of Proto-Israel happened to take place every seventh day then the prohibition of work on the seventh day would be both obeyed and efficient. This is the meaning of *unintentional random mutation*.[27]

In other words, in Proto-Israel, the egalitarian ethos prevailed because it overruled the practical constraint of uninterrupted farming. An imposition of work prohibition at the time of the periodical assemblies grew not from an Aristotelian visionary, but because against all odds,[28] in Proto-Israel the egalitarian ethos overcame settled lifestyle's demands. Proto-Israel is not the only society of settlers with an egalitarian ethos.

Typically egalitarian societies settle disputes by mediation; they need neither a clear distinction between right and wrong,[29] nor a consequential allocation of guilt.[30] However, Proto-Israel did decree what is right and what is wrong, detected the guilty, and applied corrective actions against deviations.

From the beginning of the Diaspora, the Sabbath assemblies had a primordial role in defining self-government for Jewish communities as we learn from Philo of Alexandria[31] and Josephus Flavius.[32]

The assemblies were the government; however, one needs to explain how did they fulfil their duty to provide justice? After all "justice is the bond of men in states, and the administration of justice, which is the determination of what is just, is the principle of order in political society."[33]

The theory that all covenantal societies (table 5.2) inherited the modus operandi of their parent embodiment allows understanding the justice administration of biblical Israel by examining later covenantal practices.

The coercion means of the Jewish communities of the diaspora consisted of according dignity to righteous congregants and stigmatizing offenders. This should not be seen as an on-off switch between respect and disgrace. It was rather a continuous scale ranging from high esteem through disregard[34] and banishment (*niduy*) all the way to total banishment (*cherem*).[35] Even office holders complied with the rules or else they could lose their status.[36]

Make no mistake, this is not about ritual honors at religious services. This scale of honor at the assembly served as civic certificate for every purpose; credit rating or security clearance are the closest analogy to modern American practice. One's position on the honor scale either helped or blocked the capability to purchase inventory, to ship merchandise overseas, to transfer currency. These were typical interests in medieval Jewish Diaspora; consequently, one's livelihood was linked to one's reputation in the community. The position on the respectability scale from high honor to *niduy* also served as reference for matchmaking, business partnerships and moving from one community to another. I do not claim that this started in Proto-Israel. However, the power of the assembly has been sanctioned when the first nomads settled on the Central Hill of the Land of Canaan. As soon as the decree "Remember the day of Sabbath" took off, the assemblies of Proto-Israel governed with unquestioned authority and so did the assemblies of Proto-Israel's descendants.

The community was in charge of detecting deviations. Every congregant minded other people's business (see more in the chapter 8 "Covenantal Psychology"). The Sabbath assembly gives rise to peer pressure; at the

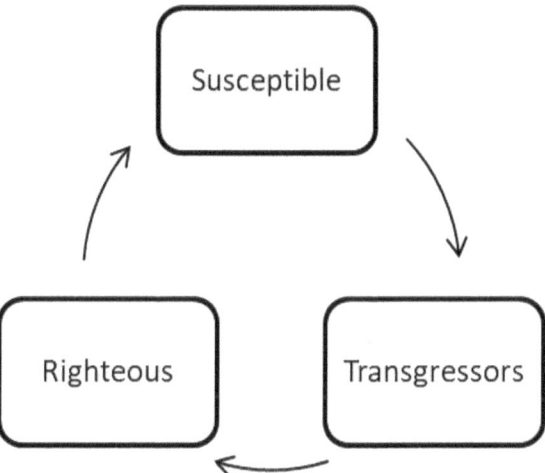

Figure 6.2 Justice Administration. As a result of corruption, certain susceptible individuals become transgressors; a correction mechanism induces repentance and a fraction of transgressors become righteous; some righteous lapse and become susceptible. Created by the author.

meeting house[37] accusations are debated, rumors are spread, guilt is attributed, and honors are given or denied and sanctions such as penalties and banishment are on the agenda. Pilgrims operated with similar means of enforcement: "If members of the congregation strayed from the true path, they were admonished; if they failed to correct themselves, they were excommunicated."[38]

Figure 6.2 describes the bio-physical model controlling social deviation in general.[39] In a covenantal system, the peer pressure of the community induces repentance; this peer pressure peaks at the weekly assembly. The mathematical model of such a covenantal justice administration is published in an earlier work.[40] A simulation of the model (figure 7.1) shows that there are three coefficients that determine the success or failure of a community. The three coefficients are as follows:

(a) The corruption coefficient measures how "contagious" is the transgression.
(b) The repentance coefficient—measures how effective is the peer pressure of the community
(c) The lapse coefficient—measures the probability of righteous to become susceptible.

There is not much a community can do about the first two coefficients. However, the lapse coefficient is community dependent. Two factors that are in the community's power may affect the lapse coefficient:

a) Influence of other cultures—Covenantal societies combat cultural diffusion of foreign values.[41] The first known covenant prohibited idolatry, pork consumption[42] and it commanded circumcision "to mark their difference."[43] We are told about the Pilgrims that "[a] sense of exclusivity was fundamental to how they perceived themselves in the world."[44] Similarly Puritans are described as "[r]igorous Calvinists, they had come a great distance to worship as they pleased; they were intolerant of those who did so differently."[45]
b) Poverty—Most covenantal societies have institutionalized anti-poverty measures[46]; for example, the poor man's box,[47] the free loan society,[48] "the very edges of your field,"[49] "fallen grapes of thy vineyard."[50] In the Puritan town, "relief of the poor was a chronic problem."[51]

To conclude this chapter, one notes that the kingless society of Proto-Israel had a workable justice administration. The biblical text is stingy in explanations how that worked. One cannot build covenantal societies by reading instructions from the Bible. Only inheriting practices, traditions, psychological attitude, and institutions from a previous covenantal society offer chances of success.

NOTES

1. Judges 21:25
2. For example, Andrey V. Korotayev, "The Chiefdom: Precursor of the Tribe?," in *The Early State, its Alternatives and Analogues*, ed. Grinin Leonid E , et al. (Volgograd: Uchitel Publishing House, 2004).
3. See, for example, Robert D. Miller, *Chieftains of the Highland Clans: A History of Israel in the 12th and 11th Centuries BC* (Eugene, Oregon: Wipf & Stock Publishers, 2012), 15; see also William G. Dever, *Who Were the Early Israelites and Where Did They Come From?* (Grand Rapids, MI: Eerdmans Publishing Company, 2006), 196.
4. a. k. a. *reverse dominance hierarchy* Cristopher Boehm, *Hierarchy in the Forest* (Cambridge, MA: Harvard University Press, 2001), 123.
5. Avraham Faust, *Israel''s Ethnogenesis: Settlement, Interaction, Expansion and Resistance* (London: Equinox Pub., 2006); Israel Finkelstein, Amihai Mazar, and Brian B. Schmidt, *The Quest for the Historical Israel: Debating Archaeology and the History of Early Israel*, Sixth Biennial Colloquium of the International Institute for Secular Humanistic Judaism (Atlanta: SBL Press, 2007); William G. Dever, *What Did the Biblical Writers Know and When Did They Know It?: What Archeology Can Tell Us About the Reality of Ancient Israel*, Kindle ed. (Grand Rapids, Michigan: Eerdmans Publishing Company, 2002).
6. Michael Chyutin, *Architecture and Utopia in the Temple Era* (New York: Bloomsbury Academic, 2006).

7. Rémi Brague, *The Law of God: The Philosophical History of an Idea* (Chicago: University of Chicago Press, 2007), 50.

8. For example, Faust, *Israel's Ethnogenesis*; Finkelstein, Mazar, and Schmidt, *The Quest for the Historical Israel*; Dever, *What Did the Biblical Writers Know and When Did They Know It?*.

9. Judges 21:25

10. Robert R. Wilson, "Israel's Judicial System in the Preexilic Period," *The Jewish Quarterly Review* 74, no. 2 (1983): 230.

11. Ibid.

12. Anthony Phillips, *Essays on Biblical Law* (London; New York: Bloomsbury Academic, 2002), 152.

13. Ibid.

14. For example, the Levite's concubine (Judges 19-21) and the poor man's lamb episode (2 Samuel 12)

15. Phillips, *Essays on Biblical Law*, 41.

16. The biblical text was not necessarily written down in Proto-Israel; reasonably, the commandments were transmitted orally until they were written down later; according to most biblical researchers, this took place during the monarchy, some advocate later dates; reasonably, prohibition of work and town assemblies were not inventions of monarchic Israel because both King and Temple were interested in centralization; sacred assemblies were kept in the Covenant not because of the new priestly elite but in spite of it; see more in Joseph Livni and Ilie Bădescu, "The Battle of the Covenantal Society against Elitism," *Romanian Journal of Sociological Studies,* (in print).

17. Leviticus 23:8.

18. For example, Ruth 4:1–11.

19. Where the elders examined evidence and pass judgment (Deuteronomy 21:18–21).

20. Leviticus 23:3

21. Exodus 20:8-10

22. Mainstream biblical theory is that the Covenant Code is the earliest portion of the Pentateuch, for example, Bernard M. Levinson, "The Birth of the Lemma: The Restrictive Reinterpretation of the Covenant Code's Manumission Law by the Holiness Code (Leviticus 25: 44–46)," *Journal of Biblical Literature* 124, no. 4 (2005): 617–639; this has been disputed John Van Seters, *A Law Book for the Diaspora: Revision in the Study of the Covenant Code* (Oxford: Oxford University Press, 2002); biblical research studies the written texts; naturally the earliest code was transmitted orally since literacy of Proto-Israel was in its infancy as evidenced by the Izbet Sarta ostracon William M. Schniedewind, *A Social History of Hebrew: Its Origins Through the Rabbinic Period* (New Haven: Yale University Press, 2013), 65. Therefore, for our purposes, the date of editing the texts is not critical.

23. Joseph Livni, "The cultural evolution of an institution: The Sabbath," *Cliodynamics* 8 (2017).

24. Ibid.

25. Some pastoralist cultures are egalitarian, some are not, for example, Peter Rigby, "Pastoralism, Egalitarianism, and the State: The Eastern African Case," *Critique of Anthropology* 7, no. 3 (1988): 17–32; Christopher Boehm et al., "Egalitarian behavior and reverse dominance hierarchy [and comments and reply]," *Current anthropology* 34, no. 3 (1993): 227–254.

26. Dmitri M Bondarenko, Leonid E Grinin, and Andrey V Korotayev, "Alternatives of social evolution," in *The Early State, Its Alternatives and Analogues*, ed. Leonid E Grinin, et al. (Volgograd: Uchitel Publishing House, 2004): 12 .

27. See, for example, in John T. Bonner, *Randomness in Evolution* (Princeton, NJ: Princeton University Press, 2013), Ch. 1.

28. *Against all odds* means an unlikely outcome, in other words, in one of many cases it will occur.

29. P. Sillitoe, *An Introduction to the Anthropology of Melanesia: Culture and Tradition* (Cambridge University Press, 1998), 148.

30. Jane Dickson-Gilmore, "Resurrecting The Peace: Traditionalist Approaches To Separate Justice In Kahnawake Mohawk Nation," in *Law & Anthropology*, ed. René Kuppe and Richard Potz (The Hague: Martinus Nijhoff Publishers, 1996), 101.

31. Jutta Leonhardt, *Jewish Worship in Philo of Alexandria* (Tübingen: Mohr Siebeck, 2001), 96.

32. John M. G. Barclay, *Jews in the Mediterranean Diaspora: From Alexander to Trajan (323 BCE–117 CE)* (Berkeley, CA: University of California Press, 1999), 417.

33. Aristotle, Benjamin Jowett, and Henry William Carless Davis, *Politics*, Kindle edition ed. (Mineola, NY: Dover Publications, 2000), 4.

34. Honors in Sabbat services can be opening the ark, carrying the Torah scroll, reading the weekly Torah portion; in many places, for example, Miskolc, Hungary these honors were attributed according to seniority Howard N. Lupovitch, *Jews at the Crossroads: Tradition and Accommodation During the Golden Age of the Hungarian Nobility, 1729–1878* (Budapest: Central European University Press, 2007), 96; often congregants in low esteem or with stigma were ruled out.

35. Renzo Toaff, "Statuti e leggi della «Nazione ebrea» di Livorno. II: La legislazione dal 1655 al 1677.(Cont. ne)," *La Rassegna Mensile di Israel* 38, no. 5 (1972): 44; Robert M Cover, "Obligation: A Jewish jurisprudence of the social order," *Journal of Law and Religion* 5, no. 1 (1987); see also Grunwald v. Bornfreund, 696 F. Supp. 838 E.D.N.Y, "Grunwald v. Bornfreund, 696 F. Supp. 838 (E.D.N.Y.)," ed. E.D. New York District Court (New York, 1988).

36. Lupovitch, *Jews at the Crossroads*, 92.

37. I deliberately used the Puritan term meeting house Robert J. Dinkin, "Seating the Meeting House in Early Massachusetts," *New England Quarterly* (1970): 450–464; the Hebrew expression Beyt-Knesset means exactly the same thing; the term synagogue is Greek and the Septuagint used it for congregation J. Gwyn Griffiths, "Egypt and the Rise of the Synagogue," *The Journal of Theological Studies* 38, no. 1 (1987): 1–5.

38. Nathanel Philbrick, *Mayflower: A Story of Courage, Community, and War*, Kindle Edition ed. (New York: Penguin Publishing Group, 2006), Kindle loc. 284.

39. Haiyun Zhao, Zhilan Feng, and Carlos Castillo-Chavez, "The Dynamics of Poverty and Crime," MTBI-02-08M (2002); Juan C Nuño, Miguel A Herrero, and Mario Primicerio, "A triangle model of criminality," *Physica A: Statistical Mechanics and its Applications* 387, no. 12 (2008); Joshua M. Epstein, *Nonlinear Dynamics, Mathematical Biology, and Social Science: Wise Use Of Alternative Therapies* (Boulder, CO: Westview Press, 1997); Zhao, Feng, and Castillo-Chavez, "The Dynamics of Poverty and Crime."

40. Joseph Livni and Lewi Stone, "The stabilizing role of the Sabbath in pre-monarchic Israel: a mathematical model," *Journal of biological physics* 41 (2015).

41. This assertion met criticism; some reviews accused me of promoting *xenophobia*; covenants decree measures that may be viewed or not of being *xenophobic*; this work studies the covenantal justice system; it promotes neither *xenophobia* nor *covenantal laws*.

42. Pork prohibition and other dietary rules hinder commensality with foreigners Jordan Rosenblum, *Food and Identity in Early Rabbinic Judaism* (Cambridge: Cambridge University Press, 2010), 141–43.; commensality enhances intercultural admixture Susan Pollock, "Between Feasts and Daily Meals. Towards an Archaeology of Commensal Spaces," *eTopoi. Journal for Ancient Studies* 2, no. Special (2011).

43. Barclay, *Jews in the Mediterranean Diaspora*; Faust, *Israel's Ethnogenesis: Settlement, Interaction, Expansion and Resistance*.

44. Philbrick, *Mayflower*. 528.

45. Stacy Schiff, *The Witches: Suspicion, Betrayal and Histeria in 1692 Salem*, Kindle Edition ed. (New York Boston London: Little Brown, 2015), 6.

46. Edwin Hatch, *The Organization of the Early Christian Churches* (London: Rivingtons, 1882).

47. Robert Halley, *Lancashire: Its Puritanism and Nonconformity* (Manchester, UK: Tubbs and Brook, 1872).

48. Michal Shekel, *Making a Difference: Commandments and Community* (Brooklyn: Ktav, 1997).

49. [Leviticus 19:9 NRSV].

50. [Leviticus 19:10 NRSV].

51. Schiff, *The Witches*, 46.

Chapter 7

Inventing a Covenantal Society Is Impossible

The third point of the thesis of this book (see pages 8,9) implies that one cannot convert hierarchical neighborhoods into covenantal communities by following biblical recipes. This chapter substantiates that all the covenantal societies (table 4) are copies of a functioning covenantal network. This point is new and contradicts previous studies of the covenantal model. An earlier quote from Elazar, (page 7) suggests that Swiss Protestantism spread due to "renewed interest in the Hebrew Bible." Chapter 6 "Justice Administration in Biblical Israel" deduces that the Hebrew Bible is not an appropriate instruction manual for setting up a successful transgression control loop; only imitating a practicing covenantal model can produce a viable conversion from stratified to rankless covenantal models. A consensus exists about the descent of all the covenantal networks of table 5.2 from copying an ancestor according to the evolution tree of figure 9.1 except for two: Calvinists and Waldensians. This chapter provides more explanations, examples, and a biophysical demonstration that both have covenantal ancestry: the Waldensians served as model for Calvinists and the Early Christians were the ancestors of the Waldensians.

As discussed earlier, one of the difficulties of transition from a hierarchy to an egalitarian structure is establishing a power flow from the people to the government. There were numerous attempts of conversion from a stratified structure to an egalitarian model; in these upheavals, power flow was not inverted and assembly governments remained practically powerless. Office holders don't yield to any assembly even if one proclaims that the power belongs to the local assembly in a revolutionary "constitution." Consider, for example, the following revolutionary promise:

1. Russia is declared to be a republic of the Soviets of Workers', Soldiers', and Peasants' Deputies. All the central and local power belongs to these soviets.
2. The Russian Soviet Republic is organized on the basis of a free union of free nations, as a federation of soviet national republics.[1]

The Bolshevik revolution was however not intended to create, defend end enforce such a constitution. This statement becomes clearer if one remembers that the American Revolution was "made to preserve the traditional order against the efforts of innovative government officials to change it."[2]

The Soviets of Workers', Soldiers', and Peasants' Deputies had no power either before or after the revolution. Before the Constitution was signed,[3] the Red Guards and not the Soviets of Workers', Soldiers', and Peasants' Deputies dispersed the Constituent Assembly.[4] Subsequently, one perceived through the dust how the Red Guard continued the previous tsarist power flow direction, provisions of constitution notwithstanding.

The reason for ineffectiveness of the assemblies of soviet deputies was not because the system had insufficient enforcement capabilities. Had the Red Guards enforce the constitution, would the assemblies gain power? Your guess is as good as mine.

This deviation substantiates by example that enforcement of a constitution is necessary but not sufficient. A constitution will have a reasonable chance to assure equality and liberty in a free and equal society. The same is applicable to the Covenant of Israel. Proto-Israel didn't come about by conversion from a stratified organization to an egalitarian one. They switched from a nomadic to a settled mode of life. The settlers of Proto-Israel inherited the spirit of freedom and equality of their nomadic ancestors. The Covenant decreed the prohibition of work on Sabbath continuing the traditions of periodic assemblies, assembly government, and conserving the settlers' egalitarian ethos.[5] Peer pressure played a role in enforcing the Covenant; nevertheless, the main factor of its survival is the adherence to ancestral legacy. Peer pressure is a necessary condition though not sufficient.

Published results of our investigation[6] indicate that peer pressure can keep deviations from the law within reasonable limits only if certain conditions are met. I shall translate the mathematical expressions of those conditions to terms bridging the interdisciplinary communication gap. Among others, the conditions require that the community assemblies are kept periodically with time intervals longer than one day but shorter than any known natural period (table 7.1). The results of the investigation showed that one week would work except it is not a natural period.[7] The reader may wonder why one rules out daily assemblies. An important aspect of covenantal egalitarianism consists of equal participation in public administration. This concept was recognized

Table 7.1 Natural Periods Known in Iron Age

Period	Duration	Natural Phenomenon
1 day	24 hours	Earth rotation around its axis
1 month	29.53 days	Moon's revolution around earth
1 year	365.25 days	Earth revolution around sun

by the earliest scholars of democracy: "For if liberty and equality, as is thought by some, are chiefly to be found in democracy, they will be best attained when all persons alike share in the government to the utmost."[8]

Aristotle speculates that everyone "may share in the government if he can find leisure."[9] No doubt *leisure* is a necessary condition for equal participation in public life. A daily assembly is ruled out because it allows only the participation of a few.

The investigation revealed more necessary conditions for the survival of a covenantal model:

a. The community customs limit socializing with foreign cultures.
b. The community limits poverty and provides at least basic support to the weak.[10]
c. Most members share a prevalent covenantal psychology inherited from one generation to the other (see more in chapter 8 "Covenantal Psychology").

There were other settled egalitarian societies in the course of history.[11] However, they were not covenantal. One of the reasons why only Proto-Israel succeeded as a covenantal model is related to the unusual condition to have a tradition of weekly compulsory assemblies. There is no natural period between one day and one month (table 7.1).

Some say that *seven* is related to the seven planets the ancient Mesopotamians thought to be orbiting around the Earth.[12] Some note that the 7th, 14th, 21st, and 28th days of a lunar month were considered unfortunate in ancient Mesopotamia.[13] Regardless, which theory one prefers, the number *seven* is not an immediate practical number and its perception requires certain intellectual effort. On the other hand, both theories are consistent with the number *seven* circulating in the Fertile Crescent and it is possible that nomadic pastoralist tribes adopted some habits related to it.

Opposed to the claim that the seven-day week is of Mesopotamian origin,[14] other sources argue that "there is no evidence that an actual seven-day cycle ever existed in ancient Mesopotamia."[15] The conflict may be explained by the fact that the 7th, 14th, 21st, and 28th day of a month do resemble to a seven-day interval; however, they are not an "actual seven day cycle" because the interval between the 28th day of a month and the 7th day of the subsequent

86   *Chapter 7*

month is nine days long. Ancient civilizations had market weeks, for example, the Roman *nundinae* of eight days.[16]

Reasonably, traditions with weekly assemblies were rare. Moreover, full participation of the community at the assemblies implies work prohibition which further reduces the chance of arriving at the covenantal arrangement.

Even covenantal societies that inherited their practices from successful societies have a surprisingly low chance of survival. The Jewish population of Judea of the first century was about two million strong.[17] At a very low growth rate of 0.2%/year, today they have about 110 million descendants. The current Jewish population size is about 14 million. Therefore, the chance of survival of a typical covenantal community is about 12.7%. The 87% of vanished Jewish communities is in a great part explained by voluntary conversions to Christianity or Islam. This indicates in many cases malfunctions of their institutions of Sabbath, dietary rules, fight against poverty, and so on.

The covenantal practice is a combination of many traditions. In this chapter, I present a biophysical demonstration proving that the covenantal repentance mechanism is one of the many essential traditions that make or break the covenantal society. I singled out this attribute of the covenantal society not necessarily because it is the most essential, but because it has been quantitatively investigated using a SIRS model; the investigation showed that any attempt of creating such a society would end in failure after a couple of months.[18]

Let me show you how mathematical simulation demonstrates the difficulty of conceiving a successful covenantal community. The key to success is partially held by the repentance procedure. Without peer pressure combined with everybody minding everybody else's business, the covenantal repentance mechanism does not function.

The strength of the repentance mechanism is represented by the ratio $w_0 = \gamma/\beta$ (see explanation of symbols in table 7.2). We called this ratio the *Basic Sabbath Number* because the peer pressure peaks at the weekly Sabbath assembly.[19] If the Basic Sabbath Number is greater than one then in spite of the initial contagion the community will settle at a transgression-free

Table 7.2   SIRS Model Symbols

Symbol	Coefficient	Meaning
S	Susceptible	
I	Wrongdoer	
R	Righteous	
N	Total population	
α	Lapse	Probability of an R→S conversion
β	Corruption	Probability of an S→I conversion
γ	Repentance	Probability of an I→R conversion

Inventing a Covenantal Society Is Impossible 87

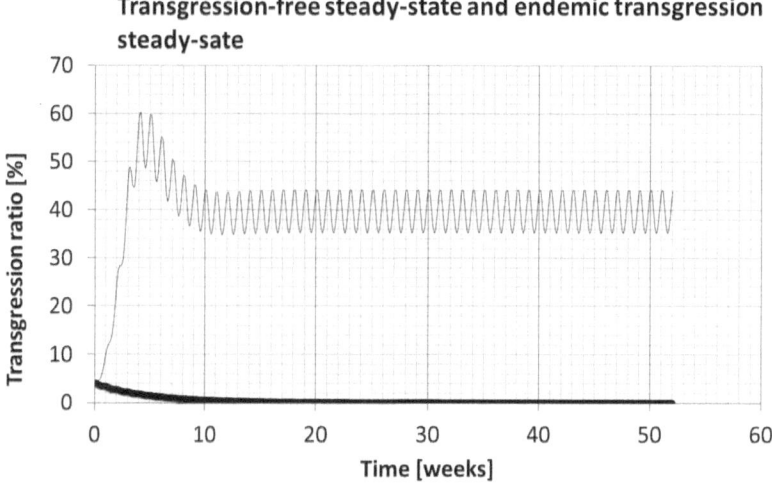

Figure 7.1 Simulation of Transgression Ratio after a Sudden Appearance of 5% Transgressors. The steady state is transgression-free if repentance exceeds corruption; if not then the steady state is tolerable at a low lapse rate. Created by the author.

equilibrium (figure 7.1). The rationale behind this axiom is that if the repentance rate exceeds the contagion rate then there are more transitions from the transgressor to the righteous category than from the susceptible to the transgressor category (figure 6.2). The contagion rate increases the number of transgressors and the repentance rate reduces it; therefore, the number of transgressors will diminish when the decrement is higher than the increment. This is similar to the balance in a bank account. If the weekly expense exceeds the weekly income then the average balance will diminish every week until it reaches zero.[20]

I mentioned earlier that the chance of survival of Jewish communities of the Diaspora was about 12.7%. This indicates that the Basic Sabbath Number of the communities very rarely exceeded the desired value of one. Therefore, the communities frequently settled at an endemic transgression ratio.

For example, figure 7.2 illustrates the results of two simulated time histories of two communities; one community features a cohesion factor $\gamma/\alpha = 1$ (see explanation of symbols in table 7.2) and the other community has a healthier cohesion factor $\gamma/\alpha = 6$. The cohesion factor is inversely proportional to the lapse coefficient; the strength of the communities is set by the factors of the lapse coefficient (see list of three key coefficients of the SIRS

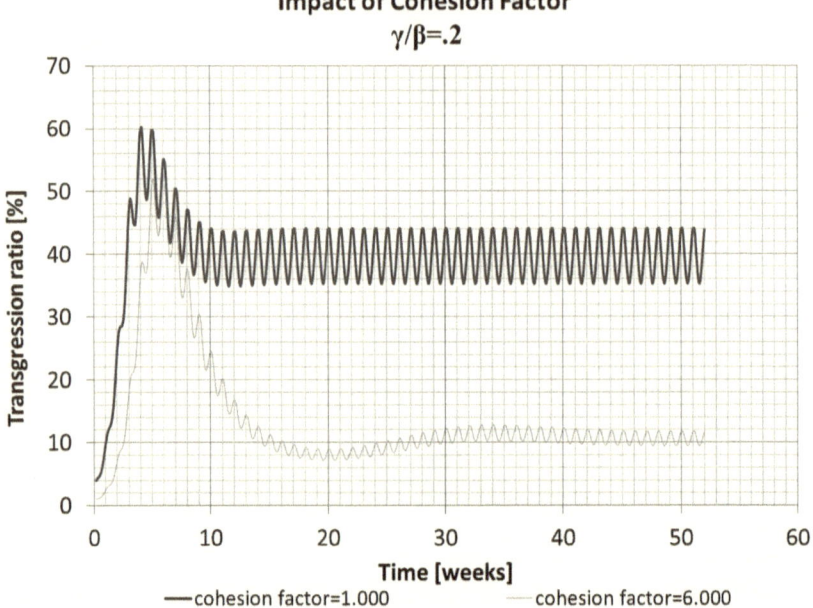

Figure 7.2 Simulation of Time History from the Appearance of a Few Transgressors. The transgression ratio increases due to contagion until it settles at equilibrium; the ratio $\gamma/\beta = .2$ is less than one; consequently at equilibrium, the transgression ratio will not be zero; for a cohesion factor $\gamma/\alpha = 1$, the average transgression ratio is about 40%; in a stronger community with a cohesion factor $\gamma/\alpha = 6$, the transgression ratio will settle at slightly more than 10%; the ripples at equilibrium reflect the weekly beat of the covenantal correction mechanism. Created by the author.

model in chapter 6 "Justice Administration in Ancient Israel"). In both communities, a small number of transgressors (initial transgressors ratio is 4%) set off an *epidemic* of transgression. The two communities react similarly; the transgression ratio reaches a peak of 50%, subsequently it decreases due to the operative repentance mechanism. However, the weaker community will settle at equilibrium at an endemic transgression ratio of 40% while in the healthier community the endemic transgression will reach only about 10% (figure 7.2).

Using the same SIRS model, one also obtains figure 7.3. This chart predicts the endemic transgression ratio of communities with different values of Basic Sabbath Number (γ/β) and different cohesion factors (γ/α). For example, the weaker community of figure 7.2 is represented by the value $\gamma/\alpha = 1$ on the horizontal axis on the curve corresponding to a Basic Sabbath Number $\gamma/\beta = .2$. The chart predicts that the community will settle at the endemic transgression ratio of 40% as predicted by the time history of figure 7.2. Similarly, the stronger community will settle at the intersection of the

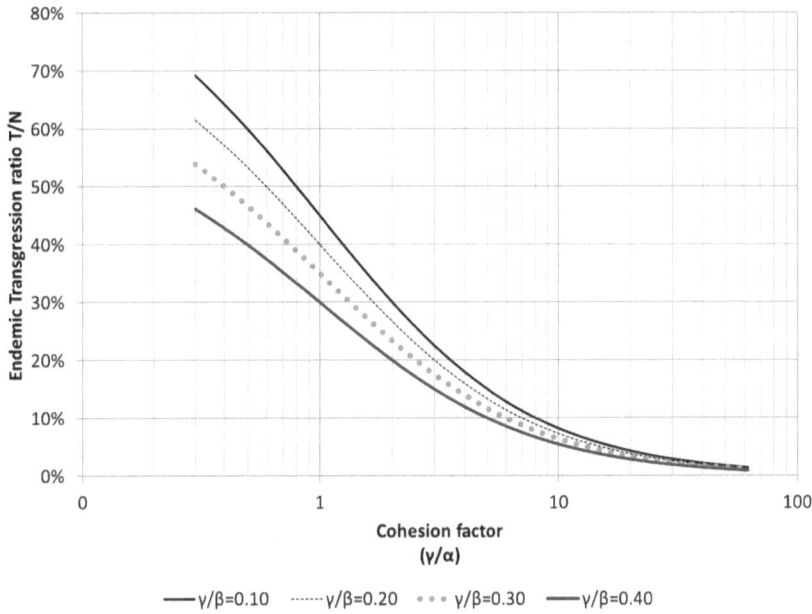

Figure 7.3 The Fate of a Covenantal Society Founded by a Valdès or Anyone Else without Copying a Living Model. The repentance to corruption ratio γ/β is low if one does not have an adequate repentance mechanism as the Waldensians had; however, how would this imaginary Waldo know how to establish covenantal repentance? The figure shows that the first attempt with a repentance to corruption ratio $\gamma/\beta < .1$ would bring his community of 70% transgressors in no time. Created by the author.

same curve with the vertical gridline corresponding to $\gamma/\alpha=6$. The predicted endemic transgression ratio is slightly exceeding 10%. Figure 7.3 therefore predicts the endemic transgression ratio of communities featuring a Basic Sabbath Number varying from 0.10 to 0.40 and a cohesion factor within the range of 0.1–50.

The curves of figure 7.3 illustrate that replacing a hierarchical repentance mechanism[21] by a new one, works only if the new mechanism is right the first time. In terms of the model, its success requires starting with a right combination of the three coefficients (table 7.2). The SIRS model predicts that cycles of trial and error lead to failure. A transition from hierarchical or oligarchical model to a covenantal model without following a live example would also fail because it requires an unsafe sequence of "repeal and replace" of correction mechanisms.

Early Christianity was a covenantal society that did grow from a hierarchical culture. The early Christians however were voluntary converts to a different sociographic reality and they had opportunity to observe and adopt practices of viable Jewish communities. After all, the Early Christian communities better succeeded in the proximity of Jewish communities of the Diaspora.[22]

However, two transitions from hierarchy to Christian covenantal models are more problematic. One of them is related to the appearance of Calvinism. Transition from covenantal to hierarchical models (e.g., the birth of post-Constantine hierarchic Christian Church) is not difficult to understand because of the multitude of viable hierarchical civilizations. As in apostolic times, in the generation of Calvin the conversion to Calvinism was voluntary. Reasonably, the converts were eager to accept the covenantal way of life with its advantages (more equality) and disadvantages (blurred power flow and consequential clashes). However, if the first communities were in a trial-and-error sequence in getting an adequate correction mechanism then the initial *Basic Sabbath Number* was bound to be low in the order of magnitude of $\gamma/\beta < .1$ or less than 0.10. The same can be said regarding the cohesion factor. This factor is related to reducing influence of hierarchic cultures and more importantly a vigorous combat of poverty. The success of Calvinism indicates that the first Calvinists adopted the model of an existing covenantal Christian society. We saw that Calvin had close relations with the Waldensians (see more in chapter 5 "The Covenantal Society, Structure, Organization, and Power Flow," page 61). Therefore, Calvinism must have copied the Waldensian model. More controversial is the alleged conversion of the Waldensians themselves to a covenantal model. If they were converted by Pierre Valdès in the twelfth century then they could not have copied a living covenantal model. Starting with a $\gamma/\beta < .1$ and with a cohesion factor of less than 0.5, the first Waldensian communities would reach a disastrous transgression ratio exceeding 70% (figure 7.3) regardless of how brilliant they were in biblical studies. The resilience of the Waldensians indicates that they inherited their covenantal practices from early Christianity as their own folklore points out.[23]

The biophysical models and their results discussed in this chapter substantiate that covenantal societies are difficult to copy and impossible to invent.

NOTES

1. The 1918 Constitution of the R.S.F.S.R.
2. Guy Chet, *The Colonists' American Revolution: Preserving English Liberty, 1607-1783* (Hoboken, NJ: Wiley, 2019), 7; Gordon S. Wood, "Rhetoric and reality in the American Revolution," in *The William and Mary Quarterly: A Magazine of Early American History* (1966): 6; Brian P. Janiskee, *Local Government in Early America: The Colonial Experience and Lessons from the Founders* (Lanham, MD: Rowman & Littlefield Publishers, 2010), 3; David C Williams, "The Constitutional Right to Conservative Revolution," *Harv. CR-CLL Rev.* 32 (1997); ibid.

3. 1 July, 1918.

4. It took place in Jan. 1918 Rex A. Wade, *The Russian Revolution, 1917* (Cambridge, UK: Cambridge University Press, 2005), 285–286.

5. The term ethos indicates a state of mind resisting stratification and not necessarily an absolute equality. Avraham Faust, *Israel's Ethnogenesis: Settlement, Interaction, Expansion and Resistance* (London: Equinox Pub., 2006), 101.; Jo Ann Hackett, "There was no King in Israel," in *The Oxford History of the Biblical World* (New York: Oxford University Press, 1998). Hackett illustrates this ethos in a powerful example: Gideon refused to become king (Judges 8.22). Ibid., 150. Hackett notes that "Gideon's answer was the correct one for the time." In other words, regardless of its historicity, the story reflects the "'politically' correct" mood of those times.

6. Joseph Livni and Lewi Stone, "The stabilizing role of the Sabbath in pre-monarchic Israel: A mathematical model," *Journal of Biological Physics* 41 (2015): 203–221.

7. One week is known to be a quarter of a lunar month; however, an Iron Age nomadic shepherd would notice the mismatch between seven days and a quarter of a month; if the two matched then every New Moon would occur on the same day of the week; The New Moon occurred in 2019 February on Monday, in March on Wednesday, and in April on Friday.

8. Aristotle, Benjamin Jowett, and Henry William Carless Davis, *Politics*, Kindle edition ed. (Mineola, NY: Dover Publications, 2000), 81.

9. Ibid., 83.

10. You shall not abuse any widow or orphan (Exodus 22:22-24).

11. For example, Creek, Choctaw, Chickasaw and Cherokee, Robert L Carneiro, "Was the chiefdom a congelation of ideas?," *Social Evolution & History* 1, no. 1 (2002); Ilgynly-depe In Turkmenistan, Y.E. Berezkin, "Alternative models of middle range society," *"Individualistic" Asia vs. "collectivistic" America* (2004); some celtic groups in the South of France, Benjamin P. Luley, "Equality, inequality, and the problem of 'Elites' in late Iron Age Eastern Languedoc (Mediterranean France), ca. 400–125 BC," *Journal of Anthropological Archaeology* 41 (2016): 33–54.

12. Eviatar Zerubavel, *The Seven Day Circle: The History and Meaning of the Week* (Chicago: University of Chicago Press, 1989), 14.

13. James.E. Smith, *Biblical Protology* (Raleigh, NC: Lulu.com, 2007), 176.

14. Ibid.; Robert Wilson, *Astronomy Through the Ages: The Story Of The Human Attempt To Understand The Universe* (Boca Raton, FL: CRC Press, 2003), 7.

15. Zerubavel, *The Seven Day Circle*, 14.

16. Ibid., 45.

17. Zvi Eckstein and Maristella Botticini, "From farmers to merchants, conversions and diaspora: Human capital and Jewish history," *Journal of the European Economic Association* 5, no. 5 (2007): 885–926.

18. Joseph Livni, "The cultural evolution of an institution: The Sabbath," *Cliodynamics* 8 (2017).

19. Livni and Stone, "The stabilizing role of the Sabbath in pre-monarchic Israel."

20. In the example of a bank account, the balance can go into the negative numbers known as overdraft; naturally, in the case of transgressors zero is the lower bound.

21. For example, the Catholic repentance mechanism consists of private confession of a congregant to a priest; the repentance in covenantal system is public therefore it takes place at the assembly; see, for example, Early Christians Roger Alling and David J. Schlafer, *Preaching as Pastoral Caring* (Harrisburg, PA: Morehouse Pub., 2005), 130., Waldensians, Jean Léger, *Histoire generale des eglises evangeliques des Vallees de Piemont ou Vaudoises* (Leiden: Jean le Carpentier, 1669), 193. and Jews of the Diaspora Howard N. Lupovitch, *Jews at the Crossroads: Tradition and Accommodation During the Golden Age of the Hungarian Nobility, 1729–1878* (Budapest: Central European University Press, 2007), 92.

22. "Very strong findings reflect the importance of Jewish diaspora communities for the rise of Christianity." Rodney Stark, "Christianizing the urban empire: An analysis based on 22 Greco-Roman cities," *Sociology of Religion* 52, no. 1 (1991): 77–88.

23. Édouard Montet, *La noble leçon: Texte original d'après le manuscrit de Cambridge, avec les variantes des manuscrits de Genéve et de Dublin, suivi d'une traduction française et de traductions en vaudois moderne* (Paris: Libraierie G. Fischbacher, 1888).

Chapter 8

Covenantal Psychology

This chapter is about a state of mind shared by constituents of covenantal communities. Ideally, as all societies, covenantal societies arrived at a *transgression-free* status. However, this is rarely the outcome of any justice system. Frequently, covenantal societies had to compromise allowing a certain amount of wrongdoing. In analogy to epidemics, we called this compromise a status of *endemic transgression*.[1] The mathematical model discussed in chapter "Inventing a Covenantal Society is Impossible" reveals that the endemic percentage of transgressors depends on the ratios between the three coefficients of table 7.. For example, all three charts (figure 7.1, figure 7.2, and figure 7.3) indicate that the endemic percentage of transgressors is lower if the repentance rate is higher. What increases the repentance rate? Unfortunately, neither the mathematical model nor the analogy between epidemic and transgression can answer the question. Fortunately, other disciplines came to the rescue. A sociologists' analysis of a covenantal system pointed at the psychological dimension determining covenantal repentance:

> It is a form of social living on a lot of land of a closed biological group, often bound by kinship, living in family households, associated in a community, (obște), which has the right to interfere with the private business of every household, by decisions taken by its general assembly, according to laws of the joint-ownership (devalmașia) and to a psychological mechanism set by diffuse traditions.[2]

The description was about unranked communities living in the Romanian Carpathian valleys. I exchanged communications with professor Bădescu, one of its authors. Subsequently, I carried out a research of this societal type concluding that they are indeed a Christian European covenantal society that claims its existence since time immemorial.³ I submit that even the term *devălmășia* indicates early Christian origins.⁴

This chapter explains how the "psychological mechanism set by diffuse traditions" improves the repentance rate and why it is essential to the survival of a covenantal society.

The previous quote of the sociological analysis resonates with anyone who grew up in a Jewish community. That is because the covenantal set of mind is coached in the first prayer a Jewish child is taught: the *Shema Israel* "probably the best known and most often repeated prayer in Judaism."⁵ According to the conventional wisdom, the prayer "proclaims the unity of God"⁶ as does its biblical source.⁷ With your permission, I will disregard this characterization not because it is not the truth but because it is not the whole truth. For the purpose of explaining the covenantal psychology, the more significant message of the *Shema Israel* is the commitment to the covenant as expressed in:

And these words, which I command thee this day, shall be upon thy heart⁸;

The unity of God is invoked earlier; no doubt it accentuates the covenant's source of authority. The prayer is daily recited reminding that:

(a) The covenant was commanded by the Lord : "These words I am commanding you."⁹
(b) The Lord commanded it directly to each faithful: "I am commanding *you*."¹⁰ This is a strong leveling principle as proven by resistance to stratification in all covenantal embodiments of table 5.2 (see more in chapter 10 "God Gave Moses the Law").
(c) The covenant shall be esteemed. [These words] are to be upon your hearts.
(d) Each individual is obliged to teach his/her off-spring the covenant: "And thou shalt teach them diligently unto thy children"¹¹; the tradition is kept alive from one generation to the next.
(e) The commandments of the covenant shall guide the congregant everywhere from early morning to late at night: "and [you] shall talk of them when you sit in your house, when you walk by the way, when you lie down, and when you rise up."¹²

One can summarize that the message of the Shema Israel is that from cradle to grave, the covenant is supreme law equal for everyone and uninterrupted practice at the same time.¹³

Another essential ingredient noticed earlier by Bădescu is "the right to interfere." I would go further and describe it as *the obligation to mind other people's business.* Covenantal culture diverges on this point from most other cultures because prevalently the virtue is "minding your own business."[14]

Not only Jews "interfere in other people's business"[15] but also the Pilgrims displayed a "clannish commitment to one another"[16] while "constantly comparing their own actions to those of others."[17] Constant peer pressure ruled in valleys of the Pyrenees.[18] In the Alps of the Waldensians, "a vigorous collective discipline assured cohesion and resilience."[19] The Puritans "joined in 'holy watchfulness' over one another."[20]

The interference in other people's business plays the role of detecting deviations illustrated by the rhombus of the diagram of figure 3.2. Since in a rankless society there is no police, everyone is a detective. The Romanian sociologists discovered this fact from observing the life of the *obște*. I provided examples how other scholars noticed the same habit in the Jewish, Gascon, Waldensian, Puritan, and Pilgrim communities. No one identified this custom from reading the Bible even though I claim that Maimonides managed to detect it in the book of Leviticus: "Directly rebuke your neighbor, so that you will not incur guilt on account of him." According to the conventional wisdom, Leviticus 19:17 teaches to discretely discuss one's conflict with a neighbor. Maimonides who was aware of the "diffuse tradition" of the covenantal practice makes it clear that if the discrete rebuke doesn't produce repentance then one has no choice but to name and shame in public.[21] Coincidentally, Pierre Valdès (1140–1205) lived contemporaneously with Maimonides (1138–1204). I wonder how could Valdès learn from Leviticus 19:17 or from anywhere else in the Bible that it takes "a collective discipline"[22] to keep the Waldensians on the right path. Maimonides is one of the most knowledgeable Judaic scholars not only of his generation but of all times. Nevertheless, I contend that Maimonides interpreted the "directly rebuke your neighbor" commandment according to the practice he saw in his community of Cordoba. I made this detour to underline again that the claim that either Valdès or anyone else founded a covenantal network is not credible.

The obligation to interfere plays an essential role in controlling transgression and keeping it within tolerable limits. The Puritan practice of New England survived because the Puritan cared not only about his own good behavior but about his neighbors' too. "Salvation depended on communal virtue"[23] was taught and practiced:

> Rigorous Calvinists, they had come a great distance to worship as they pleased; they were intolerant of those who did so differently.[24]

"Ardent, anxious, unbashful, incurably logical,"[25] Puritans didn't mind the scrutiny they were submitted to:

The Massachusetts Puritan also knew—or devoutly hoped—that he was being watched. If you inhabited a city on a hill, by definition you stood onstage. That gaze did not discomfort the settlers.[26]

True, Puritans, and Pilgrims shared "Robinson's sense of his congregation as an autonomous enclave of righteousness."[27] The bad news is that the sad proceedings of Salem prove that this minding of other peoples' business can go too far and "extreme right can blunder into extreme wrong."[28] The good news is that Salem revealed a self-correcting mechanism partially contributing to the resilience of the covenantal concept. Figure 6.2 illustrates the model of controlling evildoing. The model is a derivative of the biophysical model of controlling epidemics known as the SIR or the Kermack-McKendrick model.[29] The covenantal model is different only by the fact that the repentance mechanism is periodical[30] and therefore bounded.[31] In the special case of the witch trials of Salem, one notices two particularities:

(a) The evil disguised itself as a legitimate virtue; this feature accelerated the corruption.
(b) The lapse rate (figure 6.2) was negligible; as relatives of accused witches woke up with the awareness that the "court might have it backward"[32]

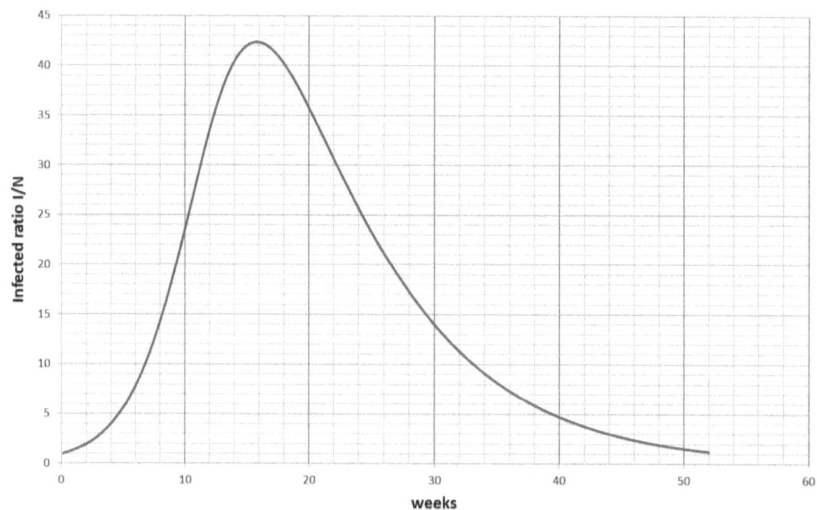

corruption coefficient=0.50; repentance coefficient=0.12

Figure 8.1 SIR Model of the Witch-Trial Epidemic—52 weeks in 1692–1693. At the beginning only 1% are affected by witch hysteria; the contagious disease takes off; then as more relatives of accused are convinced that the trials prosecute innocents, the immunity to the hysteria grows reaching 'herd immunity and the disease tapers off. Created by the author.

the proportion of recovered (**R**ighteous in figure 6.2) grew. Reasonably, these relatives would not lapse into the **S**usceptible category (figure 6.2). This type of model of negligible lapse rate predicts that the epidemic will eventually stop by itself. This is exactly the biological mechanism of fighting epidemics. As the proportion of recovered grows, the proportion of susceptible decreases.[33] The epidemic self-extinguishes because there are not enough susceptible individuals.[34] I simulated an epidemic using an SIR model and replicating a yearlong outbreak similar to the events of Salem 1692–3 (figure 8.1). The Salem witch epidemic started on 25 February 1692[35] and ended in February 1693.[36]

To my surprise, Schiff uses the same analogy of witch trials to an epidemic.[37] More importantly, she notices that after congregants "weighed in on behalf of miserable relatives,"[38] the epidemic was over.[39]

In spite of Salem, the covenantal habit to be "one another's eagle-eyed guardians"[40] was preserved albeit to a tolerable extent. In the nineteenth century, an unusually clear-sighted foreigner noticed that "in the United States everyone is personally interested in enforcing the obedience of the whole community to the law."[41]

Proto-Israel and most of its descendants (see chapter 9 "Evolution Tree") did not know the difference between law and faith. They practiced a way of life that required either faith or behavior of faithful. And that remained so in each link of the chain of covenantal arrangements (figure 6.2). The covenantal psychology described here is shared by communities belonging to several faiths; these faiths are frequently described as diagonally opposed to each other: Christianity versus Judaism, Catholicism v. Orthodoxy, and Catholicism versus Protestantism. Faith is one segment of the cultural DNA. Jews and Christians obviously differ on that segment of cultural heritage. My thesis has nothing to do with the sequence of cultural genes pointing at religious doctrines. However, the segment of cultural DNA containing this shared psychology, shared government structure, and common *Lex Rex Principle* has everything to do with the thesis of this monograph. Tocqueville, who scrutinized the spirit of the United States, observed the following:

> Amongst the Anglo-Americans, there are some who profess the doctrines of Christianity from a sincere belief in them, and others who do the same because they are afraid to be suspected of unbelief.[42]

These words of wisdom reveal the invisible link between psychology, tradition, practice, faith, and law. My thesis is that reading the Bible alone cannot reveal this hidden connection. Therefore, there is no better place to close this chapter.

NOTES

1. Joseph Livni and Lewi Stone, "The stabilizing role of the Sabbath in pre-monarchic Israel: a mathematical model," *Journal of biological physics* 41 (2015): 203–221.
2. My translation of the original Ilie Bădescu, Ozana Cucu-Oancea, and Gheorghe Șișeşte, *Dicționar de sociologie rurală* (Editura Mica Valahie, 2005).
3. Joseph Livni, "Christianity and The Romanian communities named obște," *Romanian Journal of Sociological Studies,* 1 (2016): 61–71.
4. The Romanian lexicon is Latin with a multitude of Slavic roots; I was told that the term *devălmășie* has neither Latin nor Slavic roots. In Hebrew, the expression Davar Meshiach (דבר משיח) means *the word of the Anointed*; in this context, it is a Hebrew expression, however definitely not Jewish; the idiom λόγος τοῦ Χριστοῦ (*logos tou Christou*) is found in the New Testament, for example, Colossians 3:16; by definition, no Jew would use the expression *the word of Christ.*
5. David M. Gitlitz and I. Stavans, *Secrecy and Deceit: The Religion of the Crypto-Jews* (Albaquerque: University of New Mexico Press, 2002), 461.
6. Ibid.
7. Deut. 6:4–9
8. Deut. 6.6
9. Deut. 6.6
10. Deut. 6.6
11. Deut. 6:7
12. Deut 6.7
13. This analogy between covenantal faith and constitutional faith has been outlined by Sanford Levinson, *Constitutional Faith* (Princeton, NJ: Princeton University Press, 2011), 12.
14. It is worthwhile to mention that covenantal communities are intolerant, as distinguished from the kinds of pluralistic communities that form liberal constitutionalism. For example, the Puritans were known to be intolerant and rigid. The Puritans came to America after 1630. Who was liberal and tolerant in that era? The Puritans and Pilgrims left England because of religious persecutions. That doesn't make the Puritans tolerant; however, it points at the lack of tolerance of their persecutors, that is, the Crown. In 1655, the Waldensians were submitted to the "Piedmont Easter Massacre" by the forces of the Catholic Duke of Savoy, see Alexis Muston, *The Israel of the Alps: A Complete History of the Waldenses and Their Colonies* (London: Blackie, 1875), 337.The Waldensians did mind their next neighbor's business and perhaps that qualifies them as intolerant. However, the Catholic Inquisition earlier or the Catholic Duke of Savoy and his forces in 1655 cannot be considered promoting liberalism either. Irish Catholics murdered approximately one hundred Protestants from Loughgall Parish, County Armagh, at the bridge over the River Bann near Portadown, Ulster. This atrocity occurred at the beginning of the Irish Rebellion of 1641, see Matthew Taylor, *England's Bloody Tribunal: or, Popish Cruelty Displayed, etc* (London: J. Cooke, 1770), 272–83. John Ogilvie a Jesuit priest was sentenced to death by a Glasgow court and hanged and mutilated on March 10, 1615, see Mathias

Tanner, *Societas Jesu usque ad sanguinis et vitae profusionem militans, in Europa, Africa, Asia, et America, contra gentiles, Mahometanos, Judaeos, haereticos, impios, pro Deo, fide, Ecclesia, pietate, sive, Vita, et mors eorum, qui ex Societate Jesu in causa fidei, & virtutis propugnatae, violentâ morte toto orbe sublati sunt* (Prague: Typis Universitatis Carolo-Ferdinandeae, 1675), 82–87. Brian Cansfield (1581–1643), another Jesuit priest was seized while at prayer by English Protestant authorities in Yorkshire. Cansfield was beaten and imprisoned under harsh conditions. He died on August 3, 1643, from the effects of his ordeal, see Matthias Tanner, *Die Gesellshafft Jesu biss zur vergiessung ihres Blutes wider den Gotzendienst Unglauben und Laster* (Prague: Carlo Ferdinandeischen Universitat Buchdruckeren., 1683). It appears that in about 1650, persecution was the rule, tolerance the exception. Curiously, Calvinist Holland was the first society practicing religious tolerance. Their religious toleration comprised not only the Catholics their main opponent, but also Anabaptists and "even the despised Jews." Douglas Campbell, *The Puritan in Holland, England, and America: An Introduction to American History* (London: Harper, 1892).

15. Leo. Lowenthal, *False Prophets: Studies on Authoritarianism* (New York: Taylor & Francis, 2017), 236.

16. Nathanel Philbrick, *Mayflower: A Story of Courage, Community, and War*, Kindle Edition ed. (New York: Penguin Publishing Group, 2006), Kindle loc. 333.

17. Ibid., Kindle Loc. 265.

18. Frédéric Le Play, *L'organisation de la famille selon le vrai modèle signalé par l'histoire de toutes les races et de tous les temps* (Mame, 1895), 128

19. Pierrette Paravy, *De la chrétienté romaine à la Réforme en Dauphiné. Évêques, fidèles et déviants (vers 1340-vers 1350)*, vol. 1, COLLECTION DE L'ÉCOLE FRANÇAISE DE ROME (Rome: École française de Rome, 1993), 1026.

20. Stacy Schiff, *The Witches: Suspicion, Betrayal and Histeria in 1692 Salem*, Kindle Edition ed. (New York Boston London: Little Brown, 2015), 97.

21. Leviticus 19:17 Maimonides explains the verse teaching that "in heavenly i.e. religious matters [Covenant! my note] if he (the sinner) doesn't turn after a secret [rebuke], we may put him to shame in multitude [public] , make his sins public, reprove him in his presence, abuse and curse him until he turns for the better" Moses Maimonides and Hermann H. Bernard, *The Main Principles of the Creed and Ethics of the Jews, Exhibited in Selections from the Yad Hachazakah of Maimonides* (Cambridge: Deighton, 1832), 186.

22. *De la chrétienté romaine à la Réforme en Dauphiné. Évêques, fidèles et déviants (vers 1340-vers 1350)*, 1:1026

23. Schiff, *The Witches*, 97.

24. Ibid., 6.

25. Ibid., 33.

26. Ibid., 48.

27. Philbrick, *Mayflower*, 529.

28. Schiff, *The Witches*, 13.

29. William O. Kermack and Anderson G. McKendrick, "A contribution to the mathematical theory of epidemics" (paper presented at the Proceedings of the Royal Society of London A: mathematical, physical and engineering sciences, 1927).

30. A periodical magnitude varies in time; however, it repeats itself after a defined period; for example, the balance in the checking account of a salaried employee is a periodical value; if the salary is paid monthly then the period is one month.

31. If the period is τ then the repentance coefficient cannot exceed $1/\tau$, see Livni and Stone, "The stabilizing role of the Sabbath in pre-monarchic Israel."

32. Schiff, *The Witches*, 342.; see also p. 357.

33. Figure 12.P.1 of Joshua M. Epstein et al., "Generating Epidemics Dynanics," in *Generative Social Science: Studies in Agent-Based Computational Modeling*, ed. Joshua M. Epstein (Princeton, NJ: Princeton University Press, 2012), 272.

34. The model of Justice Administration (see previous chapter) is slightly different because the **R**ecovered don't acquire permanent immunity. It is called *SIRS* model. The typical epidemic model with permanent immunity of the recovered is called *SIR* model; The Salem witch case is a practical example of the SIR variant; see theoretical description in literature how the disease takes off, reaches a peak and self-extinguishes, for example, Ibid., 271–72.

35. Schiff, *The Witches*, 45.

36. Ibid., 353.

37. Ibid., 209, 281, 340.

38. Ibid., 342.

39. Ibid., 352.' see also David K. Fremon, *The Salem Witchcraft Trials in United States History* (Berkley Height, NJ: Enslow Publishers, Incorporated, 2014), 59.

40. Schiff, *The Witches*, 104.

41. Alexis de Tocqueville, *Democracy in America*, trans. Henry Reeve, Kindle Edition ed., vol. 1 (Project Gutenberg, 2006), 198.

42. Ibid., 244.

Chapter 9

Evolution Tree

As mentioned earlier, this work is about the genealogical ancestry of the American constitution. The term *genealogical* indicates that the work searches for the cultural lineage of the modern constitutional framework. As in bio-genetics, the study results arrive at an ancestry tree; the tree is a branching diagram showing the parent to child succession of various sociopolitical entities. Figure 9.1 illustrates the evolution tree of American constitutionalism from Proto-Israel to the Pilgrims from the covenant to the Mayflower Compact.

The tree doesn't mention every possible Christian or Jewish denomination; its main purpose is to follow the route from early Proto-Israel to Pilgrims and Puritans. For example, the Pilgrims (figure 9.1) are cultural descendants of Calvinists. This means that their practices, community psychology, government structure, and power-flow direction have been directly inherited from Calvinist communities. Similarly, the Calvinists descend from Waldensians; the ancestry arrives at Proto-Israel through similar transmission by vertical inheritance following the path from Waldensians to Early Christians who adopted their community organizations and traditions from Roman Palestine which is a descendant of Proto-Israel.

The tree is slightly different from the conventional family tree of Christian denominations (figure 9.2). First, the two charts represent two different aspects. Figure 9.2 represents relationships of *denominations*. Denomination category is a faith descriptor. A denomination is a subgroup of a major religion; the subgroups reciprocally distinguish each other as being "us" or "them." For example, the Calvinists are a Protestant Christian denomination. The fact that they are not hierarchical or that they subscribe to the "Lex, Rex" direction of authority flow (figure 4.1) doesn't make them less Christian or less Protestant.

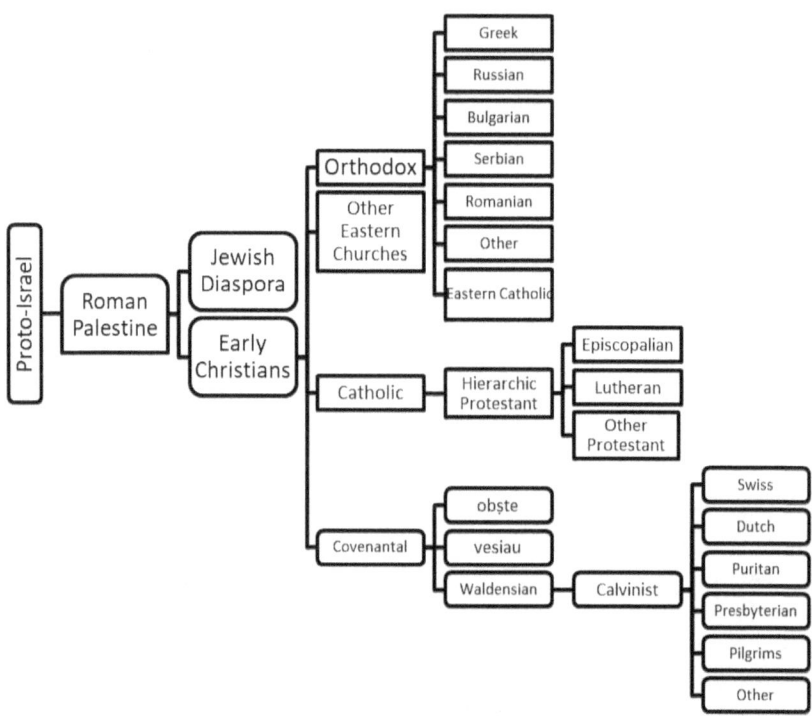

Figure 9.1 Evolution Tree from Proto-Israel to Pilgrims. Sharp-corner modules represent hierarchic organizations and round-corner modules represent rankless congregations and networks; Roman Palestine is mixed: covenantal (Pharisee) and hierarchic (Sadducee); the obște is a covenantal congregation type in the Carpathian region of Romania[1]; the vesiau is a similar congregation type in the Pyrenees[2]. Created by the author.

The evolution tree (figure 9.1) follows the sociopolitical heritage of the Calvinists; they are rankless and covenantal. The previous chapters demonstrated that covenantal traditions cannot be learned from a book. Therefore, Calvinists copied their covenantal practice, "Lex, Rex" model of power flow (figure 4.1), community structure (figure 5.3), repentance mechanism (pp. 84–88), and covenantal psychology from another covenantal organization.

Early Christianity was covenantal (table 5.2); only the church Fathers (fourth century)[3] "started its movement toward pyramidal governance."[4]

Thus, the covenantal nature of Early Christians and of Calvinists is not news. The novelty of this work consists of the three medieval covenantal networks. The Romanian covenantal network of communities (*obște*) and the similar network of Gascony (*vesiau*) are not considered denominations and rightly so. Therefore, they are not mentioned in figure 9.2. The Orthodox Romanian box contains the Romanian *obște*. Similarly, the Roman Catholic box contains the *vesiau* of Gascony. Neither the members of these

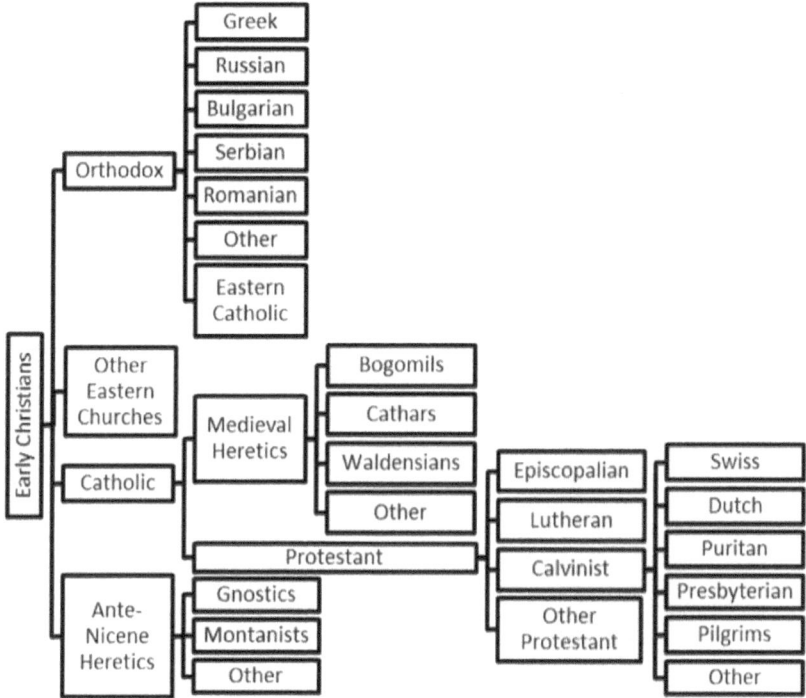

Figure 9.2 **Family Tree of Christian Denominations.** Created by the author.

communities nor the two Churches claim otherwise. The distinction of their sociopolitical life, mostly their autonomous justice administration, was detected not by the church but by scholars of sociology, history, and law. This point emphasizes that figure 9.1 illustrates the evolution of the covenantal sociological type, its understanding of the legal term covenant, its traditions of law enforcement, and its legacy of equality under law and not their theological philosophy.

The Waldensians however are present in both charts. No doubt the Waldensians were excommunicated from the Roman Catholic Church as illustrated in the family tree of denominations (figure 9.2). That is because the church hierarchy regarded them as Catholics until the Synod of Verona (1184) when they were excommunicated. As the Romanian and Gascon networks, the Waldensians opposed hierarchy. However, in Romania and Gascony, the local rulers arrived at an agreed modus vivendi allowing the communities living by their ancient customs, traditions, laws, and law enforcement.

Unfortunately for the Waldensians, their clash against hierarchy was not with a prince, but with the Vatican and the Inquisition. The reasons why a similar arrangement of reciprocal understanding was not achieved with the church is out of scope. The conflict slid into a theological battle; the church branded the Waldensians heretics; only recently the church termed them as a denomination.[5] Therefore, in the chart of figure 9.2 they appear as heretics.

Table 9.1 lists differences between Catholics and Waldensians. Some of the divergences can be interpreted as differences in faith. Table 9.1 lists them because they also represent divergence in practice. Some people associate religiosity more with practice than with faith, while others judge faith and practice equally important.[6] Let me illustrate the difference with an example. The first item of table 9.1 is "against purgatory." Admittedly, some believe and some don't in the existence of purgatory; we don't try to distinguish the believers from skeptic participants at practices of confession, communion, holy mass, and extreme unction which serve among others to avoid

Table 9.1 Practice Divergences of Waldensians

#	Waldensian-Catholic Practice Discord	Pre-Nicaean Practice
1	Against purgatory[7]	Saint-Augustine denies the existence of purgatory[8]
2	Against lent[9]	The church introduced the Lent as early as the eighth century[10]
3	Against matins[11]	Saint Benedict decreed the matins[12]
4	Against decrees of the church[13]	The first Decrees were in Nicaea
5	God alone can absolve from sin[14]	Tertullian harshly criticizes innovation[15]
6	Against long fasts[16]	Spiritual fasting was voluntary in Early Christian times[17]
7	Against images[18]	Pre-Nicaean Christianity opposed images[19]
8	Against prayers for the dead[20]	Saint-Augustine opposes the practice[21]
9	Against saints[22]	One cannot talk about a cult of saints in apostolic times
10	Against priests' celibacy[23]	Saint Paul "urges the bishop to be 'the husband of one wife'"[24]
11	Against Distinction of clergy[25]	Reasonably, Early Christians had no inclination for distinction of clergy[26]
12	Against Hierarchy[27]	Early Christians were against hierarchy[28]
13	Against the wood of the True Cross[29]	The legend originated in the fourth century[30]
14	for sacerdotal succession[31]	Early Christians didn't yet broadly agree to apostolic succession[32]
15	Jurisdiction Rome, Antioch, Alexandria[33]	Canon 6 of the Council of Nicaea provided special jurisdiction to Rome, Antioch, and Alexandria[34]
16	Against levitical pomp[35]	Reasonably, the simplistic organization of the Early Christians had no room for Levitical pomp

purgatory. They are practiced by Catholics regardless of their religious belief in purgatory.

The distinction between faith and practice is important for the purpose of clarifying the thesis of this book. The thesis submits that the roots of American constitutionalism are in the Covenant of Israel. Many scholars linked the constitution with its biblical roots.[36] One reads that the Pilgrims were "imbued with the heritage of covenant."[37] The term *imbued* indicates faith; however, the term heritage points at practice. Levinson's book is about constitutional *faith* as its title confirms. However, Levinson knows the distinction. Two examples of Levinson are helpful. Talking about conversion to Judaism Levinson distinguishes between "propositional content of Judaism"[38] and the "willingness of the convert to take on the behavioral duties attached to Judaism, the performance of the commandments."[39] The thesis of this monograph is about the latter. The second example of Levinson requires less constitutional expertise because it talks about the covenant of marriage; most of the human race is familiar with this bond.

The "wedding vows, by which . . . two individuals join together in constituting a special kind of common enterprise" are a covenant and a leap of *faith*. To put it concisely, the wedding is *faith* the marriage is practice. In most cases, the practice of marriage is inherited from our parents. Frequently we do what our parents did; in some case, we intentionally do the opposite. Either way, the daily practice of marriage is a result of cultural inheritance from earlier generations of ancestors. This monograph is about covenantal practice. That said, this book doesn't deny either the existence or the importance of constitutional faith. This thesis is about practice because the evolution tree of figure 9.1 connecting the Pilgrims to Israel of the Judges is about the transmission of practice, that is, social structure, respecting equality and opposing inequality, reciprocal responsibility, and so on. This segment of shared cultural DNA can be explained only by the evolution tree (figure 9.1). The similarity between covenantal faith and constitutional faith could be explained by the Pilgrims knowledge of the Scriptures and their reliance on the covenant; however, the practice requires faithful copying of a living model.

The Catholic practices of table 9.1 also known as *sacraments* are observed by the Catholic tradition and they are very much consistent with a hierarchic philosophy. The doctrine of apostolic succession authorizes only ordained priest to administer *sacraments*. The authority of these priests flows from top to bottom in a ranked order: Pope, cardinal, archbishop, bishop, priest, and deacon.

The Waldensians did not practice confession and extreme unction because their heritage gave no human the authority to forgive sins. The Inquisition accused the Waldensians not only of not believing in purgatory but most importantly for spreading the view that the Roman church thought up the purgatory because of its greed.[40] This accusation reveals that the conflict was

Table 9.2 Waldensian Practices Conforming to Catholic Doctrine

#	Practice
1	For trinity[41]
2	For Sabbath on Sunday[42]
3	For Incarnation of the Son of God[43]
4	For resurrection of the dead[44]
5	For the Last Judgment[45]
6	For the Resurrection of Christ[46]
7	Election of church by Christ[47]
8	Christian date of celebration of Easter[48]
9	There is an after-world[49]
10	Love thy enemy[50]
11	Mary, "the noble Virgin of royal descent"[51]
12	Original sin[52]

less about believing in purgatory and more about opposing the practice of administering means to avoid purgatory. This point generates another question: how did the alleged founder(s) of the Waldensians know that the church introduced the concept of purgatory?

This question is important because the conventional wisdom claims that Pierre Valdès founded the Waldensian sect in Lyon at about 1170[53] or in 1173.[54] According to the conventional wisdom, this hypothesis that Valdès is the founder of the Waldensians "is not seriously challenged anymore."[55] Chapter 7 "Inventing a Covenantal Society is Impossible" not only challenges this unopposed theory but demonstrates that Pierre Valdès couldn't devise a proper repentance mechanism which is essential to the survival of the covenantal model. This chapter brings an additional proof that Pierre Valdès could not found the Waldensian sect this time showing that he had no chance to arrive at the divergences of table 9.2. I dwell on disproving the theory claiming that Valdès founded the Waldensians, not for the sake of having a debate, but because by proving the hereditary link between Early Christians and Waldensians I prove the validity of the tree of figure 9.1. Let us return to discuss first the practices related to purgatory. Let me show that it is not likely that Valdès knew that by removing these practices one returns closer to the Early Christian tradition.

There is some technical fault in admitting that Valdès knew about the history of purgatory while portraying him as insufficiently educated.[56] Even if he were educated in church history, he would reasonably not know Saint-Augustine's objection to purgatory. On the other hand, inferring that Valdès didn't know about the invention of purgatory casts doubt on this "unchallenged theory" that he founded the Waldensian sect. For the sake of argument, let me assume that Valdès guessed that the church invented the purgatory and that early

Christianity practiced nothing to avoid expiatory purification. The probability of guessing right the answer to a dual choice test question is 50%. However, table 9.2 lists sixteen divergences; its right-hand column indicates that in all sixteen divergences, the Roman Catholic practice conflicted not only with the Waldensian practice but also with the pre-Nicaean Christian practice. Therefore, in all sixteen deviations, the Roman Catholic Church modified earlier practices.

The unadjusted curve of figure 9.3 considers that Valdès guessed correctly not one but sixteen deviations. This implies that Valdès introduced sixteen dissidences and succeeded in all of them to return to Early Christian practice. The horizontal axis represents the probability of correctly guessing one divergence, that is, closer to Early Christians. The intersection of the unadjusted curve with the vertical grid line crossing the horizontal axis at point .5 is 1.53×10^{-5}. Figure 9.3 illustrates that even if the probability were an exaggerated 50%, even then the probability to get sixteen dissidences correctly would be less than one to sixty-five thousand.[57]

Admittedly, Luther did not intend to revive Early Christian practice, yet some of Luther's dissidences coincide with Early Christian practice. Examination of the deviations indicates trivial opposition to unpopular doctrines: purgatory, long fasts, priests' celibacy, a legend about the wood of the true cross and pomposity. Therefore, Valdès also had a good chance to correctly adopt these five innovations. The "adjusted curve" of figure 9.3 calculates Valdès' chances of correctly guessing only $16 - 5 = 9$ dissidences. Even in that case, the probability of success is below one in two thousand. The confidence that Valdès didn't found the Waldensians practice is therefore 99.95%.

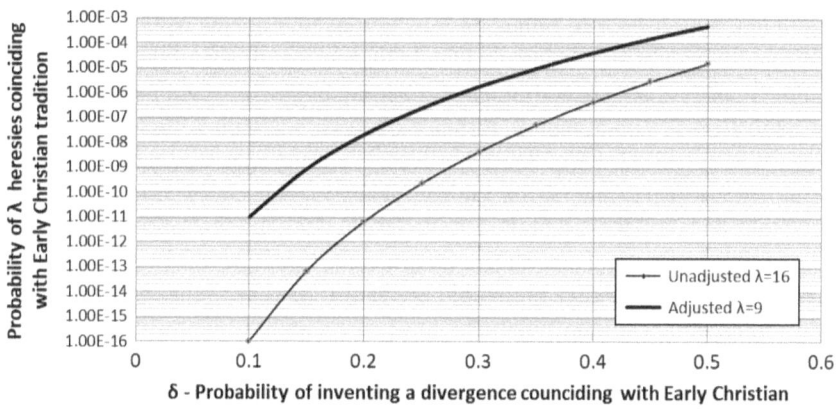

Figure 9.3 Probability of Valdès Guessing Correctly Nine to Sixteen Practices of Early Christianity. Created by the author.

It is worthwhile to note that some proponents of the hypothesis that Valdès is the founder of the Waldensians admit that the Waldensian practice is "drawn from the Sacred Scriptures"[58] implying, that the Waldensians revived Early Christian practice using the Scripture as recipe. The previous debate disproves this argument on grounds that none of the sixteen conformances of the Waldensian practices to Early Christian practice are in the Scriptures. Moreover, chapter "Inventing a Covenantal Society is Impossible" demonstrates that Valdès could not arrive at a proper repentance mechanism by a trial-and-error sequence. Moreover, he could not guess such a mechanism the first time right because the adequate mechanism requires at least five essential features (items 5–9 of table 5.1). None of these features become obvious from reading the Scripture. The easiest example for illustrating this is the Sabbath institution. The conventional wisdom equates the Sabbath with a day of rest. One can read the Bible time and again and the Sabbath will remain a day of rest. However, in the covenantal practice, the Sabbath is a day when work is prohibited. The difference is that a person is *allowed to refuse* to work on a rest day; however, work prohibition *obligates* the congregant *to refuse* to work. Neither Valdès nor Calvin could learn from the Bible the essential role of the Sabbath in maintaining a covenantal society. This role is not obvious even if one witnesses the practice.[59] Calvin must have had an exceptional perception; he observed the practice and detected the crucial role of the weekly assemblies:

> But unless these meetings are stated and have fixed days allotted to them how can they be held? . . . So impossible, however, would it be to preserve decency and order without this politic arrangement that the dissolution of it would instantly lead to disturbance and ruin of the church.[60]

A hierarchy will not be ruined because some congregants work on Sabbath. Unlike Calvin, Valdès, the alleged Catholic founder of the Waldensian faith, couldn't watch a covenantal practice. Consequently, he could not detect that the Sabbath is of paramount importance. Another example of Scripture ambiguity is in verses 83–84 of La noble leçon[61] stating that God gave the commandments to each one of the faithful. The Waldensians learned this from the Bible because they inherited their covenantal interpretation from their covenantal parents and ancestors. Chapter 10 "God Gave Moses the Law" explains why people with hierarchic education read the same Scripture and arrive at an opposite interpretation.

This chapter doesn't claim that the Waldensian practice is identical to Early Christians' practice. Table 9.2 shows Waldensian practices that may come either from apostolic times or the Catholic Church. I detected one practice that positively comes from the Catholic Church: the date of

Easter. The great majority of the practices of table 9.1 cannot be explained without a succession of traditional heritage. Therefore, it is safe to conclude that the Waldensian covenantal structure, the inverted power flow, and the philosophy allowing the survival of the Waldensian communities had been inherited from Early Christians and had been transmitted by tradition from one generation to the next.

NOTES

1. Henri H. Stahl, *Traditional Romanian Village Communities* (Cambridge: Cambridge University Press, 1980); Henri H. Stahl, *Sociologia satului devălmaș românesc* [Sociology of communal Romanian village], vol. 3 (Bucharest: Fundația Regele Mihai I, 1946); Ilie Bădescu, Ozana Cucu-Oancea, and Gheorghe Șișeşte, *Dicționar de sociologie rurală* (Editura Mica Valahie, 2005); Joseph Livni, "Christianity and The Romanian communities named obște," *Romanian Journal of Sociological Studies*, 1 (2016): 61–71.

2. Hélène Couderc-Barraud, *La violence, l'ordre et la paix: résoudre les conflits en Gascogne du XIe au début du XIIIe siècle* (Presses universitaires du Mirail, 2008); Gustave Bascle de Lagrèze, *Histoire du droit dans les Pyrénées—comté de Bigorre* (1867); *La féodalité dans les Pyrénées, comté de Bigorre*, mémoire lu à l'Académie des sciences morales et politiques (Paris: A. Durand, 1864); Frédéric Le Pay, *La Réforme sociale en France déduite de l'observation comparée des peuples européens*, 3 vols. (Paris: Tours, 1874).

3. Ambrose was still elected by the people in 374 Carlo Locatelli, *Vita di S. Ambrogio* (Milano: S. Majocchi, 1874), 54.

4. Daniel J. Elazar, *Covenant & Commonwealth: From Christian Separation through the Protestant Reformation* (New Brunswick, NJ: Transaction Publishers, 1995), 38.

5. In 2015, Pope Francis, asked Waldensian Christians for forgiveness for their persecution.

6. Adam B. Cohen, Joel I. Siegel, and Paul Rozin, "Faith versus practice: Different bases for religiosity judgments by Jews and Protestants," *European Journal of Social Psychology* 33, no. 2 (2003): 287–295.

7. Monastier, *Histoire de l'Eglise vaudoise - Tome I*, Vol. 1 (Geneva: Kessmann, 1847), 14, 19; Paravy, *De la chrétienté romaine à la Réforme en Dauphiné*, Vol. 1, 939, 44, 1158; Audisio, "Des Pauvres de Lyon aux vaudois réformés," 49, 50; Adam Blair, *History of the Waldenses: With an Introductory Sketch of the History of the Christian Churches in the South of France and North of Italy, Till these Churches Submitted to the Pope, When the Waldenses Continued as Formerly Independent of the Papal See* (Edinborough: A. & C. Black, 1832), 161.

8. Jacques Le Goff, *The Birth of Purgatory* (Chicago: University of Chicago Press, 1986), 36,66.

9. Monastier, *Histoire de l'Eglise vaudoise—Tome I*, 1, 15; Léger, *Histoire generale des eglises evangeliques des Vallees de Piemont ou Vaudoises*, 124.

10. Adrien Baillet, *Les vies des Saints et histoire des festes et des mysteres de l'Eglise* (Paris: Nully, 1710), 11.

11. Monastier, *Histoire de l'Eglise vaudoise—Tome I*, 1, 15; Audisio, "The Waldensian Dissent: Persecution and Survival c. 1170-c. 1570, trans," 55.

12. Roy Hammerling, *A History of Prayer: The First to the Fifteenth Century* (Leiden: Brill, 2008), 210; Geoffrey Wainwright, *The Oxford History of Christian Worship*, ed. Geoffrey Wainwright and Karen B Westerfield Tucker (Oxford: Oxford University Press, USA, 2006), 110.

13. Vedder, "Origin and Early Teachings of the Waldenses," 481.

14. Blair, *History of the Waldenses*, 140; Alexis, *L'Israël des Alpes: première histoire complète des Vaudois du Piémont et de leurs colonies*, Vol. I (Paris: Libr. de Marc Ducloux, 1851), 12; Allix, *Some Remarks Upon the Ecclesiastical History of the Ancient Churches of Piedmont* (Clarendon, 1821), 236.

15. C. Danley, *Peter: Friend and Apostle of Jesus, Failure and Finally Greatness* (New York: iUniverse, 2008), 139–40.

16. Léger, *Histoire generale des eglises evangeliques des Vallees de Piemont ou Vaudoises*, 96.

17. Johannes Behm, "Nestis," in *Theological Dictionary of the New Testament: Abridged in One Volume*, ed. G. Kittel, G. Friedrich, and G.W. Bromiley (Grand Rapids, MI: Eerdmans Publishing Company, 1985), 633.

18. Monastier, *Histoire de l'Eglise vaudoise - Tome I*, 1, 2, 17, 30; Paravy, *De la chrétienté romaine à la Réforme en Dauphiné*, Vol. 1, 1158.

19. The Second Council of Nicaea (787) triggered the proliferation of Christian images in the West mostly in the form of sculpture Beate Fricke, "Fallen Idols and Risen Saints: Western Attitudes Towards the Worship of Images and the 'Cultura Veterum Deorum,'" in *Negating the Image: Case Studies in Iconoclasm*, ed. Ann McClanan and Jeffrey Johnson (New York: Routledge, 2016), 67. However, the Council of Frankfurt (797) and the Libri Carolini ibid. still oppose the rulings about tolerance of images of the Second Council of Nicaea; one concludes that the permissive attitude toward images was fixated in about the 8th century.

20. Vedder, "Origin and Early Teachings of the Waldenses," 482; William Stephen Gilly, *Waldensian Researches During a Second Visit to the Vaudois of Piemont* (London: Rivington, 1831), 140.

21. James B. Gould, *Understanding Prayer for the Dead: Its Foundation in History and Logic* (Eugene, Oregon: Cascade Books, 2016), 27.

22. Monastier, *Histoire de l'Eglise vaudoise—Tome I*, 1, 17, 30; Paravy, *De la chrétienté romaine à la Réforme en Dauphiné*, Vol. 1, 1158; Audisio, "The Waldensian Dissent: Persecution and Survival c. 1170-c. 1570, trans," 55; Vedder, "Origin and Early Teachings of the Waldenses," 483; Allix, *Some Remarks upon the Ecclesiastical History*, 236.

23. Léger, *Histoire generale des eglises evangeliques des Vallees de Piemont ou Vaudoises*, 96.

24. Charles A. Frazee, "The origins of clerical celibacy in the Western church," *Church History* 41, no. 2 (1972): 150. The "first thinker to champion clerical celibacy over matrimony is Tertullian (c. 150-225)." Nevertheless, in 325, St. Paphnutius "was mainly instrumental in preventing the rule of celibacy being forced on the clergy by the Council of Nicea" Edgar C. S. Gibson, "John Cassian," in *A Select Library of Nicene and Post-Nicene Fathers of the Christian Church: Sulpitius Severus. Vincent of Lerins. John Cassian*, ed. Philip Schaff and Henry Wace (New York: Christian Literature Company, 1894), 319. claiming that "marriage itself is honorable and the bed is undefiled" (Parish 2016, 68, Bauduer 1827).

25. Monastier, *Histoire de l'Eglise vaudoise—Tome I*, 1, 12; Paravy, *De la chrétienté romaine à la Réforme en Dauphiné*, Vol. 1, 932.

26. Early Christianity is ambivalent regarding this question; according to Edward Gibbon, *The History of the Decline and Fall of the Roman Empire* (Boston: Little, Brown, 1854) the terms *laity* and *clergy* antedate Tertullian (155–240). Nevertheless, Tertullian was "outspokenly critical of bishops who based their authority solely on their office, rather than their spiritual qualities and resolve" John Potts, *A History of Charisma* (London: Palgrave Macmillan UK, 2009), 71.

"The whole body of Christians was upon a level: 'all ye are brethren'. The distinctions which St. Paul makes between Christians are based not upon office, but upon varieties of spiritual power" Edwin Hatch, *The Organization of the Early Christian Churches* (London: Rivingtons, 1882), 121.

27. Monastier, *Histoire de l'Eglise vaudoise—Tome I*, 1, 12; Audisio, "The Waldensian Dissent: Persecution and Survival c. 1170-c. 1570, trans," 16.

28. The study of the actual Early Christian organization indicates that the administration of the communities was taken care by local community councils usually named *gerousia* and the officers of the councils were called *presbyters* Hatch, *The Organization of the Early Christian Churches*, 65. The initial job description of these officers varied in time and space; however, by the second century it became more uniform and it coincided with the one of the Jewish *elders* ibid., 67. Moreover, the Early Christian communities of Palestine continued the organization of the Jewish communities and "there is . . . a strong presumption, which subsequent history confirms . . . that the *elders* of the Jewish communities which had become Christian were, like the *elders* of the Jewish communities which remained Jewish, officers of administration and of discipline." Since the Christian communities had the power to remove elders of the council ibid., 119–20., one concludes that the Early Christians were *against hierarchy*.

29. Allix, *Some Remarks upon the Ecclesiastical History*, 236; William Stephen Gilly, *Narrative of an Excursion to the Mountains of Piemont, and Researches Among the Vaudois, Or Waldenses, Protestant Inhabitants of the Cottian Alps: With an Appendix Containing Copies of Ancient Manuscripts and Other Interesting Documents* (London: C. and J. Rivington, 1824), 167.

30. Jan Willem Drijvers, *Helena Augusta* (Leiden: E.J. Brill, 1992), 5; Barbara Baert, *A Heritage Of Holy Wood: The Legend Of The True Cross In Text And Image* (Leiden: Brill, 2004), x.

31. Paravy, De la chrétienté romaine à la Réforme en Dauphiné. Évêques, fidèles et déviants (vers 1340-vers 1350), 1, 937, 39., footnote 69; Allix, Some remarks upon the ecclesiastical history of the ancient churches of Piedmont, 282–83.

32. Early Christian communities had a governing body of presbyters (elders); Hatch, The Organization of the Early Christian Churches, 39 provides evidence that they were also called επισκοποι (bishops) a function that slowly passed "into the hands of a single officer" named bishop, see also George Herbert Dryer, History of the Christian Church (Cincinnati: Curts & Jennings, 1896), 191. As mentioned earlier Tertullian criticised bishops who based their authority on their office Potts, A History of Charisma, 71. This proves that in the first two centuries the authority of the bishop was questioned and the notion of apostolic succession was not yet popular.

33. Paravy, De la chrétienté romaine à la Réforme en Dauphiné. Évêques, fidèles et déviants (vers 1340-vers 1350), 1, 1036; Gilly, Waldensian Researches During a Second Visit to the Vaudois of Piemont, 470.

34. Hefele and Clark, A History of the Councils of the Church: from the Original Documents, to the close of the Second Council of Nicaea A.D. 787, 389.

35. Monastier, Histoire de l'Eglise vaudoise - Tome I, 1, 13.

36. See endnote 27 of the introduction "Nice to meet you . . ."

37. Sanford Levinson, *Constitutional Faith* (Princeton, NJ: Princeton University Press, 2011), 11.

38. Ibid., 91.

39. Ibid.

40. Point XI Léger, *Histoire generale des eglises evangeliques des Vallees de Piemont ou Vaudoises*, Vol. II (Leiden: Jean le Carpentier, 1669), 23.

41. Paravy, *De la chrétienté romaine à la Réforme en Dauphiné*, Vol. 1, 931; Gilly, *Waldensian Researches During a Second Visit to the Vaudois of Piemont*, 141; Comba, *History of the Waldenses of Italy*, 265–66, 69.

42. Léger, *Histoire generale des eglises evangeliques des Vallees de Piemont ou Vaudoises*, 96; Paravy, *De la chrétienté romaine à la Réforme en Dauphiné*, Vol. 1, 1076; Gilly, *Waldensian Researches During a Second Visit to the Vaudois of Piemont*, 217; Comba, *History of the Waldenses of Italy*, 284.

43. Paravy, *De la chrétienté romaine à la Réforme en Dauphiné*, Vol. 1, 931; Comba, *History of the Waldenses of Italy*, 265–66.

44. Paravy, *De la chrétienté romaine à la Réforme en Dauphiné*, Vol. 1, 931; Comba, *History of the Waldenses of Italy*, 265–66.

45. Paravy, *De la chrétienté romaine à la Réforme en Dauphiné*, Vol. 1, 931; Comba, *History of the Waldenses of Italy*, 265–66.

46. La Noble Leçon verse 62 Montet, *La noble leçon*.

47. Paravy, *De la chrétienté romaine à la Réforme en Dauphiné*, Vol. 1, 931; Comba, *History of the Waldenses of Italy*, 265–266.

48. Paravy, *De la chrétienté romaine à la Réforme en Dauphiné*, Vol. 1, 1077; Jean Jalla, "Un precursore del puseismo nelle Valli al Secolo XVII," *Bollettino della società di studi valdesi*, no. 9 (1884): 39.

49. Point XI Léger, Histoire generale des eglises evangeliques des Vallees de Piemont ou Vaudoises, 23, Vol. II.

50. La Noble Leçon verse 252 Montet, La noble leçon: Texte original d'après le manuscrit de Cambridge, avec les variantes des manuscrits de Genéve et de Dublin, suivi d'une traduction française et de traductions en vaudois moderne.

51. La Noble Leçon verse 208.

52. La Noble Leçon verses 56–58.

53. Philippe Pouzet, "Les origines lyonnaises de la secte des Vaudois," *Revue d'histoire de l'Église de France* 22, no. 94 (1936): 11; Olivier Legendre and Michel Rubellin, "Valdès: un «exemple» à Clairvaux? Le plus ancien texte sur les débuts du Pauvre de Lyon," *Revue Mabillon* 11 (2000): 189.

54. Anonymous chronicler cited by Pouzet, "Les origines lyonnaises de la secte des Vaudois," 8; H.C. Vedder, "Origin and Early Teachings of the Waldenses, according to Roman Catholic Writers of the Thirteenth Century," *The American Journal of Theology* 4, no. 3 (1900): 475; Legendre and Rubellin, "Valdès: un «exemple» à Clairvaux?," 191; Dennis McCallum, "The Waldensian Movement From Waldo to the Reformation," (American Waldesian Society, History: Founded in the Middle Ages, Waldenses, Global Anabaptist Mennonite Encyclopedia, 2014).

55. Gabriel Audisio, "Des Pauvres de Lyon aux vaudois réformés," *Revue de l'"histoire des religions* (2000): 157; see also Pouzet, "Les origines lyonnaises de la secte des Vaudois," 8.

56. "Les origines lyonnaises de la secte des Vaudois," 33; Gabriel Audisio, The Waldensian Dissent: Persecution and Survival c. 1170–c. 1570, trans. Claire Davison (Cambridge: Cambridge University Press, 1999), 24.

57. That is because $1/1.53 \times 10^{-5} = 65536$.

58. Pierrette Paravy, *De la chrétienté romaine à la Réforme en Dauphiné. Évêques, fidèles et déviants (vers 1340-vers 1350)* [in Français]. Collection De L'école Française De Rome. Vol. 1 (Rome: École française de Rome, 1993), 1148.; also "the first forefathers of the Waldensian Church were quite anxious to appeal to apostolic tradition unpracticed, but unforgotten" Emilio Comba, *History of the Waldenses of Italy: From Their Origin to the Reformation*, trans. Teofilo Comba (London: Truslove & Shirley, 1889), 9.

59. Comba suggests that unpracticed tradition can be "unforgotten" *History of the Waldenses of Italy*, 9; if a tradition is not practiced it is forgotten.

60. John Calvin and Henry Beveridge, *Institutes of the Christian Religion* (Peabody, MA: Hendrickson, 2008), 463–64.

61. Édouard Montet, *La noble leçon: Texte original d'après le manuscrit de Cambridge, avec les variantes des manuscrits de Genéve et de Dublin, suivi d'une traduction française et de traductions en vaudois moderne* [in French] (Paris: Libraierie G. Fischbacher, 1888).

Chapter 10

God Gave Moses the Law

This chapter further rationalizes why one cannot design a covenantal society using biblical recipes. The biblical text is valuable information. The reader of the text processes the information into meaning. Information is objective; however, meaning is subjective.[1] In a jury trial, the jurors receive the same information; for some the information means guilty and for some not guilty. Individuals don't store information; they rather accumulate previously interpreted meaning.[2] This chapter will discuss two examples. The examples illustrate why the biblical text predictably means one thing for readers with hierarchical background and something else for readers with an egalitarian background.

Fournier the Inquisitor dedicated ten sessions of questioning the Waldensian suspect named Raymond de La Côte to clear the thorny interpretation of the precept: *God gave Moses the law*.[3] All three monotheistic religions teach this lesson. Both the Inquisitor and his victim accepted it because it is in the Hebrew Bible [Exodus 19:3]. However, there are two ways to recite the sentence:

1. God gave *Moses* the law (emphasis on *Moses*).
2. God gave Moses the *law* (emphasis on *law*).

Fournier's model of social order is hierarchy; for him, Exodus 19:3 teaches that God gave *authority to Moses*, the Levite priest; through a succession of biblical figures one arrives at Christ and subsequently at the Catholic doctrine of Apostolic Succession.[4]

I chose this example not because the phrase "God gave Moses the law" is deep; quite the contrary I chose to discuss it because it is obviously clear. Its ambiguity has nothing to do with its language and everything to do with the background of the reader of the phrase. It is not a coincidence that Paravy perfectly explains Fournier's meaning. Her background, education, and undeniable knowledge of the subject allow her to interpret the meaning of the phrase:

> The faith concerning the law given to Moses actually implied, from the point of view of the Catholic hierarchy, the examination of the delegation of authority by God and thus posed the essential problem of obedience to the Church.[5]

Similarly, a covenantal society cannot exist unless its congregants' persuasion sets the focus on the message and not on the messenger. For example, verses 148–150 of "La noble leçon"[6] illustrate how the Waldensian Raymond de La Côte interpreted the phrase "God gave Moses the law." The verses say "God gave his people the Law; He transmitted it by Moses."

As Early Christians, Waldensians opposed hierarchy. Nevertheless, inquisitors such as Rainier Sacconi[7] and Jacques Fournier "thoroughly explored" the Waldensian hierarchy and found its three ranks of ministry: bishop, priest, and deacon.[8] Born, educated, and living in a world of ranks and elitist bias, an Inquisitor is blind to notions like assembly government, no ranks and supremacy of law.

However, scholars who grew up with Waldensians know better. "The statement of Rainier in the thirteenth century, that the Waldenses had a bishop who alone ordained, is false."[9] Similarly, Léger[10] points out that the three "ranks" detected by the inquisitor are subordinated to the people they teach, and that they need consent of the "Council of Brothers" for any initiative.

No one disputes that the Church is indeed a descendant of Apostolic Christians. However, the Church inherited the model of *hierarchy* from the Roman civilization. In evolutionary terms, the concept of Christian hierarchy is a *mutation* of the fourth century.[11] The Roman aristocracy resisted conversion to Christianity precisely because Early Christianity practiced "love for one's neighbor and humility, with strictures on wealth and notions of equality."[12] Salzman[13] convincingly substantiates that only a faith respecting the privileges of the aristocrats and honoring their status could lead to the conversion of the Roman aristocracy. Aristocrats converted to Christianity only after Christianity adopted "fundamental aristocratic concepts such as *nobilitas*, an attribute derived from birth."[14] The peasantry followed their patrons opening the gates to a massive Christianization.[15]

In a hierarchical world, one cannot reconstruct apostolic egalitarian structure by learning the Scriptures. One needs to see a covenantal practice, understand how it is different, and inherit its vital elements to arrive at a new descendant. Apostolic Christianity and Calvinism followed this path.

The simple statement "God gave Moses the Law" produced ten interrogations of Raymond de La Côte. Imagine the length of the hypothetical discussion of the verses from which our story began:

> In those Days there was no King in Israel; Every man did what was right in his own eyes.[16]

Google Scholar found 1260 works citing "In those Days there was no King in Israel." According to the prevalent opinion of biblical researchers, the intention of the verses is to convince us that "monarchy is a good idea."[17] Let me add my own commentary because it is relevant to my thesis. Needless to say, the second verse produced the royalist interpretation. However, the word "right" casts doubt on this interpretation. Without claiming that the verse was wrongly translated, the original Hebrew term is not *right* but *straight*. My background of exact sciences suggests that the word *straight* doesn't imply anarchy. If the verse were intended to advocate monarchy then the use of the word *straight* would be counterintuitive. In geometry, *straight* and *right* indicate a unique answer: a straight line is the shortest trajectory between two points; a right angle is unique by generating the two equally big angles (figure 10.1).

On this matter, exact sciences and the study of law and policy merge. Both are searching for one solution which is unique, optimal, agreeable, or simply the only practical one. Intriguingly, the origin of the English word *right* is the Proto-Indo-European root *reg*.[18] The root means to move in a

Figure 10.1 **Both Sides of a Right Angle Are Equal Angles.** Created by the author.

straight line,[19] that is, it came from the wisdom of ancient geometry. Yet from this root also grew words describing both legal-political notions of my thesis: Rex and Lex (see Latin *regula* or English regulation[20]). Therefore, this consideration is relevant to the history of law in general. Reasonably, in the beginning of settled existence most disputes were about land and land boundaries. Boundaries were often marked by stones.[21] How many stones one needs to determine a straight line, or a straight angle? Ancient fundamental axioms of Euclidian geometry answer these questions. No wonder concepts of *Law* and *Geometry* provided the wisdom determining the settlement of such disputes. This easily explains why the geometric notion *straight* became related to *law* and *king*. In modern German language, judge is *Richter* (also from the root *reg*) and its meaning is *righter* or the *one who straightens things out*. Therefore, I suggest that the expression *did what was right in his eyes* could also imply that everyone judged what is right and acted accordingly. The fact that Israel of the Judges existed for a couple of centuries and its covenantal spirit survived until our days indicates that this interpretation has merit.

Returning to "God gave Moses the law," the disagreement was not about God, but about Moses and the Law, not about faith but about political authority. Often, I was misunderstood as if I talk about faith. I never do because I understand very little about faith. When saying that one cannot copy a covenantal society, I mean the practice of learning, obeying, and enforcing the covenant. The difficulty of inventing a covenantal society consists of concepts of structure and institutions. For adequate organization and tradition reconcile justice with absence of ruler and allow each congregant to feel equal to his/her peers. Surprisingly, a Catholic aristocrat saw such a practice, perceived it, understood that its particularity is not necessarily its faith and explained it better:

> I do not know whether all the Americans have a sincere faith in their religion, for who can search the human heart? but I am certain that they hold it to be indispensable to the maintenance of republican institutions. This opinion is not peculiar to a class of citizens or to a party, but it belongs to the whole nation, and to every rank of society.[22]

NOTES

1. John C Mingers, "Information and meaning: Foundations for an intersubjective account," *Information Systems Journal* 5, no. 4 (1995): 285–306.

2. Ibid.

3. Pierrette Paravy, *De la chrétienté romaine à la Réforme en Dauphiné. Évêques, fidèles et déviants (vers 1340-vers 1350)*, vol. 1, COLLECTION DE L'ÉCOLE FRANÇAISE DE ROME (Rome: École française de Rome, 1993), 931.

4. See details in Arnold Ehrhardt, *The Apostolic Succession: In the First Two Centuries of the Church* (Eugene, OR: Wipf & Stock Publishers, 2009).

5. My translation of Paravy, *De la chrétienté romaine à la Réforme en Dauphiné*, vol. 1, 931–932.

6. The founding document of the Waldensian creed Édouard Montet, *La noble leçon: Texte original d'après le manuscrit de Cambridge, avec les variantes des manuscrits de Genéve et de Dublin, suivi d'une traduction française et de traductions en vaudois moderne* (Paris: Libraierie G. Fischbacher, 1888), 39.

7. Paravy, *De la chrétienté romaine à la Réforme en Dauphiné*, vol. 1, 1037; Jean Léger, *Histoire generale des eglises evangeliques des Vallees de Piemont ou Vaudoises* (Leiden: Jean le Carpentier, 1669), 199.

8. Paravy, *De la chrétienté romaine à la Réforme en Dauphiné*, vol. 1, 932–34.

9. Emilio Comba, *History of the Waldenses of Italy: From Their Origin to the Reformation*, trans. Teofilo Comba (London: Truslove & Shirley, 1889), 222.

10. Léger, *Histoire generale des eglises evangeliques des Vallees de Piemont ou Vaudoises*, 190.

11. Ambrose of Milan was the first aristocratic bishop ordained in December 374, Carlo Locatelli, *Vita di S. Ambrogio* (Milano: S. Majocchi, 1874), 58; he was still elected in 374, ibid., 45–51.

12. Michele Renee Salzman, *The Making of a Christian Aristocracy: Social and Religious Change in the Western Roman Empire*, Kindle Edition ed. (Cambridge, MA: Harvard University Press, 2002), Kindle loc. 114–15.

13. Ibid.

14. Ibid., Kindle loc. 323–24.

15. Ibid., Kindle loc. 113; Peter Heather, *The Fall of the Roman Empire: A New History* (Hampshire, UK: Pan Books, 2010), 127.

16. Judges 21:25

17. Israel Knohl, *How was the Hebrew Bible Born? Talks with Shmuel Shir* (Tel Aviv: Dvir, 2018).

18. Calvert Watkins, *The American Heritage Dictionary of Indo-European Roots* (Boston; New York: Houghton Mifflin, 2000), 70.

19. Ibid.

20. Ibid.

21. For example, 1 Samuel 6:14.

22. Alexis de Tocqueville, *Democracy in America*, trans. Henry Reeve, Kindle Edition ed., vol. 1 (Project Gutenberg, 2006), 245.

Chapter 11

The Supremacy of the Law

Chapter "God Gave Moses the Law" discussed how people from a hierarchic background cannot envisage a society without hierarchy. Not only were the Inquisitors convinced that the Waldensians had their own hierarchy, but even prominent scholars took at face value such findings of the Inquisition.[1] However, there were a few exceptional thinkers such as A. de Tocqueville and others, (see list of researchers on page 53 in chapter 4 "The Covenantal Society: Lex Rex"), who in spite of their hierarchic background detected, studied, and understood this perplexing model of rule with practically no ruler. Most stimulating is the astonishment of Tocqueville as he unveils a reality that for him is mysterious, yet for the typical American is as trivial as baseball rules[2]:

> In America the principle of the sovereignty of the people is not either barren or concealed, as it is with some other nations; it is recognized by the customs and proclaimed by the laws.[3]

This chapter deals with the supremacy of the Law under the sovereign authority of "we the people." The consensus in America is that the framers of the constitution spoke in the name of "we the people". How has this been embedded in the national consciousness? Similarly, why did Proto-Israel and its Jewish descendants believe that the Covenant expressed the will of the Sovereign?[4] The answer is the same for both questions: the law proclaimed the customs of "we the people." Centuries ago, Aristotle, the ancient sage correlated law obedience with customs: "the law has no power to command obedience except that of habit."[5]

An important conclusion of this wisdom is that not all custom is law and not all law is custom. Custom is law if it is enforceable. Chapter 3 "The

Covenant of Israel: Customary Law or Law" demonstrates that Israel of the Judges enforced its customs substantiating point b) of my thesis (page 8 in the introduction "Nice to Meet You . . ."). At the same time, the first point of the thesis claims that the roots of American constitutionalism are in biblical Israel. That doesn't mean that American constitutional practice consists of the customs of Israel of the Judges. The Israelite root of American constitutionalism is "that agreement on a common text"[6] serving as unique reference to justify "all practices, beliefs, or institutions"[7] of the community and of the network of communities signatories to the agreed common text.[8] As in the American constitutional democracy in all the covenantal heirs of Israel of the Judges, one can establish the following:

> "[w]hile members of the community may disagree about specific beliefs and practices, they do agree about what is the proper way of justifying them."[9]

This significance of the term "supremacy of law" saw light in Israel of the Judges and was inherited by each covenantal society including the Pilgrims.[10] The Pilgrims formulated the Mayflower Compact. The short text was not intended to make world history. However, this important document became the embryo of the constitution because its principle of sovereignty of the people and its message regarding the supremacy of the law have been put into practice as the little colony began its struggle for survival:

> Despite Bradford's lament, his vision of a compact, self-contained community of fellow worshippers remained the organizing principle behind each of the colony's new towns.[11]

This "organizing principle" of Bradford (figures 5.1 and 5.3) had lived for almost three millennia when Bradford and his companions landed in Cape Cod.[12] Neither the Mayflower passengers nor Proto-Israel invented it. Proto-Israel continued its previous nomadic pastoralist traditions; these traditions penetrated its practice of administering justice and keeping internal peace. Both attempts ended up in success, for both it is true that:

> they had taken it upon themselves to found a self-governing republic while no one was looking.[13]

The descendants of both commencements grew into a nation. Naturally, these two nations viewed these inherited rules of organization including its inverted power flow (figure 5.3) as the will of the Sovereign. The designation of the Sovereign evolved along the centuries from "I am the Lord" to "we the people."[14] However, the message of the inviolability of the Sovereign's statute remained the same.

As mentioned above, this message is trivial for the American reader and easily understandable by readers who grew up in a covenantal environment (round cornered boxes of figure 9.1). However, Old World cultures that evolved from the sharp-cornered boxes have kept something of their "ruler makes rules" philosophy. The Enlightenment removed absolute monarchy and replaced obligatory dogmas of the Church with the principle of freedom of religion. Subsequently, the political debate of part of the Old World transitioned into democratic organizations; however, the principle of the law being the supreme source of authority was not directly implemented. The power of the King was replaced by the power of democratically elected parliaments. The democratic parliament inherited the authority to decree the law.

Rousseau attributes absolute sovereignty to the "general will" identifying it with the legislative branch.[15] This contrasts with the view of the American framers of the constitution who insisted on protecting "personal and property rights even against the legislative authority."[16] This contradiction has consequences: French constitutions replaced one another without providing judicial checks on legislative power.[17] Similarly, constitutions in Latin America, replaced previous ones to fit economic visions of rulers or ruling parties.[18]

This emphasis on the difference between the two constitutional concepts should not be read as criticism of either of the two philosophies. The objective of this discussion is rather to illustrate how cultural evolution produced two politically similar systems, each maintaining cultural DNA from its predecessor. This work repeatedly mentions the Aristotelian wisdom that laws are obeyed if they reflect previous practice. Therefore, the democratization of the Old World maintained the concept that rules decreed by the Sovereign, albeit the sovereign became a democratically elected organ. Similarly, in other Old World cultures in which the oligarchic model prevailed before the Enlightenment (e. g., England), democratization did not completely demolish the concept of ruling class and its privileges.

Democracy has many roots and in Europe it inherited concepts of sovereignty from its Christian predecessors (figure 9.1). The American democracy also inherited some European ideas from Athens, Rome, London, and Paris. However, the idea that the Law is Sovereign and that the constitution "is antecedent to government" evolved from the customs of some pastoralist tribes of the Near East, which settled in the Highland of the Holy Land and obstinately resisted the concept of mortal rulers even when they turned to farming.

True, these tribes became a nation which produced a valuable literature culminating with the Hebrew Bible. The Hebrew Bible does contain laws and statutes; however, reading the Bible cannot lead to the concept of Supremacy of law so deeply engraved in the Mayflower Compact. Figure 9.1 illustrates that the route consisted of a process of evolution. Each link inherited the essential practices of its predecessor and conserved them while adopting other cultural mutations from neighboring cultures as the changing circumstances required.

NOTES

1. For example, we read in a study that "the *majorals* or the bishops are at the top of the [Waldensian] hierarchy," my translation of Pierrette Paravy, *De la chrétienté romaine à la Réforme en Dauphiné. Évêques, fidèles et déviants (vers 1340-vers 1350)*, vol. 1, COLLECTION DE L'ÉCOLE FRANÇAISE DE ROME (Rome: École française de Rome, 1993), 933. This is not a note of the inquisitor, but rather Paravy's description of the Waldensian organization.

2. Yours truly still struggles with strikes, foul balls, tag outs, force outs, and strikeouts.

3. Alexis de Tocqueville, *Democracy in America*, trans. Henry Reeve, Kindle Edition ed., vol. 1 (Project Gutenberg, 2006), 33.

4. Judah Halevi (died in 1141) is quoted "The Law is the true King in Israel" Rémi Brague, *The Law of God: The Philosophical History of an Idea* (Chicago: University of Chicago Press, 2007), 50.

5. Aristotle, Benjamin Jowett, and Henry William Carless Davis, *Politics*, Kindle edition ed. (Mineola, NY: Dover Publications, 2000), 38.

6. Moshe Halbertal, *People of the Book: Canon, Meaning, and Authority* (Cambridge, MA: Harvard University Press, 2009), 8.

7. Ibid.

8. Halbertal calls this feature of covenantal existence "text centeredness" ibid., 6–8.

9. Ibid., 8.

10. The term "rule of law" has been utilized to describe many other meanings; for example in a debate the term advocates for abolishing patriarchal laws: "Turkey is called upon to abolish the practice of reduced sentences in the case of so-called honour crimes and to abolish the reference in the penal code to women's virginity. Customs and tradition cannot take precedence over the rule of law" Anna Karamanou, *Progress towards accession by Turkey* (Strasbourg: EU Parliamentary Debates; Apr. 1st, 2004).

I am for erasing reference to female virginity from the penal code; however, I underline here that in this work the term "rule of law" doesn't mean changing the law; it means that the law is above the ruler (Lex Rex model of figure 4.1).

11. Nathanel Philbrick, *Mayflower: A Story of Courage, Community, and War*, Kindle Edition ed. (New York: Penguin Publishing Group, 2006), 2636.

12. Puritans, Pilgrims and Proto-Israel shared the view that "the only biblically sanctioned organizational unit was the individual congregation" ibid., 257. and "a congregation began with a covenant" ibid.

13. Stacy Schiff, *The Witches: Suspicion, Betrayal and Histeria in 1692 Salem*, Kindle Edition ed. (New York Boston London: Little Brown, 2015), 99.

14. How can one mix religion with politics? In ancient time, this distinction didn't exist. In ancient Israel, the covenant was first politics then religion. "It was only later with the rise of Christianity and the beginning of the long exile of the Jews from their lands that covenant took on a more strictly religious character for some, in which the political dimension was downplayed, if not downright ignored by Christian theologians, on the one hand, and diminished by Jewish legists on the other." Daniel J. Elazar, *The Covenant Tradition in Politics*, vol. 1 (Transaction Publishers, 1995), Ch. 1.

15. Jeremy Rabkin, "Revolutionary visions in legal imagery: Constitutional contrasts between France and America," in *The Legacy of the French Revolution*, ed. Ralph C. Hancock and L. Gary Lambert (Lanham, MD: Rowman & Littlefield, 1996), 228.

16. Ibid.

17. Ibid.; Noel B. Reynolds, "The Rule of Law in Eighteenth Century Revolutions," in *The Legacy of the French Revolution*, ed. Ralph C. Hancock and L. Gary Lambert (Lanham, MD: Rowman & Littlefield, 1996), 195.

18. Mario Sznajder, Luis Roniger, and Carlos Forment, *Shifting Frontiers of Citizenship: The Latin American Experience* (Leiden—Boston: Brill, 2012).

Chapter 12

Evolution, Customs, and Law

Throughout this work, I presented evidence that covenantal societies (table 5.2) are similar to each other. The similarities encompass their structure (figures 5.2 and 5.3), their Lex Rex flow of authority (figure 4.1), their mode of operation of the justice administration (chapter 6 "Justice Administration in Biblical Israel"), and their psychological manifestations prevailing in the community (chapter 8 Covenantal Psychology).

The similarities between Jewish Palestine under Romans and Early Christianity described earlier (chapter 5 "The Covenantal Society, Structure, Organization, and Power Flow") are not surprising. More intriguing are the similarities among medieval covenantal societies. The scholars of the Waldensian, Romanian, and Gascon communities worked independently, and they were not aware that they discuss the same social taxonomic identity. Nevertheless, they describe their subject communities in similar terms; the investigations identify not only the same static sociographic pattern, but they also come across identical dynamics of their history, namely traditions that have been transmitted from time immemorial.[1]

Traditions are not invented; they are practiced and inherited.[2] This brings us to evolution. The scientific theory of evolution was introduced to explain the history of inheritable characteristics of living organisms. Scientific research concluded that the giraffe, the elephant, the cockroach, and even the spinach are what they are as a result of evolution. The term evolution has often been loosely borrowed (e.g., quotation about Greek tragedy on page 7 in the introduction "Nice to Meet You . . ."); however, this work associates the evolution of the constitution with biological evolution in the same scientific connotation at least as far as the theory's mathematical substantiation is concerned.[3]

The constitution is a document. Cynical minds would even remark that before it appeared, the constitution was paper and ink. That is not however what makes the constitution worthy of so many serious writings.[4] The constitution is an extraordinary innovation carefully crafted by wise thinkers:

> The Framers of the American Constitution were visionaries. They designed our Constitution to endure. They sought not only to address the specific challenges facing the nation during their lifetimes, but to establish the foundational principles that would sustain and guide the new nation into an uncertain future.[5]

Then, doesn't this idea of evolution of the constitution contradict the creative initiative of the founders? Most people I met would opine that neither the cockroach nor the spinach was conceived by visionaries. Please allow me a little bit of a sidebar here because this cockroach analogy may be deplorably misinterpreted.

There are many ways to describe the history of an innovation. For example, the conventional way is stating that Dr. Fleming discovered antibiotic treatment. Let us hear now how Dr Fleming himself describes the event:

> When I woke up just after dawn on September 28, 1928, I certainly didn't plan to revolutionize all medicine by discovering the world's first antibiotic, or bacteria killer. But I guess that was exactly what I did.[6]

Dr. Fleming researched a bug.[7] He noticed that a dirty mold left by negligence on his desk stopped the growth of his bug colony. Rather than getting upset about this negative outcome of his intended research on September 28, 1928, Dr. Fleming saw the full half of the glass and that revolutionized the treatment of infectious diseases. In evolutionary terms, biological science knew before this event that there are invisible creatures that damage the health of humans. Science made them visible, classified them, and knew that this particular suspect is involved in serious damages. Science also knew something about the mold in question; at least we can deduce that it was known to be a specific type of mold because it had a scientific name.[8] Was Dr. Fleming a visionary or a lucky scientist? He was both!

Skill and luck determine the success of an endeavor. In mathematical jargon skill is deterministic and luck is related to probability. Darwin proposed the evolution theory mentioned earlier; it indeed explains how one arrived at the giraffe, elephant, and all other living creatures.

There is however one aspect of this theory that is often forgotten and that is the role of probabilities involved in evolution. The chapter will explain later why this is relevant; for the time being, let me survey what a mathematician contributed to understanding what evolution is about.

Evolution, Customs, and Law 129

As mentioned earlier, Fisher formulated the mathematical justification of Darwin's theory of evolution.[9] One can explain Fisher's explanation without his algebra using common interdisciplinary language. Evolution is related to genetics and genetics is about inheritance of features from one's parents. Every living creature has at least one parent; we humans belong to the lucky ones that have two parents. Very often children inherit features from their parents: height, eye color, sometimes health disorders, and so on. This is because there is a material component that is identical in our cells and our parent's cells. You guessed correctly it is the material in the nucleus of the cell called DNA. We are different from our parents, not because the copying of the cells is not perfect, but because some segments of the DNA is copied from one parent and others from the other parent. The distribution is random and diversity comes from the huge number of possibilities to combine the various segments.

However, wrong copying from a parent DNA does occur (figure 12.1). It takes place rarely; this phenomenon of wrong copying is well researched and geneticists gave it a name: *mutation*. These mutations are unintentional mistakes. I devote so many words to mutations' lack of intention not to defend these deviations but because often one reads that mutations come about to improve our survival chance when environmental changes endanger us. This is maybe because evolution is often called *survival of the fittest*.

Mutations are random changes. The best analogy to mutations is inadvertent errors found in a term paper copied from someone else.[10] Some of

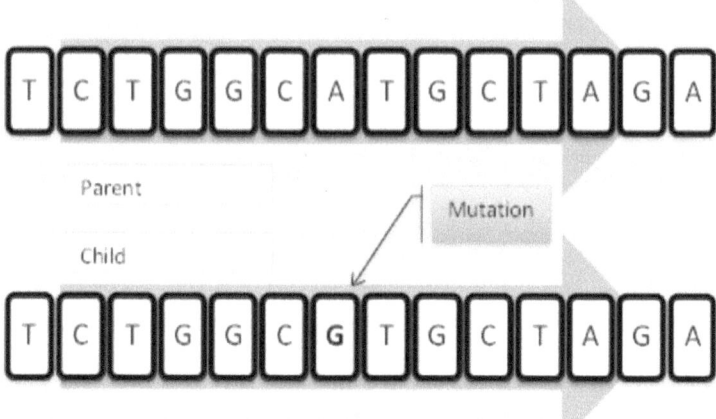

Figure 12.1 Mutation in DNA Code. The DNA code of more than 3 million-long sequence of similar repetitions of four possible choices: A, C, G, T. The image represents a tiny segment. When DNA replicates itself, every location on the copy is identical to the original; here, a random error miscopied the parent DNA at the indicated location and it replaced A with G; this is a mutation. Created by the author.

these mutations have little effect on our survival. Mutations that improve our survival are hard to detect because such mutations reduce the chance of survival of the DNA that carries no such mutation. Reasonably, the carriers of unfit features face extinction and thus the mutated copy is the only one in existence. The original DNA may be discovered by paleo-geneticist, a specialization dedicated to examine genetic material from remains of early creatures. The extinction of the less fit original explains why evolution is associated with *survival of the fittest*. A mutation which diminishes one's fitness has a short life expectancy; consequently, they give little opportunity to be detected.

The mathematics of Fisher calculates probabilities of mutations and quantitatively evaluates how genes with favorable features propagate, and how they replace older versions. For example, it calculates how fast the ratio of individuals carrying an advantageous mutation grows. Naturally, this growth rate increases with a magnitude that expresses how advantageous the mutation is. Another important magnitude expresses the average radius of *random migration*. Random migration is the interchange of population between adjacent towns. People move from one town to the other mostly for purpose of marriage and work. Some move within the neighborhood, some move longer distances. Statisticians overcame long time ago this type of disarray and introduced the notion of average, in our case average distance of random migration.

Now the discussion can leave genetics and return to cultural evolution in general and of tradition in particular. The mathematical principles of genetic inheritance have been extended to cultural evolution.[11] Random mutations are biological analogue to cultural innovations.[12] Similarly, to the biological outcome, an innovation faces three possible fates:

1. General acceptance or fixation, for example, agriculture,[13] or alphabet.[14]
2. Extinction.
3. Equilibrium with the older version, for example, covenantal Proto-Israel (innovation) and oligarchic Canaan (older version).[15]

The notion of covenant between a victorious sovereign and a defeated nation had been in existence long before our story of a kingless people began.[16] Consequently, the innovation of the term covenant is out of scope. However, its interpretation as a covenant between an immortal Sovereign and a people, that interpretation is an innovation; it qualifies as random mutation. In my view, the idea of preferring an immortal very powerful Sovereign over a monarch originated from the egalitarian ethos many pastoralists share. This innovation would have faced extinction had it not been accompanied by another random mutation consisting of compulsory weekly assemblies.[17]

I dwell on this point of random mutations because there are scholars who claim that cultural evolution involves *intentional* innovations which are the "closest analog to biological mutations."[18] Abrutyn proposes an alternative evolution theory, that is, an evolution consisting of waves of "institutional entrepreneurs."[19] According to this theory, the entrepreneurs provided adaptive solutions to the needs of the times.

A study of validity of extending the evolution theory to intentional innovations is out of scope. For the sake of discussion, I will admit that in most cases the difference is negligible; however, in a few situations, the difference invalidates the extrapolation. I shall use an example in which intentional innovations need special care.

Abrutyn's interest in the survival of Jewish culture is because "no religious group has survived long without being in control of territory and having political autonomy." In general, when a political system falls down its culture vanishes. For example, the Egyptian, Babylonian, Byzantine, Roman, and Hun empires collapsed and their heritage acculturated into the replacing polities. Didn't these cultures have cultural entrepreneurs also? Why were the intentional innovations of Jewish entrepreneurs adaptive and why did Pharaoh's counsellors fail? The most accepted theory explaining the reason why those empires collapsed is the theory of growing complexity. I provided a socio-physical substantiation explaining what complexity means and why pre-industrial empires were bound to collapse because of growing complexity.[20]

For our purposes, let us illustrate the example of pharaonic Egypt. Pharaoh maintained an army, a navy, police, and jails; he built pyramids, roads, and bridges. My investigation demonstrates that in a pre-industrial society, such a complex system ultimately arrives to the thin edge between stability and instability[21] and then intentional innovations of wise advisors, not only don't help but they rather make things worse.[22] Under these circumstances, intentional adaptive innovations of cultural entrepreneurs are not the "closest analog to mutations"[23]; consequently, the extension of evolution theory to intentional measures is not cautious.[24] The careful approach is sticking with evolution by random mutation:

> Humiliating to human pride as may be, we must recognize that the advance and even the preservation of civilization are dependent upon a maximum of opportunity for accidents to happen.[25]

This debate is relevant to following the evolution path of the constitution from "I am the Lord" to "We the people."

As described earlier, the innovation of covenanting with the Lord was accidental and its analogy to random mutation does not require explanation.

As the framers of the constitution, the editors of the covenant were practically "we the people" because the covenant articulated the customary laws of the settlers. The initial text was orally transmitted and reasonably, as any oral literature, it followed an evolutionary process of replication and alterations.

The history of when the authors of the Hebrew Bible wrote it down and the question who were they is controversial, irrelevant, and out of scope. The key is to understand that the concept of a covenant between each individual and the immortal Sovereign survived the monarchy.[26] This survival entailed a struggle for keeping the customary law and its traditional enforcement methods.[27]

Both Proto-Israel and the Pilgrims adopted covenantal structures not because some visionary charismatic leaders designed for them beneficial social organizations; evolution theory explains that they survived because they happened to embrace a social structure that in those conditions was beneficial.

> While the "great man" theory of leadership has fallen out of fashion, the more general theoretical orientation, of which the "great man" approach is only a variant, remains dominant.[28]

The great man approach envisages that the great man's decisions will be followed and successfully implemented regardless of organizational structure. As mentioned in chapter "The Difference between Political Concessions and Constitutional Liberties," the point of view of this monograph predicts that a choice stemming from existing practice and supported by existing structural processes has a better chance to prevail than arbitrary propositions regardless of the charisma of its proponents.

This inversion of cause and effect is not intended to convert readers from the great man approach to cultural evolution methodology; nevertheless, it will make a case that evolution theory arrives at the roots of the *predictable* statutes of the constitution. The study of the background of its Framers helps to explain the *unpredictable* outcomes of the 1787 Constitutional Convention.

The next turn of evolution of the covenant was the appearance of Christianity. The most important mutation was the extension of the "chosen people," that is, the cosignatories to the covenant to anyone who accepts the covenant and its new spiritual Christian narrative. The converts subscribed to keep a covenant, and were organized in egalitarian covenantal structure (see chapters "The Covenantal Society: Lex Rex" and "The Covenantal Society, Structure, Organization, and Power Flow"). All across the Roman Empire, many inhabitants converted to this new sociopolitical way of life. This massive conversion was accelerated by a few modifications, for example, the relaxation of dietary rules and of circumcision. That doesn't mean that these innovations caused the conversions. The reasons for the conversions during apostolic times are beyond the scope of this thesis.

The Roman Empire became a large territory covered by an almost continuous multitude of Christian communities with covenantal structure, inverted power flow, a justice administration pulsating at a weekly tempo, and covenantal psychology deeply rooted in practices that became tradition.

Christianity turned hierarchical during the third and fourth centuries. Yet in some remote valleys of mountainous regions traditions survived. The reasons why in those areas is open to future research. My hypothesis is related to the magnitude described earlier as the average radius of migration. The exchange of population in these valleys could have covered significantly less area than in the lowlands.

The covenantal tradition of the Alpine villages[29] was picked up by Calvinism when times were right for the expansion of protestant traditions. Calvin's gamble has paid off. The next phase in the evolution brings us to the Pilgrims and Puritans.

> The fundamental principles of American constitutionalism developed naturally out of covenant theology. Combined with other intellectual, economic, political, and social influences, covenant theology generated and nurtured the principles of popular sovereignty, limited government, the written constitution, supreme law, inalienable rights, and republican virtue.[30]

This chapter showed how "The fundamental principles of American constitutionalism" evolved from the first covenant the one conceived when "there was no King in Israel." That doesn't mean that the framers of the constitution were not visionaries. They inherited those principles from a tradition practiced and inherited along many generations; they also made sure that the constitution reflects actual government practices of "we the people" which by itself is a remarkable achievement. For "in social evolution, the decisive factor is not the physical and inheritable properties of the individuals, but the selection by imitation of successful institutions and habit."[31]

The legacy of earlier covenants and constitutions doesn't diminish the foresight of future clashes and the ingenuity of finding within the tradition practical solutions involving government structure and conflict resolving procedures. This approach gave in to reality even as far as "truths to be self-evident, that all men are created equal" are concerned. It is important to discuss some of them here. Ignoring two of these blatant constitutional slip-ups would leave a mistaken impression; one could conclude that this thesis claims that the evolution from "I am the Lord" to "We the people" took no turns against the very noble principles the covenantal approach advocates. The two aspects that I ask to discuss are slavery and gender equality. These two aspects are similar in the sense that they negate the very essence of equality before the law. However, they diverge in their evolutionary history.

Consenting to slavery was an appalling constitutional compromise; it was appropriately characterized as "the [n]emesis of Constitution."[32] No doubt, approval of slavery did not come to America on the Mayflower. Puritans settled New England with the persuasion that "[e]very person within this Jurisdiction, whether Inhabitant or forreiner shall enjoy the same justice and law."[33] True, the contagion of slavery had tainted this persuasion as reflected by their equivocal opposition to this inexcusable institution in article 91 of the first Puritan legal code of New England:

> There shall never be any bond slaverie, villinage or Captivitie amongst us unles it be lawfull Captives taken in just warres, and such strangers as willingly selle themselves or are sold to us. And these shall have all the liberties and Christian usages which the law of god established in Israell concerning such persons doeth morally require. This exempts none from servitude who shall be Judged thereto by Authoritie.[34]

Nevertheless, scholars recognize that "throughout the Constitutional Convention the northern delegates made numerous compromises over slavery."[35] It was a painful compromise; to illustrate the northern opposition to slavery one notes that Gouverneur Morris of Pennsylvania declared that slavery was a "curse of heaven."[36] Was the compromise necessary? Knowing that the Southern States "would not accept the Constitution without protection for slavery,"[37] the answer is yes. In evolution terms, mutations opposed to survival lead to extinction.

Only later, the 13th amendment abolished slavery in the United States. The subject of constitutional concession to preserve slavery and the high cost to abolish it has been amply debated by scholars.[38] This work touches the subject only to underline that in this evolutionary process, the constitution was not the result of an ideological theory of a perfect society but of a practical implementation of the reality in the colonies. The process balanced the preservation of traditional arrangement against constraints generated by the need to survive. Survival required defeating the threat of war with the British Crown and victory against the most powerful empire of that time necessitated achieving a functioning Union.

The subject of gender equality was not a narrative about compromise; gender inequality of the original constitution was a result of cultural forces that for centuries had maintained practices of ignoring women in public deliberations. Unlike slavery, gender inequality equally prevailed in the covenantal model of the North and the more oligarchic tendencies of the South. There is evidence that women were excluded from the public debate already by the Pilgrims of the Mayflower.[39] All the other evolutionary links of the covenantal society excluded women from formal participation in public debates, with two exceptions: in Early Christian communities women held office,[40] and in the Pyrenees, women of communities named *vesiau* were full participants in the town assembly, expressed their opinion and voted.[41]

As far as gender is concerned, the tendency to preserve tradition upheld the inequality in spite of the fact that reasonably close to half of the population opposed it.[42]

Gender inequality took longer to remove; however, the bright side of this episode was that the cost of the change for equality was significantly lower. Passed by Congress June 4, 1919, and ratified on August 18, 1920, the 19th amendment granted women the right to vote.

It is useful to mention a less thorny, however, equally relevant illustration of the constitutional approach to conserve the actual governing institutions rather than inventing an idealized revolutionary one. This example is about the balance between state sovereignty and federal power. Chapter "The Covenantal Society, Structure, Organization, and Power Flow" discussed that the covenantal ancestors had a common community structure (figure 5.2) and intercommunity network (figure 5.3). The power source in the community was the assembly and it delegated authority to the office holders. The communities of a region formed a rather tight regional network. The several regional networks formed a loose national alliance. The national alliance mostly served as a forum of harmonizing the covenantal life, discuss divergences, and agree or disagree on common practice. The first settlements of New England followed the pattern. For example, towns such as Plymouth, Boston, Quincy, Salem, Lexington, and Concord clustered into the colony of Massachusetts; Hartford, New Haven, Wethersfield, and Windsor were linked into the Connecticut colony. For better or worse (see Salem in chapter "Covenantal Psychology"), the town had judicial authority over its inhabitants. The power flow from assembly to office holders and to individuals was maintained. Therefore, it is not surprising that in 1777 the colonies sought to maintain their sovereignty. By default, federal institutions had no power except powers expressly granted by Congress:

> Each state retains its sovereignty, freedom and independence, and every Power, Jurisdiction and right, which is not by this confederation expressly delegated to the United States, in Congress assembled.[43]

However, the Union had to wage war, defend commerce, and manage diplomacy. This needed a certain reduction of state sovereignty in favor of central power, leaving Congress leeway to make decisions and take action. The thorny issue became representation in Congress. A proportional representation of each state according to its population would lead to a national Congress inherently being identified as the spokesmen of "we the people." However, the covenantal tradition proposed that each state is represented by the same number of delegates protecting state sovereignty against federal encroachment. We all know that the gap was finally bridged by a compromise: the House of Representatives was to be proportional to the population and the Senate was to maintain equal representation to each State. This concession known as Sherman's compromise[44] illustrates how mutation after mutation the constitution arrived at its current formulation. On American soil, this process started in Plymouth, with the Mayflower Compact. However, in the beginning there was the Covenant.

This story started with a people that once upon a time had no king. The story then went on and encountered other people who managed to live without a king. The story ends with the most powerful nation on Earth consisting of men and women of various origins, races, and faiths who promised to never have a king. May they live happily ever after.

NOTES

1. Ilie Bădescu, Ozana Cucu-Oancea, and Gheorghe Şişeşte, *Dicționar de sociologie rurală* (Editura Mica Valahie, 2005), 539; Iancu Filipescu, "Din contribuțiile profesorului Henri H. Stahl la dezvoltarea sociologiei istoriei," [Contributions of Professor Henti Stahl to the development of history's sociology.] *Sociologie Romanească* IV, no. 3 (2006): 27–33; Frédéric Le Pay, *La Réforme sociale en France déduite de l'observation comparée des peuples européens,*, 3 vols. (Paris: Tours, 1874), 127; Gustave Bascle de Lagrèze, *Histoire du droit dans les Pyrénées - comté de Bigorre* (1867), 88–90, 126, 29; Jean Léger, *Histoire generale des eglises evangeliques des Vallees de Piemont ou Vaudoises* (Leiden: Jean le Carpentier, 1669), 125.

2. Scholars such as Hobsbawm teach that some traditions are invented. For example, singing the National Anthem at certain occasion is an "invented tradition." This disagreement is a matter of semantics. In this work, tradition is what Hobsbawm defines as *"convention or routine, which has no symbolic function as such, though it may acquire it incidentally"* see Eric Hobsbawm and Terence Ranger, *The Invention of Tradition* (Cambridge, UK: Cambridge University Press, 2012), 3. Thus, the conflict is reconciled.

3. Biological genetic (haploid) vertical transmission is a particular case of cultural transmission, see Table 2.3.1 Luigi Luca Cavalli-Sforza and Marcus W. Feldman, *Cultural Transmission and Evolution* (Princeton, NJ: Princeton University Press, 1981), 84.

4. I googled 171 *popular* books on goodreads.com.

5. Geoffrey R Stone and William P Marshall, "The Framers' Constitution," *Democracy: A Journal of Ideas* 21 (2011).

6. Howard Markel, "The real story behind penicillin," in *Health* (US: PBS Newshour, 2013).

7. More precisely, he studied an ugly microbe with an innocent name *Staphylococcus aureus* that is specialized in causing skin infections but is also guilty of causing pneumonia, heart valve infections, and bone infections.

8. The mold's scientific name is *Penicillium notatum*.

9. Ronald A. Fisher, *The Genetical Theory of Natural Selection* (Oxford, UK: Oxford University Press, 1999); "The Wave of Advance of Advantageous Genes," *Annals of Eugenics* 7 (1937): 355–369.

10. In my student years, one of my assistant professors recognized that a lab report submitted to him was actually authored by him many years earlier; I can only imagine how upset he was by the unintentional "mutations" that were introduced along the years by the long chain of students that copied and "improved" the original.

11. Cavalli-Sforza and Feldman , *Cultural Transmission and Evolution*.

12. Seth Abrutyn, "Pollution-purification rituals, cultural memory and the evolution of religion: How collective trauma shaped ancient Israel," *AJCS* 3, no. 1 (2015):113-55; Cavalli-Sforza and Feldman, *Cultural Transmission and Evolution, 10, 22*; Jenni E. Pettay et al., "Heritability And Genetic Constraints of Life-History Trait Evolution in Preindustrial Humans," *PNAS* 102 no. 8 (2005): 2838-43; Joel Mokyr, "Induced technical innovation and medical history: an evolutionary approach," in *Technological Change and the Environment*, ed. Arnulf Grübler, Nebojsa Nakicenovic, and William D. Nordhaus (Washington, DC: Resources for the Future, 2002)

13. Ron Pinhasi, Joaquim Fort, and Albert J Ammerman, "Tracing the origin and spread of agriculture in Europe," *PLoS biology* 3, no. 12 (2005):

14. Orly Goldwasser, "Canaanites Reading Hieroglyphs. Horus is Hathor? - The Invention of the Alphabet in Sinai," Egypt and the Levant, no. 16 (2006): 121-60; John F. Healey, The Early Alphabet (Oakland. CA: University of California Press, 1990):.

15. António Augusto Tavares, "Quelques termes bibliques relatifs à des institutions anciennes: problèmes de traduction et d'histoire," *Didaskalia* 15.2 (1985):257-66

16. For example, the Hittite covenant in George E. Mendenhall, *Law and Covenant in Israel and the Ancient Near East* (Pittsburgh: Biblical Colloquium, 1955), 29.

17. Joseph Livni, "The cultural evolution of an institution: The Sabbath," *Cliodynamics* 8 (2017).

18. Seth Abrutyn, "Pollution-purification rituals,".

19. Ibid.

20. Joseph Livni, "Investigation of collapse of complex socio-political systems using classical stability theory," *Physica A: Statistical Mechanics and its Applications* 524 (2019): 532–562.

21. Joseph A. Tainter, The Collapse of Complex Societies (Cambridge: Cambridge University Press, 1990).

22. Not surprisingly, the effect of random mutations appearing at the brink of collapse is . . . . random.

23. Abrutyn, "Pollution purification rituals".

24. In mathematical terms, instability renders extinction to certainty while fixation and equilibrium have no chance; therefore, evolution theory predicting probabilities of survival is not useful.

25. Fridrich A. Hayek, *The Constitution of Liberty* (University of Chicago Press, 1978), 29.

26. Not only it survived but the priestly editors of Deuteronomy had no choice, but leave untouched this thorny issue in their written code: "Face to face the LORD spoke to you on the mountain out of the fire" (Deut. 5.4).

27. Joseph Livni and Ilie Bădescu, "The Battle of the Covenantal Society against Elitism," *Romanian Journal of Sociological Studies* (in print).

28. Richard J. Ellis, *A Theory of Charismatic Leadership in Organizations* (Berkley: UC Berkley. Institute og Govenmental Studies, 1986).

29. Alexis Muston called these valleys "Israel of the Alps," see Alexis Muston, *L'Israel des Alpes: Première histoire complète des Vaudois du Piémont et de leurs colonies*, vol. II (Paris: Marc Ducloux, 1851). His reason was that Jews and Waldensians endured similar persecution. This work substantiates a more profound analogy: the common covenantal tradition.

30. Lynn D. Wardle, "The constitution as covenant," *Brigham Young University Studies* 27, no. 3 (1987): 11–28.

31. Hayek, *The Constitution of Liberty*, 59.

32. Harold .M. Hyman and William .M. Wiecek, *Equal Justice Under Law: Constitutional Development, 1835–1875* (New York: Harper & Row, 1982), 86.

33. "The Massachusetts Body of Liberties" (Massachusetts General Court, 1641), article 2.

34. Ibid., article 91.

35. Paul Finkelman, "The cost of compromise and the covenant with death," *Pepperdine Law Review*. 38 (2010): 845.

36. "The Constitution and the Intentions of the Framers: The Limits of Historical Analysis," *University of Pittsburgh Law Review* 50 (1988): 382.

37. Ibid., 379.

38. For example, "The cost of compromise and the covenant with death," 846.

39. Mary Beth Norton, "The Constitutional Status of Women in 1787," *Law and Inequality* 6 (1988): 9.

40. Kevin Madigan and Carolyn Osiek, *Ordained Women in the Early Church: A Documentary History* (Baltimore, MD: Johns Hopkins University Press, 2005).

41. de Lagrèze, *Histoire du droit dans les Pyrénées - comté de Bigorre*.

42. See, for example, the letter of Abigail Adams to John Adams noting men's tendency to behave like tyrants, Norton, "The Constitutional Status of Women in 1787."

43. "Articles of Confederation 1777," in *Papers of the Continental Congress, 1774–1789;*, ed. Continental Congress (National Archives, 2003).

44. Aaron N. Coleman, *The American Revolution, State Sovereignty, and the American Constitutional Settlement, 1765–1800* (Lanham, MD: Lexington Books, 2016).

Bibliography

Abbott, Frank F. *A History and Description of Roman Political Institutions*. Boston and London: Ginn, 1901.
Abrutyn, Seth. "Pollution-Purification Rituals, Cultural Memory and the Evolution of Religion: How Collective Trauma Shaped Ancient Israel." *AJCS* 3, no. 1 (February 2015): 123–155.
Achard, Guy. "L'emploi De Boni, Boni Viri, Boni Cives, Et Leurs Formes Superlatives Dans L'action Politique De Cicéron." *Les Études Classiques* 41 (1973): 207–221.
Adams, John. "A Dissertation on the Canon and Feudal Law." In *The Works of John Adams*, edited by Charles Francis Adams, 447–456. Boston: Little, Brown, 1851.
Adams, John Quincy. "Oration at Plymouth - Delivered at Plymouth Mass. December 22, 1802 in Commemoration of the Landing of the Pilgrims." *The Daily Republican*, Dec 22, 2002 1802.
Alexis, Muston. *L''israël Des Alpes: Première Histoire Complète Des Vaudois Du Piémont Et De Leurs Colonies*. Vol. *I*, Paris: Libr. de Marc Ducloux, 1851.
Alling, Roger, and David.J. Schlafer. *Preaching as Pastoral Caring*. Harrisburg, PA: Morehouse Pub., 2005.
Allix, Pierre. *Some Remarks Upon the Ecclesiastical History of the Ancient Churches of Piedmont*. Oxford: Clarendon, 1821.
Aristotle. *The Athenian Constitution*. Start Publishing LLC, 2013.
Aristotle, Benjamin Jowett, and Henry William Carless Davis. *Politics*. Kindle edition ed. Mineola, NY: Dover Publications, 2000.
Arnaldo, Momigliano, and Cornell Tim. *Senatus Consultum*. Oxford: Oxford University Press.
"Articles of Confederation 1777." In *Papers of the Continental Congress, 1774-1789;*, edited by Continental Congress: National Archives, 2003.
Audisio, Gabriel. "Des Pauvres De Lyon Aux Vaudois Réformés." *Revue de l''histoire des religions* (2000): 155–66.

———. *The Waldensian Dissent: Persecution and Survival C. 1170-C. 1570*, Cambridge: Cambridge University Press, 1999.

Bădescu, Ilie. "Communal Society and the "Dual System" Equality and Inequality in the Carpathian Valleys. "Revista română de sociologie anul XXX, no. 3–4 (2019): 179–221.

Bădescu, Ilie, Ozana Cucu-Oancea, and Gheorghe Şişeşte. *Dicţionar De Sociologie Rurală*. Bucharest: Editura Mica Valahie, 2005.

Bădescu, Ilie, and Darie Cristea. *Elemente Pentru Un Dictionar De Sociologie Rurala: Concepte - Teme - Teorii*. Bucharest: Editura Mica Valahie, 2011.

Baert, Barbara. *A Heritage of Holy Wood: The Legend of the True Cross in Text and Image*. Leiden: Brill, 2004.

Baillet, Adrien. *Les Vies Des Saints Et Histoire Des Festes Et Des Mysteres De L''eglise*. Paris: Nully, 1710.

Bar Yosef, Yaakov. *Netzari Emunah Rashi*. Raleigh, NC: Lulu.com.

Barceló, Juan A., and Florencia Del Castillo. "Simulating the Past for Understanding the Present. A Critical Review." In *Simulating Prehistoric and Ancient Worlds*, edited by Juan A Barceló and Florencia Del Castillo, 1–140. Cham, Switzerland: Springer, 2016.

Barclay, John M. G. *Jews in the Mediterranean Diaspora: From Alexander to Trajan (323 Bce - 117 Ce)*. Berkeley, CA: University of California Press, 1999.

Barkan, Steven E. "Sociology Comprehensive Edition V. 1.0." Retrieved from http://2012books.lardbucket.org/pdfs/sociology-comprehensiveedition.pdf on October 24 (2012): 2016.

———*Theological Dictionary of the New Testament: Abridged in One Volume*. Grand Rapids, MI: Eerdmans Publishing Company, 1985.

Berezkin, Y.E. "Alternative Models of Middle Range Society."." *Individualistic" Asia vs."collectivistic" America* (2004): 75–83.

Bickerman, Elias. "The Edict of Cyrus in Ezra." In *Studies in Jewish and Christian History, Volume 1*, edited by Amram Troper, 71–107. Leiden Boston: Brill, 2007.

Bidot-Germa, Dominique. "The Specific Features of Medieval Notaries North and South of the Pyrenees: The Example of Béarn." *Imago temporis: medium Aevum* 5 (2011): 175–91.

Blair, Adam. *History of the Waldenses: With an Introductory Sketch of the History of the Christian Churches in the South of France and North of Italy, Till These Churches Submitted to the Pope, When the Waldenses Continued as Formerly Independent of the Papal See*. Edinborough: A. & C. Black, 1832.

Bloch, Marc. *Feudal Society*. London, New York: Routledge, 2014.

Blum, Jerome. "The European Village as Community: Origins and Functions." *Agricultural History* 45, no. 3 (1971): 157–78.

Bodenmann, Reinhard. "Les Vaudois Et La Production Du Livre Évangélique Français (1525-1550)." *Revue Littératures| Université McGill* 24, no. 24 (1) (2017): 25–30.

Boehm, Christopher, Harold B. Barclay, Robert Knox Dentan, Marie-Claude Dupre, Jonathan D. Hill, Susan Kent, Bruce M. Knauft, Keith F. Otterbein, and Steve Rayner. "Egalitarian Behavior and Reverse Dominance Hierarchy [and Comments and Reply]." *Current anthropology* 34, no. 3 (1993): 227–54.

Boehm, Cristopher. *Hierarchy in the Forest*. Cambridge, MA: Harvard University Press, 2001.

Bondarenko, Dmitri M., Leonid E. Grinin, and Andrey V. Korotayev. "Alternatives of Social Evolution." In *The Early State, Its Alternatives and Analogues*, edited by Leonid E. Grinin, Robert L. Carneiro, Dmitri M. Bondarenko, Nikolay N. Kradin and Andrey V. Korotayev, 3–27. Volgograd: Uchitel Publishing House, 2004.

Bonner, John T. *Randomness in Evolution*. Princeton, NJ: Princeton University Press, 2013.

Bourin, Monique. "Historiographie Des Communautés De La France Méridionale." In *La formation des communautés d''habitants au Moyen Âge. Perspectives historiographiques*, edited by Ludolf Kuchenbuch, Dieter Scheler and Joseph Morsel. Xanten, Germany, 2003.

Bowie, Nikolas. "Why the Constitution Was Written Down." *Stanford Law Review* 71 (2019): 1397.

Boyd, Robert, and Peter J. Richerson. "The Evolution of Ethnic Markers." *Cultural Anthropology* 2, no. 1 (1987): 65–9.

Bragg, Melvyn, Tom Healey, Justin Champion, and Clare Jackson "The Divine Right of Kings." In *In Our Time*, edited by Melvyn Bragg, 45 min. London: BBC Radio 4, 2007.

Brague, Rémi. *The Law of God: The Philosophical History of an Idea*. Chicago: University of Chicago Press, 2007.

Britannica, The Editors of Encyclopaedia. "Habeas Corpus." In *Encyclopaedia Britannica*, 77–88. Chicago: Encyclopædia Britannica, inc., 2019.

Bunimovitz, Shlomo, and Zvi Lederman. "A Border Case: Beth-Shemesh and the Rise of Ancient Israel." *Israel in Transition: From the Late Bronze II to Iron IIa (c. 1250–850 bce)* 1 (2008): 21–31.

Burgess, Michael. *Comparative Federalism: Theory and Practice*. London and New York: Taylor & Francis, 2006.

Burrill, Alexander Mansfield. *A New Law Dictionary and Glossary*. New York: J. S. Voorhies, 1859.

Calvin, John, and Henry Beveridge. *Institutes of the Christian Religion*. Peabody, MA: Hendrickson, 2008.

Campbell, Douglas. *The Puritan in Holland, England, and America: An Introduction to American History*. London: Harper, 1892.

Cantemir, Dimitrie. *Descrierea Moldovei*. Grup Editorial Litera, 2016.

Carmi, Shai, Ken Y. Huy, Ethan Kochav, Xinmiu Liu, James Xue, and Filan Grady. "Sequencing an Ashkenazi Reference Panel Supports Population-Targeted Personal Genomics and Illuminates Jewish and European Origins." *Nature Communications* 5, no. 1 (2014).

Carneiro, Robert L. "Was the Chiefdom a Congelation of Ideas?". *Social Evolution & History* 1, no. 1 (2002): 80–100.

Cavalli-Sforza, Luigi Luca, and Marcus W. Feldman. *Cultural Transmission and Evolution*. Princeton, NJ: Princeton University Press, 1981.

Chaniotis, Angelos. "The Divinity of Hellenistic Rulers." *A Companion to the Hellenistic World* (2003): 431–45.

Chéruel, Adolphe. *Dictionnaire Historique Des Institutions, Moeurs Et Coutumes De La France, 1*. Paris: Libr. de L. Hachette, 1865.

Chet, Guy. *The Colonists'' American Revolution: Preserving English Liberty, 1607-1783*. Hoboken, NJ: Wiley, 2019.

Chyutin, Michael. *Architecture and Utopia in the Temple Era*. New York: Bloomsbury Academic, 2006.

Coffin, Charles Carleton. *The Story of Liberty*. New York: Harper & brothers, 1879.

Cohen, Adam B, Joel I. Siegel, and Paul Rozin. "Faith Versus Practice: Different Bases for Religiosity Judgments by Jews and Protestants." *European Journal of Social Psychology* 33, no. 2 (2003): 287–95.

Coleman, Aaron .N. *The American Revolution, State Sovereignty, and the American Constitutional Settlement, 1765–1800*. Lanham, MD: Lexington Books, 2016.

Comba, Emilio. *History of the Waldenses of Italy: From Their Origin to the Reformation*. Translated by Teofilo Comba. London: Truslove & Shirley, 1889.

Congress, First Continenal. "Friday, October 14, 1774.", edited by United States. Continental Congress. Edited from the original records in the Library of Congress ... Washington Journals of the Continental Congress, 1774–1789, 1774.

Couderc-Barraud, Hélène. *La Violence, L'ordre Et La Paix: Résoudre Les Conflits En Gascogne Du Xie Au Début Du Xiiie Siècle*. Presses universitaires du Mirail, 2008.

Cover, Robert M. "Obligation: A Jewish Jurisprudence of the Social Order." *Journal of Law and Religion* 5, no. 1 (1987): 65–74.

D'Acci, Luca. "Simulating Future Societies in Isobenefit Cities: Social Isobenefit Scenarios." *Futures* 54 (2013): 3–18.

Danley, C. *Peter: Friend and Apostle of Jesus, Failure and Finally Greatness*. New York: iUniverse, 2008.

De Freitas, Shaun A. "Samuel Rutherford on Law and Covenant: The Impact of Theologico-Political Federalism on Constitutional Theory." University of the Free State, 2003.

de Lagrèze, Gustave Bascle. *Histoire Du Droit Dans Les Pyrénées - Comté De Bigorre*. 1867.

———. *La Féodalité Dans Les Pyrénées, Comté De Bigorre*. Mémoire Lu À L'académie Des Sciences Morales Et Politiques. Paris: A. Durand, 1864.

Dershowitz, Alan M. *The Genesis of Justice*. New York: Warner Books, 2000.

Dever, William .G. *What Did the Biblical Writers Know and When Did They Know It?: What Archeology Can Tell Us About the Reality of Ancient Israel*. Kindle ed. Grand Rapids, Michigan: Eerdmans Publishing Company, 2002.

———. *Who Were the Early Israelites and Where Did They Come From?* Grand Rapids, MI: Eerdmans Publishing Company, 2006.

Dianda, Bas. *A History of the Seventies: The Political, Cultural, Social and Economic Developments That Shaped the Modern World*. Wilmington, DE: Vernon Press, 2019.

Dickson-Gilmore, Elizabeth Jane. "Resurrecting the Peace: Separate Justice and the Invention of Legal Tradition in the Kahnawake Mohawk Nation." London School of Economics and Political Science (United Kingdom), 1996.

Dickson-Gilmore, Jane. "Resurrecting the Peace: Traditionalist Approaches to Separate Justice in Kahnawake Mohawk Nation." In *Law & Anthropology*, edited by René Kuppe and Richard Potz, 83–106. The Hague: Martinus Nijhoff Publishers, 1996.

Dinkin, Robert J. "Seating the Meeting House in Early Massachusetts." *New England Quarterly* (1970): 450–64.

Dossat, Yves, and Marcelin Defourneaux. "Les Dossiers De L'universalis, L'inquisition." In *Encyclopedia Universalis*. Boulogne-Billancourt, 2015.

Drijvers, Jan Willem. *Helena Augusta*. Leiden: E.J. Brill, 1992.

Dryer, George Herbert. *History of the Christian Church*. Cincinnati: Curts & Jennings, 1896.

Du Boulay, Francis Robin Houssemayne. "Law Enforcement in Medieval Germany." *History* 63, no. 209 (1978): 345–55.

Dueppen, Stephen .A. "Reinventing Equality: The Archaeology of Kirikongo, Burkina Faso." University of Michigan, 2008.

E.D.N.Y. "Grunwald V. Bornfreund, 696 F. Supp. 838 (E.D.N.Y)." edited by E.D. New York District Court. New York, 1988.

Eckstein , Zvi, and Maristella Botticini. "From Farmers to Merchants, Conversions and Diaspora: Human Capital and Jewish History." *Journal of the European Economic Association* 5, no. 5 (2007): 885–926.

Edmonds, Christopher A., Anita S. Lillie, and L. Luca Cavalli-Sforza. "Mutations Arising in the Wave Front of an Expanding Population." *Proceedings of the National Academy of Sciences* 101, no. 4 (2004): 975–79.

Ehrhardt, Arnold. *The Apostolic Succession: In the First Two Centuries of the Church*. Eugene, OR: Wipf & Stock Publishers, 2009.

Elazar, Daniel J. "Judaism and Democracy: The Reality." *Jerusalem Letter*, no. 48 (1986).

Elazar, Daniel J. *Covenant & Commonwealth: From Christian Separation through the Protestant Reformation*. New Brunswick, NJ: Transaction Publishers, 1995.

———. *Covenant & Constitutionalism: The Great Frontier and the Matrix of Federal Democracy*. New Brunswick, NJ: Transaction Publishers, 1997.

———. *Covenant and Polity in Biblical Israel*. New Brunswick, NJ: Transaction Publishers, 1998.

———. *The Covenant Tradition in Politics*. Vol. 1: Transaction Publishers, 1995.

———. "Switzerland as a Model in the Commonwealth Tradition." In *Commonwealth: The Other Road to Democracy– The Swiss Model of Democratic Self-Government*, edited by D.J. Elazar, J.W. Baker, G. Lehmbruch and M. Frenkel, 243–64. Lanham, MD: Lexington Books, 2001.

Elazar, Daniel J., and Stewart Cohen. *The Jewish Polity: Jewish Political Organization from Biblical Times to the Present*, . Bloomington, IN: Indiana University Press, 1985.

Ellis, Richard J. *A Theory of Charismatic Leadership in Organizations*. Berkley: UC Berkley. Institute og Govenmental Studies, 1986.

Epstein, Joshua M. *Nonlinear Dynamics, Mathematical Biology, and Social Science: Wise Use of Alternative Therapies*. Boulder, CO: Westview Press, 1997.

Epstein, Joshua M., Derek A.T. Cummings, Shubha Chakravarti, Ramesh N. Singha, and Donald S. Burke. "Generating Epidemics Dynanics." In *Generative Social Science: Studies in Agent-Based Computational Modeling*, edited by Joshua M. Epstein, 271–77. Princeton: Princeton University Press, 2012.

Faust, Avraham. *Israel's Ethnogenesis: Settlement, Interaction, Expansion and Resistance*. London: Equinox Pub., 2006.

———. "Pigs in Space (and Time): Pork Consumption and Identity Negotiations in the Late Bronze and Iron Ages of Ancient Israel." *Near Eastern Archaeology* 81, no. 4 (2018): 276–99.

———. "The Rural Community in Ancient Israel During Iron Age II." *Bulletin of the American Schools of Oriental Research* 317 (2000): 17–39.

Faust, Avraham, and Justin Lev-Tov. "The Constitution of Philistine Identity: Ethnic Dynamics in Twelfth to Tenth Century Philistia." *Oxford Journal of Archaeology* 30, no. 1 (2011): 13–31.

Field, Andy, Jeremy Miles, and Zoë Field. *Discovering Statistics Using R*. Los Angeles, London SAGE Publications, 2012.

Filipescu, Iancu. "Din Contribuțiile Profesorului Henri H. Stahl La Dezvoltarea Sociologiei Istoriei." [In Romanian]. *Sociologie Romanească* IV, no. 3 (2006): 27–33.

Finkelman, Paul. "The Constitution and the Intentions of the Framers: The Limits of Historical Analysis." *University of Pittsburgh Law Review* 50 (1988): 349.

———. "The Cost of Compromise and the Covenant with Death." *Pepperdine Law Review* 38 (2010): 845.

Finkelstein, Israel. "Pots and People Revisited: Ethnic Boundaries in the Iron Age I." In *The Archaeology of Israel: Constructing the Past, Interpreting the Present*, edited by N.A. Silberman and D.B. Small, 216–37. Sheffield, UK: Bloomsbury Publishing, 1997.

Finkelstein, Israel, Amihai Mazar, and Brian. B. Schmidt. *The Quest for the Historical Israel: Debating Archaeology and the History of Early Israel*. Sixth Biennial Colloquium of the International Institute for Secular Humanistic Judaism. Atlanta: SBL Press, 2007.

Finkelstein, Israel, and N.A. Silberman. *The Bible Unearthed: Archaeology's New Vision of Ancient Israel and the Origin of Sacred Texts*. New York: Simon & Shuster, 2002.

Fisher, Ronald A. *The Genetical Theory of Natural Selection*. Oxford, UK: Oxford University Press, 1999.

———. "The Wave of Advance of Advantageous Genes." *Annals of Eugenics* 7 (1937): 355–69.

Frank, Richard Ira. "Ammianus on Roman Taxation." *The American Journal of Philology* 93, no. 1 (1972): 69–86.

Frazee, Charles A. "The Origins of Clerical Celibacy in the Western Church." *Church History* 41, no. 2 (1972): 149–67.

Fremon, David K. *The Salem Witchcraft Trials in United States History*. Berkley Height, NJ: Enslow Publishers, Incorporated, 2014.

Fricke, Beate. "Fallen Idols and Risen Saints: Western Attitudes Towards the Worship of Images and the 'Cultura Veterum Deorum'." In *Negating the Image:*

Case Studies in Iconoclasm, edited by Ann McClanan and Jeffrey Johnson, 67–95. New York: Routledge, 2016.

Gagarin, Michael. *Early Greek Law*. Berkley, Los Angeles, London: University of California Press, 1989.

Gavrilets, Sergey, David G. Anderson, and Peter Turchin. "Cycling in the Complexity of Early Societies." *Issue: Cliodynamics*, 1, no. 1 (2010).

Gibbon, Edward. *The History of the Decline and Fall of the Roman Empire*. Boston: Little, Brown, 1854.

Gibson, Edgar C.S. "John Cassian." In *A Select Library of Nicene and Post-Nicene Fathers of the Christian Church: Sulpitius Severus. Vincent of Lerins. John Cassian*, edited by Philip Schaff and Henry Wace, 183–621. New York: Christian Literature Company, 1894.

Gidney, William Thomas. *The Jews and Their Evangelization*. London: Student Volunteer Missionary Union, 1899.

Gilly, William Stephen. *Narrative of an Excursion to the Mountains of Piemont, and Researches among the Vaudois, or Waldenses, Protestant Inhabitants of the Cottian Alps: With an Appendix Containing Copies of Ancient Manuscripts and Other Interesting Documents*. London: C. and J. Rivington, 1824.

———. *Waldensian Researches During a Second Visit to the Vaudois of Piemont*. London: Rivington, 1831.

Gitlitz, David M., and I. Stavans. *Secrecy and Deceit: The Religion of the Crypto-Jews*. Albaquerque: University of New Mexico Press, 2002.

Godelier, Maurice. "Systèmes De Parenté, Formes De Famille Quelques Problèmes Contemporains Qui Se Posent En Europe Occidentale Et En Euro-Amérique." *La revue lacanienne*, 3, no. 8 (2010): 37–48.

Goff, Jacques Le. *The Birth of Purgatory*. Chicago: University of Chicago Press, 1986.

Goitein, Shlomo Dov, and Jacob Lassner. *A Mediterranean Society: An Abridgment in One Volume*. Berkley: University of California Press, 1999.

Gottwald, Norman. *Tribes of Yahweh: A Sociology of the Religion of Liberated Israel, 1250-1050 Bce*. Sheffield: Bloomsbury Publishing, 1999.

Gould, James B. *Understanding Prayer for the Dead: Its Foundation in History and Logic*. Eugene, OR: Cascade Books, 2016.

Griffiths, J. Gwyn. "Egypt and the Rise of the Synagogue." *The Journal of Theological Studies* 38, no. 1 (1987): 1–15.

Hackett, Jo Ann. "There Was No King in Israel." In *The Oxford History of the Biblical World*, 132–64. New York: Oxford University Press, 1998.

Hadeler, K.P., and F. Rothe. "Travelling Fronts in Nonlinear Diffusion Equations." *Journal of Mathematical Biology* 2, no. 3 (1975): 251–63.

Halbertal, Moshe. *People of the Book: Canon, Meaning, and Authority*. Cambridge, MA: Harvard University Press, 2009.

Halley, Robert. *Lancashire: Its Puritanism and Nonconformity*. Manchester, UK: Tubbs and Brook, 1872.

Hammerling, Roy. *A History of Prayer: The First to the Fifteenth Century*. Leiden: Brill, 2008.

Hanks, Sharon .L. *Ecology and the Biosphere: Principles and Problems*. Boca Raton, FL: Taylor & Francis, 1996.

Hatch, Edwin. *The Organization of the Early Christian Churches*. London: Rivingtons, 1882.

Hayek, Fridrich A. *The Constitution of Liberty*. Chicago: University of Chicago Press, 1978.

Hazeltine, Harold Dexter. "The Influence of Magna Carta on American Constitutional Development." *Columbia Law Review* 17, no. 1 (1917): 1–33.

Heather, Peter. *The Fall of the Roman Empire: A New History*. Hampshire, UK: Pan Books, 2010.

Hefele, C.J., and W.R. Clark. *A History of the Councils of the Church: From the Original Documents, to the Close of the Second Council of Nicaea A.D. 787*. Eugene, OR: Wipf & Stock Publishers, 2007.

Hesse, Brian. "Pig Lovers and Pig Haters: Patterns of Palestinian Pork Production." *Journal of Ethnobiology* 10, no. 2 (1990): 195–225.

Hesse, Brian, and Paula Wapnish. "Can Pig Remains Be Used for Ethnic Diagnosis in the Ancient near East?". *Journal for the Study of the Old Testament Supplement Series* (1997): 238–70.

Hirschman, Elizabeth C., and Donald N. Yates. *When Scotland Was Jewish: DNA Evidence, Archeology, Analysis of Migrations, and Public and Family Records Show Twelfth Century Semitic Roots*. Jefferson, NC and London: McFarland, Incorporated, Publishers, 2015.

Hobsbawm, Eric, and Terence Ranger. *The Invention of Tradition*. Cambridge, UK: Cambridge University Press, 2012.

Houston, Stephen, and David Stuart. "Of Gods, Glyphs and Kings: Divinity and Rulership among the Classic Maya." *Antiquity* 70, no. 268 (1996): 289–312.

Hyman, Harold .M., and William .M. Wiecek. *Equal Justice under Law: Constitutional Development, 1835- 1875*. New York: Harper & Row, 1982.

Innes, William C. *Social Concern in Calvin's Geneva*. Eugene, OR: Pickwick Publications, 1983.

Iorga, Nicolae. "Scrisori De Boieri Scrisori De Domni." In *Din publicațiile casei școalelor*, edited by Casa școalelor. Vălenii de Munte, Romania: Editura casei școalelor; Datina Românească, 1925.

Ireland, Clive.R. *Experimental Statistics for Agriculture and Horticulture*. Cambridge: CABI, 2010.

Jacobsohn, Gary J. *Apple of Gold: Constitutionalism in Israel and the United States*. Princeton, NJ: Princeton University Press, 2017.

Jalla, Jean. "Un Precursore Del Puseismo Nelle Valli Al Secolo Xvii." *Bollettino della società di studi valdesi*, May, no. 9 (1884): 24–40.

Janiskee, Brian P. *Local Government in Early America: The Colonial Experience and Lessons from the Founders*. Lanham, MD: Rowman & Littlefield Publishers, 2010.

Karamanou, Anna. *Progress Towards Accession by Turkey*. Strasbourg: EU Parliamentary Debates; Apr. 1st, 2004.

Kempinski, Aharon. "Tel Masos." *Expedition* 20, no. 4 (1978): 29.

Kermack, William O., and Anderson G. McKendrick. "A Contribution to the Mathematical Theory of Epidemics." Paper presented at the Proceedings of the Royal Society of London A: mathematical, physical and engineering sciences, 1927.

King, Philip J., and Lawrence E. Stager. *Life in Biblical Israel*. Louisville, KY: Westminster John Knox Press, 2001.

Klein, Philip A. *Beyond Dissent: Essays in Institutional Economics*. Armonk, NY: M.E. Sharpe, 1994.

Knohl, Israel. *How Was the Hebrew Bible Born? Talks with Shmuel Shir* [in Hebrew]. Tel Aviv: Dvir, 2018.

———. "The Priestly Torah Versus the Holiness School: Sabbath and the Festivals." *Hebrew Union College Annual* (1987): 65–117.

———. *The Sanctuary of Silence: The Priestly Torah and the Holiness School*. Winona Lake, IN: Eisenbrauns, 2007.

Kopel, David B. "The Scottish and English Religious Roots of the American Right to Arms: Buchanan, Rutherford, Locke, Sidney, and the Duty to Overthrow Tyranny." *Bridges* 12 (2005): 291.

Korotayev, Andrey V. "The Chiefdom: Precursor of the Tribe?". In *The Early State, Its Alternatives and Analogues*, edited by Grinin Leonid E. , Robert L. Carneiro, Dmitri M. Bondarenko, Nikolay N. Kradin and Andrey V. Korotayev, 300–24. Volgograd: Uchitel Publishing House, 2004.

Kurun, Ismael. *The Theological Origins of Liberalism*. Lanham, MD: Lexington Books, 2016.

Latham, Stephen R. "Medical Professionalism." *Mount Sinai Journal of Medicine* 69 (2002): 363–9.

Le Pay, Frédéric. *La Réforme Sociale En France Déduite De L'observation Comparée Des Peuples Européens*, . 3 vols Paris: Tours, 1874.

———. *L'organisation De La Famille Selon Le Vrai Modèle Signalé Par L'histoire De Toutes Les Races Et De Tous Les Temps*. Mame, 1895.

Legendre, Olivier, and Michel Rubellin. "Valdès: Un «Exemple» À Clairvaux? Le Plus Ancien Texte Sur Les Débuts Du Pauvre De Lyon." *Revue Mabillon* 11 (2000): 187–95.

Léger, Jean. *Histoire Generale Des Eglises Evangeliques Des Vallees De Piemont Ou Vaudoises*. Leiden: Jean le Carpentier, 1669.

Leonhardt, Jutta. *Jewish Worship in Philo of Alexandria*. Tübingen: Mohr Siebeck, 2001.

Levinson, Bernard M. "The Birth of the Lemma: The Restrictive Reinterpretation of the Covenant Code's Manumission Law by the Holiness Code (Leviticus 25: 44–46)." *Journal of Biblical Literature* 124, no. 4 (2005): 617–39.

Levinson, Sanford. *Constitutional Faith*. Princeton, NJ: Princeton University Press, 2011.

Livni, Haim, and Joseph Livni. "Interpretation of Findings of Founder Population Genetics Studies Applying Lineage Extinction Theory." *Physica A: Statistical Mechanics and its Applications* 462 (2016): 641–53.

Livni, Joseph. "Christianity and the Romanian Communities Named Obşte." [In Romanian]. *Romanian Journal of Sociological Studies,* 1 (2016): 61–71.

———. "The Cultural Evolution of an Institution: The Sabbath." *Cliodynamics* 8 (2017): 59–74.

———. "Investigation of Collapse of Complex Socio-Political Systems Using Classical Stability Theory." *Physica A: Statistical Mechanics and its Applications* 524 (2019): 553–62.

———. "Investigation of Population Growth of Ancient Israel." [In English]. *Ugarit Forschungen*, no. 46 (2015): 213–34.

———. "Testing Competing Archaeological Theories of Israel's Origins Using Computation Techniques." *Archeologia e Calcolatori* 28, no. 1 (2017): 109–28.

Livni, Joseph, and Ilie Bădescu. "The Battle of the Covenantal Society against Elitism - an Overlooked Chapter in the History of Social Inequality." *Romanian Journal of Sociological Studies, New Series,* no. 1 (2020): 3–36.

Livni, Joseph, and Lewi Stone. "The Stabilizing Role of the Sabbath in Pre-Monarchic Israel: A Mathematical Model." *Journal of Biological Physics* 41 (2015): 203–21.

Llewelyn, Stephen .R., and Alana M. Nobbs. "The Earliest Dated Reference to Sunday on Papyri." In *New Documents Illustrating Early Christianity, 9: A Review of the Greek Inscriptions and Papyri Published in 1986-87*, edited by Stephen R. Llewelyn. Grand Rapids, MI: Eerdmans Publishing Company, 2002.

Lobban, Richard A. "Pigs and Their Prohibition." *International Journal of Middle East Studies* 26, no. 1 (1994): 57–75.

Locatelli, Carlo. *Vita Di S. Ambrogio*. Milano: S. Majocchi, 1874.

Lowenthal, Leo. *False Prophets: Studies on Authoritarianism*. New York: Taylor & Francis, 2017.

Luley, Benjamin P. "Equality, Inequality, and the Problem of "Elites" in Late Iron Age Eastern Languedoc (Mediterranean France), Ca. 400–125 BC." *Journal of Anthropological Archaeology* 41 (2016): 33–54.

Lupovitch, Howard N. *Jews at the Crossroads: Tradition and Accommodation During the Golden Age of the Hungarian Nobility, 1729-1878*. Budapest: Central European University Press, 2007.

Lutz, Donald S. *The Origins of American Constitutionalism*. Baton Rouge, Louisiana: Louisiana State University Press, 1988.

Lutz, H.F. "Kingship in Babylonia, Assyria, and Egypt." *American Anthropologist* 26, no. 4 (1924): 435–53.

Madigan, Kevin, and Carolyn Osiek. *Ordained Women in the Early Church: A Documentary History*. Baltimore, MD: Johns Hopkins University Press, 2005.

Maeir, Aren M., and Louise A. Hitchcock. ""And the Canaanite Was Then in the Land"? A Critical View on the "Canaanite Enclave" in Iron I Southern Canaan." In *Alphabets, Texts and Artifacts in the Ancient near East: Studies Presented to Benjamin Sass*, edited by Israel Finkelstein, Christian Robin and Thomas Römer, 209–26. Paris: Van Dieren, 2016.

Maimonides, Moses, and Hermann H. Bernard. *The Main Principles of the Creed and Ethics of the Jews, Exhibited in Selections from the Yad Hachazakah of Maimonides,* . Cambridge: Deighton, 1832.

Markel, Howard. "The Real Story Behind Penicillin." In *Health*. US: PBS Newshour, 2013.

"The Massachusetts Body of Liberties." Massachusetts General Court, 1641.
Mathieu, Jacques. *La Nouvelle-France: Les Français En Amérique Du Nord, Xvie-Xviiie Siècle*. Saint-Nicolas, Quebec, Canada: Presses de l'Université Laval, 2001.
Mazar, Amihai. "The Israelite Settlement." In *The Quest for the Historical Israel: Debating Archaeology and the History of Early Israel*, edited by Israel Finkelstein and Amihai Mazar, 85–98, Atlanta, GA: Society of Biblical Lit, 2007.
McCallum, Dennis. "The Waldensian Movement from Waldo to the Reformation." American Waldesian Society, History: Founded in the Middle Ages, Waldenses, Global Anabaptist Mennonite Encyclopedia, 2014.
McCoy, Charles S., and Wayne J. Baker. *Fountainhead of Federalism: Heinrich Bullinger and the Covenantal Tradition*. Louisville, KY: Westminster John Knox Press, 1991.
McIlwain, Charles Howard. *Constitutionalism: Ancient and Modern*. Clark, NJ: Lawbook Exchange, 2005.
Mendenhall, George E. *Law and Covenant in Israel and the Ancient near East*. Pittsburgh: Biblical Colloquium, 1955.
Middleton, Conyers. *The Life and Letters of Marcus Tullius Cicero*. London: Henry G. Bohn, 1848.
Miller, Geoffrey P. "Monarchy in the Hebrew Bible." *NYU School of Law, Public Law Research Paper*, no. 10–76 (2010).
Miller, Robert .D. *Chieftains of the Highland Clans: A History of Israel in the 12th and 11th Centuries Bc*. Eugene, OR: Wipf & Stock Publishers, 2012.
Mingers, John C. "Information and Meaning: Foundations for an Intersubjective Account." *Information Systems Journal* 5, no. 4 (1995): 285–306.
Misra, Krishna .B. *Handbook of Performability Engineering*. London: Springer 2008.
Moller, William .E., and Gustav. Kawerau. *History of the Christian Church ...: A. D. 1517-1648, Reformation and Counter-Reformation; Ed. By Dr. G. Kawerau ... Tr. By J. H. Freese*. New York: S. Sonnenschein & Company, limited, 1900.
Monastier, Antoine. *Histoire De L'eglise Vaudoise - Tome I*. Vol. 1. Geneva: Kessmann, 1847.
Money, Jeannette, and George Tsebelis. "Cicero's Puzzle: Upper House Power in Comparative Perspective." *International Political Science Review* 13, no. 1 (1992): 25–43.
Montet, Édouard. *La Noble Leçon: Texte Original D'après Le Manuscrit De Cambridge, Avec Les Variantes Des Manuscrits De Genéve Et De Dublin, Suivi D'une Traduction Française Et De Traductions En Vaudois Moderne* [in French]. Paris: Libraierie G. Fischbacher, 1888.
Moore, Sally Falk. *Law as Process: An Anthropological Approach*. Hamburg: Lit Verlag, 2000.
Moots, G.A. *Politics Reformed: The Anglo-American Legacy of Covenant Theology*. Columbia, MO: University of Missouri Press, 2010.
Mosheim, John Laurence, and Archibald Maclaine. *An Ecclesiastical History Antient and Modern from the Birth of Christ to the Beginning of the Eighteenth Century, in Which the Rise, Progress, and Variations of Church Power Are Considered in Their Connexion with the State of Learning and Philosophy and the Political History of Europe During That Period*. London: Strahan and Preston, 1811.

Mousnier, Mireille, Roland Viader, and Guilhem Ferrand. "Le Rempart De La Coutume." *Archéologie du Midi médiéval* 25, no. 1 (2007): 123–33.

Mullett, Michael. "Reviews : Euan Cameron, the Reformation of the Heretics. The Waldenses of the Alps 1480-1580, Oxford, Clarendon Press, Xviii + 291pp; £22.50." *European History Quarterly* 16, no. 2 (1986): 219–21.

Murphy, James Bernard. *Habit and Convention at the Foundation of Custom*, edited by Amanda Perreau-Saussine and James Bernard Murphy, 53–129. Cambridge: Cambridge University Press, 2007.

———. *The Philosophy of Customary Law*. Oxford New York: Oxford University Press, 2014.

Muston, Alexis. *The Israel of the Alps: A Complete History of the Waldenses and Their Colonies*. London: Blackie, 1875.

———. *L'israel Des Alpes: Première Histoire Complète Des Vaudois Du Piémont Et De Leurs Colonies*. Vol. II. Paris: Marc Ducloux, 1851.

Neal, Daniel, Joshua Toulmin, and John Overton Choules. *The History of the Puritans*. New York: Harper & Brothers, 1844.

Nelson, Eric. *The Hebrew Republic*. Cambridge, MA: Harvard University Press, 2010.

———. "'Talmudical Commonwealthsmen' and the Rise of Republican Exclusivism." *The Historical Journal* 50, no. 4 (2007): 809–35.

Norton, Mary Beth. "The Constitutional Status of Women in 1787." *Law and Inequality* 6 (1988): 7.

Nuño, Juan C., Miguel A. Herrero, and Mario Primicerio. "A Triangle Model of Criminality." *Physica A: Statistical Mechanics and its Applications* 387, no. 12 (2008): 2926–36.

Paine, Tomas, and Gordon S. Wood. *Common Sense and Other Writings*. New York: Modern Library, 2003.

Paravy, Pierrette. *De La Chrétienté Romaine À La Réforme En Dauphiné. Évêques, Fidèles Et Déviants (Vers 1340-Vers 1350)* [in Français]. Collection De L'école Française De Rome. Vol. 1, Rome: École française de Rome, 1993.

Pauley, Mathew A. *Athens, Rome, and England: America's Constitutional Heritage*. New York: Intercollegiate Studies Institute (ORD), 2014.

Peyran, Jean Rodolphe, and Thomas Sims. *An Historical Defence of the Waldenses or Vaudois: Inhabitants of the Valleys of Piedmont*. London: C. & J. Rivington, 1826.

Philbrick, Nathanel. *Mayflower: A Story of Courage, Community, and War*. Kindle Edition ed. New York: Penguin Publishing Group, 2006.

Phillips, Anthony. *Essays on Biblical Law*. London; New York: Bloomsbury Academic, 2002.

Plumptre, Edward H. *The Bible Educator*, edited by E.H. Plumptre. Vol. 1, London Paris New York: Cassell, Petter & Galpin, 1877.

Pollock, Susan. "Between Feasts and Daily Meals. Towards an Archaeology of Commensal Spaces." *eTopoi. Journal for Ancient Studies* 2, no. Special (2011): 1–20.

Potts, John. *A History of Charisma*. London: Palgrave Macmillan UK, 2009.

Pouzet, Philippe. "Les Origines Lyonnaises De La Secte Des Vaudois." *Revue d'histoire de l'Église de France* 22, no. 94 (1936): 5–37.

Rabkin, Jeremy. "Revolutionary Visions in Legal Imagery: Constitutional Contrasts between France and America." In *The Legacy of the French Revolution*, edited by Ralph C. Hancock and L. Gary Lambert. Lanham, MD: Rowman & Littlefield, 1996.

Rabushka, Alvin. *Taxation in Colonial America*. Princeton: Princeton University Press, 2015.

Radford, Robert T. *Cicero: A Study in the Origins of Republican Philosophy*. Amsterdam: Rodopi, 2002.

Rainey, Anson F. "Whence Came the Israelites and Their Language?" *Israel Exploration Journal* 57, no. 1 (2007): 41–64.

Rehm, Rush. *Greek Tragic Theatre*. London: Routledge, 2003.

Reynolds, Noel B. "The Rule of Law in Eighteenth Century Revolutions." In *The Legacy of the French Revolution*, edited by Ralph C. Hancock and L. Gary Lambert, 189–98. Lanham, MD: Rowman & Littlefield, 1996.

Rigby, Peter. "Pastoralism, Egalitarianism, and the State: The Eastern African Case." *Critique of Anthropology* 7, no. 3 (1988): 17–32.

Romme, A. Georges L. "Unanimity Rule and Organizational Decision Making: A Simulation Model." *Organization Science* 15, no. 6 (2004): 704–18.

Rosenblum, Jordan. *Food and Identity in Early Rabbinic Judaism*. Cambridge: Cambridge University Press, 2010.

Rossi, Carla. "The Role of Dynamic Modelling in Drug Abuse Epidemiology." *Bulletin on Narcotics* LIV, no. 1 and 2 (2002): 33–44.

Rutherford, Samuel. *Lex, Rex, or, the Law and the Prince*. Penn Laird, VA: Sprinkle Publications, 1982.

Sabine, George H, and Thomas L. Thorson. *A History of Political Theory*. Oxford: Oxford and IBH Publishing, 2018.

Safrai, Zeev. *The Economy of Roman Palestine*. London - New York: Taylor & Francis, 2003.

Salzman, Michele Renee. *The Making of a Christian Aristocracy: Social and Religious Change in the Western Roman Empire*. Kindle Edition ed. Cambridge, MA: Harvard University Press, 2002.

Samson, Steven Alan. "Covenant Origins of the American Polity." *Faculty Publications and Presentations. 5.* Liberty University (1994).

———. "Theological Sources of American Constitutionalism." *Faculty Publications and Presentations. 54.* Liberty University (1991).

Sandnes, Karl Olav "Equality within Patriaichal Structures." In *Constructing Early Christian Families: Family as Social Reality and Metaphor*, edited by Halvor Moxnes, 150–65. London: Taylor & Francis, 2002.

Santoro L'Hoir, Francesca. *The Rhetoric of Gender Terms: 'Man', 'Woman', and the Portrayal of Character in Latin Prose*. Leiden: Brill, 1992.

Sapir-Hen, Lidar, Guy Bar-Oz, Yuval Gadot, and Israel Finkelstein. "Pig Husbandry in Iron Age Israel and Judah." ZDPV, 2013.

Sapir-Hen, Lidar, Meirav Meiri, and Israel Finkelstein. "Iron Age Pigs: New Evidence on Their Origin and Role in Forming Identity Boundaries." *Radiocarbon* 57, no. 2 (2015): 307–15.

Sawyer, James M. *The Survivor's Guide to Theology*. Eugene, OR: Wipf & Stock Publishers, 2016.

Schane, Sanford. "Ambiguity and Misunderstanding in the Law." *Thomas Jefferson Law Review* 25 (2002): 167.

Schiff, Stacy. *The Witches: Suspicion, Betrayal and Histeria in 1692 Salem*. Kindle Edition ed. New York Boston London: Little Brown, 2015.

Schloss, Chaim. *2000 Years of Jewish History: From the Destruction of the Second Bais Hamikdash until the Twentieth Century*. Jerusalem: Feldheim Publishers, 2002.

Schniedewind, William M. *A Social History of Hebrew: Its Origins through the Rabbinic Period*. New Haven: Yale University Press, 2013.

Schweizer, Eduard. *The Good News According to Matthew*. Atlanta: John Knox Press, 1975.

Shavit, Yaacov, and Barbara Harshav. "Cyrus King of Persia and the Return to Zion: A Case of Neglected Memory." *History and Memory* 2, no. 1 (1990): 51–83.

Shekel, Michal. *Making a Difference: Commandments and Community*. Brooklyn: Ktav, 1997.

Sillitoe, P. *An Introduction to the Anthropology of Melanesia: Culture and Tradition*. Cambridge University Press, 1998.

Silver, Morris. *Economic Structures of Antiquity*. Westport, CT, London: Greenwood Press, 1995.

Smith-Christopher, Daniel .L., and Katherine Southwood. *The Religion of the Landless: The Social Context of the Babylonian Exile*. Eugene, OR: Wipf and Stock, 2015.

Smith, James.E. *Biblical Protology*. Raleigh, NC: Lulu.com, 2007.

Soussen Max, Claire. *"Iudei Nostri," Pouvoir Royal, Communautés Juives Et Société Chrétienne Dans Les Territoires De La Couronne D'aragon Au Xiiie Et Première Moitié Du Xive Siècle."* St Quentin en Yvelines, 2005.

Spencer, Charles. *Killers of the King: The Men Who Dared to Execute Charles I*. New York: Bloomsbury Publishing, 2015.

Staar, Richard Felix. *Communist Regimes in Eastern Europe*. Stanford: Hoover Press, 1971.

Stager, Lawrence E. "Forging an Identity, the Emergence of Ancient Israel." In *The Oxford History of the Biblical World*, edited by Michael D. Coogan, 132–64. New York: Oxford University Press, 1998.

Stahl, Henri H. *Sociologia Satului Devălmaş Românesc* [in Romanian] [Sociology of communal Romanian village]. Vol. 3, Bucharest: Fundaţia Regele Mihai I, 1946.

Stahl, Henri H. *Traditional Romanian Village Communities*. Cambridge: Cambridge University Press, 1980.

Stark, Rodney. "Christianizing the Urban Empire: An Analysis Based on 22 Greco-Roman Cities." *Sociology of Religion* 52, no. 1 (1991): 77–88.

Stone, Geoffrey R, and William P. Marshall. "The Framers' Constitution." *Democracy: A Journal of Ideas* 21 (2011): 61.

Stone, John R. *The Routledge Dictionary of Latin Quotations: The Illiterati's Guide to Latin Maxims, Mottoes, Proverbs, and Sayings*. New York and London: Taylor & Francis, 2013.

Stone, Jon.R. *More Latin for the Illiterati: A Guide to Medical, Legal and Religious Latin*. London and New York: Taylor & Francis, 2003.

Sulzberger, Mayer. *The Polity of the Ancient Hebrews*. Philadelphia: J.H. Greenstone, 1912.

Sznajder, Mario, Luis Roniger, and Carlos Forment. *Shifting Frontiers of Citizenship: The Latin American Experience*. Leiden, Boston: Brill, 2012.

Tainter, Joseph A. *The Collapse of Complex Societies*. Cambridge: Cambridge University Press, 1990.

Tanner, Mathias. *Societas Jesu Usque Ad Sanguinis Et Vitae Profusionem Militans, in Europa, Africa, Asia, Et America, Contra Gentiles, Mahometanos, Judaeos, Haereticos, Impios, Pro Deo, Fide, Ecclesia, Pietate, Sive, Vita, Et Mors Eorum, Qui Ex Societate Jesu in Causa Fidei, & Virtutis Propugnatae, Violentâ Morte Toto Orbe Sublati Sunt*. Prague: Typis Universitatis Carolo-Ferdinandeae, 1675.

Tanner, Matthias. *Die Gesellshafft Jesu Biss Zur Vergiessung Ihres Blutes Wider Den Gotzendienst Unglauben Und Laster*. Prague: Carlo Ferdinandeischen Universitat Buchdruckeren., 1683.

Tavares, António Augusto. "Quelques Termes Bibliques Relatifs À Des Institutions Anciennes: Problèmes De Traduction Et D'histoire." (1985).

Taylor, Matthew. *England's Bloody Tribunal: Or, Popish Cruelty Displayed, Etc.* London: J. Cooke, 1770.

Thies, Roger, Kirk W. Barron, Robert C. Beesley, Siribhinya. Benyajati, Robert W. Blair, Kenneth J. Dormer, Jay P. Farber, et al. *Physiology*. New York: Springer 1995.

Toaff, Renzo. "Statuti E Leggi Della «Nazione Ebrea» Di Livorno. Ii: La Legislazione Dal 1655 Al 1677.(Cont. Ne)." *La Rassegna Mensile di Israel* 38, no. 5 (1972): 33–48.

Tocqueville, Alexis de. *Democracy in America*. Translated by Henry Reeve. Kindle Edition ed. Vol. 1: Project Gutenberg, 2006.

———. *Democracy in America. :* . Kindle ed. Vol. 1, Chicago: The University of Chicago Press, 2000.

Trebilco, Paul. *The Early Christians in Ephesus from Paul to Ignatius*. Grand Rapids, MI: Eerdmans Publishing Company, 2007.

Unknown. *Revue De Gascogne: Bulletin Bimestral De La Société Historique De Gascogne*. AUCH: Imprimerie et Litographie Foix, 1901.

Urdan, Timothy C. *Statistics in Plain English*. Mahwah, NJ and London: Lawrence Erlbaum Associates, 2005.

Van Seters, John. *A Law Book for the Diaspora: Revision in the Study of the Covenant Code*. Oxford: Oxford University Press, 2002.

Vedder, Henry C. "Origin and Early Teachings of the Waldenses, According to Roman Catholic Writers of the Thirteenth Century." *The American Journal of Theology* 4, no. 3 (1900): 465–89.

Volterra, Vito. "Variations and Fluctuations of the Number of Individuals in Animal Species Living Together." *ICES Journal of Marine Science* Vol. 3, no. 1 (1928): 3–51.

Wade, Rex A. *The Russian Revolution, 1917*. Cambridge, UK: Cambridge University Press, 2005.

Wainwright, Geoffrey. *The Oxford History of Christian Worship*, edited by Geoffrey Wainwright and Karen B. Westerfield Tucker Oxford: Oxford University Press, USA, 2006.

Wardle, Lynn D. "The Constitution as Covenant." *Brigham Young University Studies* 27, no. 3 (1987): 11–28.

Watkins, Calvert. *The American Heritage Dictionary of Indo-European Roots*. Boston; New York: Houghton Mifflin, 2000.

Watt, Isabella M., Thomas A. Lambert, Robert M. Kingdon, Jeffrey R. Watt, Paule H. Dubuis, and Sandra Coram-Mekkey. *Registres Du Consistoire De Genève Au Temps De Calvin. Tome I, 1542-1544*. Geneva: Librairie Droz, 1996.

Weber, Max. *Ancient Judaism*. New York & London: Free Press, 2010.

Whiteway, Augustine Robert. "The Pyrenean Neighbour; or, the Vicinal System in the Western Pyrenees." *Archaeological Journal* 58, no. 1 (1901): 182–98.

Wilkinson, Benjamin G. *Our Authorized Bible Vindicated*. Fort Oglethorpe, GA: Teach Services, 2014.

Williams, David C. "The Constitutional Right to Conservative Revolution." *Harvard Civil Rights-Civil Liberties Law Review* 32 (1997): 413.

Wilson, Nigel Guy. *Encyclopedia of Ancient Greece*. New York: Routledge, 2006.

Wilson, Robert. *Astronomy through the Ages: The Story of the Human Attempt to Understand the Universe*. Boca Raton, FL: CRC Press, 2003.

Wilson, Robert R. "Israel's Judicial System in the Preexilic Period." *The Jewish Quarterly Review* 74, no. 2 (1983): 229–48.

Winter, Irene. "Touched by the Gods: Visual Evidence for the Divine Status of Rulers in the Ancient near East." Paper presented at the Oriental Institute Seminars 4, Chicago, 2008.

Wood, Gordon S. "Rhetoric and Reality in the American Revolution." *The William and Mary Quarterly: A Magazine of Early American History* (1966): 4–32.

Zerubavel, Eviatar. *The Seven Day Circle: The History and Meaning of the Week*. Chicago: University of Chicago Press, 1989.

Zhao, Haiyun, Zhilan Feng, and Carlos Castillo-Chavez. "The Dynamics of Poverty and Crime." MTBI-02-08M (2002): 225–35.

Zoekauer, Ludovico. "Sui Framenti I Piu Antichi Del Constituto Di Pistoia." In *Rivista Italiana Per Le Scienze Giuridiche*, edited by G. Fusinato and F. Schupfer, 72–81. Roma: E. Loescher & Company, 1892.

Index

Alexander II, 50
Alps, 3, 50, 70, 95, 98, 139
Analysis of Variance, 39
ancestry tree, 3, 101
Andover, 64, 71
ANOVA. *See* Analysis of Variance
apostolic Christianity, 53, 62–64
apostolic succession, 63, 71, 106, 115, 119
Aragon, 50, 54
arbitration, 48
archon, 63
Aristotelian, 48, 76, 123
Aristotle, 15–17, 20, 21, 53, 75, 80, 85, 91, 121, 124, 140
Articles of Confederation, 52, 139, 140
Athenian Constitution, 15, 20, 140
Athens, 4, 9, 15, 16, 48, 123
Audisio, 61, 69, 70, 105, 113, 140
Augustine, 55, 107
Austerfield, 13
authority, 16; apostolic succession, 115, 116; of assembly, 76; Catholic priests, 106, 118; Cicero, 16; covenant's source of, 94; Diaspora Egypt, 59; direction of flow, 101, 127; Early Christians, 63; of elders, 30, 49; in the electoral procedure, 27; to forgive sins, 106; France, 66; in Gouroun chiefdom, 47; judicial, 135; of kings in monarchic Israel, 49; legislative, 123; limiting government, 18; limits of, 4, 5, 16, 17, 18; Mayflower Compact, 52; of office holders, 6, 60, 135; Old World democracies, 123; of parliament, 123; of the people, 121; in Proto-Israel, 36; of Roman Senate, 17; royal, 47, 53; of ruling class, 48; of taxation, 14; Waldensian community, 63; Weber, 16; which the people commits to its government, 4, 17
autorictas patrum, 17

Babylon, 49, 50
Babylonian, 49, 54, 131
Bădescu, 3, 51, 53, 55, 57, 65, 66, 70, 79, 93, 94, 98, 102, 137, 139
banishment, 76, 77
besiau, 33, 50
Beth-Shemesh, 36, 41–43, 46
Bigorre, 50, 52, 55, 63, 70, 71, 102, 137, 139
boier, 51
Bolshevik, 84
boni homines, 65, 71
boni viri, 65
Boston, 60, 71, 135

Bowie, 19, 22
Bradford, 122
Brewster, 52
Byzantine, 131

Cairo Geniza, 59, 66
Calvin, 61, 68, 90, 110, 113, 133
Calvinism, 62, 64, 90, 116, 133
Calvinists, 9, 19, 61, 78, 83, 90, 95, 99, 101, 102
Cambridge, 71
Canaanites, 14, 28, 39, 41, 46
Cantemir, 51, 53, 55
Carpathians, 35, 50
Catholic Church. See Roman-Catholic Church
Charlemagne, 50
Charlestown, 71
Charter Constitutionalism, 19
Chelmsford, 71
cherem, 76
chiefdom, 35, 47, 91
chiefdoms, 28, 35, 73, 75
Cicero, 16, 17, 20, 26, 65
clan, 14, 58
commensality, 81
communalist, 57
Concord, 135
congregation, 57–60, 124; Ecclesia, 71; *obște*, 102; Pilgrims, 77; Presbyterian, 66; Puritan, 60, 96; synagogue, 80; term, 57; *vesiau*, 102
Connecticut, 135
Constantin, 61
constitutional faith, 105
Continental Congress, 24, 139, 140
control law, 41
Cordoba, 95
corrective action, 41
Couderc-Barraud, 53, 55, 70, 102
Council of Brothers, 116
Covenant Code, 15, 75, 79
covenantal society, 6, 29, 57, 78, 86, 89, 93, 94, 110, 115, 116, 118, 122

credit rating, 76
Cursente, 53
custom, 37
customary law, 5, 10, 15, 29, 37, 132
customary rules, 15, 48
Cyrus, 50, 54
czar, 47

Darwin, 7, 128, 129
de La Côte, 115–17
de Lagrèze, 53, 55, 70, 71, 102, 137, 139
Declaration of Independence, 52
Declaration of Rights and Grievances, 24–26
decorated pottery, 36
Dedham, 71n109
denominations, 101–4
Dictum of Kenilworth, 27
dietary rules, 81, 86, 132
Dorchester, 71
Dorislaus, 18, 21
Dover, 71
Draco, 15

Early Christianity, 62, 89, 102, 116
Early Christians, 55, 71, 81, 83, 89, 101, 102, 107, 108, 110, 111, 135; disputes, 50; hierarchy, 116; organization, 63; organization, 63; presbyter, 65
ecclesiae, 63
Edict of Tolerance, 50
egalitarian, 57, 75, 84, 115; chiefdoms, 75; disputes, 76; ethos, 15, 49, 75, 76, 84, 130; farmers, 15; four room house, 44; networks, 52; pastoralists, 10, 80; Proto-Israel, 36; settled societies, 85; structure, 83, 116, 132
Egypt, 47, 53, 80, 131
Egyptian, 14, 28, 66, 131
Elazar, 3, 5–8, 10, 48, 53, 57, 65, 66, 83, 112, 125
elders, 30, 49, 54, 60, 63, 74

endemic, 87–89, 93
England, 4, 5, 8, 18, 98
Enlightenment, 123
epidemics, 2, 9, 88, 93, 96, 97, 99, 100
equality, 31, 48; Aristotle, 85; article 3, 27; before the law, 29, 48, 103; constitution, 84; Early Christians, 90, 116; in the eyes of the Lord, 9, 14; gender, 134, 135; Hayek, 29; Iron Age Languedoc, 91; monarchic Israel, 30; nomads, 84; Pilgrims, 105; Proto-Israel, 30, 36, 48, 91; Puritans, 31; *vesiau*, 135
evolution tree, 83, 101, 102, 105
Exeter, 71
extinction, 130
eye for an eye, 29

Fisher, 7, 10, 129, 130, 138
fixation, 130, 139
Fleming, 128
Florentine Republic, 48
Fors, 51
Fournier, 115, 116
framers of the constitution, 64, 123, 132, 133
France, 58
fundamental law, 15
Fundamental Orders of Connecticut, 52

Gascon, 95, 103, 127
Gascony, 63, 102, 103
gender equality, 133
general will, 123
George III (king), 18, 24
Gordon, 50, 56, 90
Gouroun, 47
Gratian, 23
Great Council of Venice, 48
great man, 132
Greece, 7, 15, 47, 53
Guilford, 71
Gusti, 53

habeas corpus, 23, 25
Halevi, 50, 124
Hamilton, 64
Hampton, 71
Hartford, 71, 135
Haverhill, 71n109
Hayek, 31, 33, 139
Hellenistic, 47, 53
heretics, 63
hierarchical, 6, 7, 9, 51, 83, 89, 90, 101, 115, 116, 133
hierarchy, 48, 49, 59, 61, 63, 64, 66, 73, 78, 80, 83, 90, 103, 110, 115, 116, 121, 124
Holiness School, 30, 33, 45
HS. *See* Holiness School

immutable law, 26
inequality: Athens, 48; gender, 134, 135; Gouroun, 47; Iron Age Languedoc, 91; Pilgrims, 105, 135; slavery, 134
Inquisition, 63, 98, 103, 106, 121
Inquisitor, 69, 115, 116

Jefferson, 20, 23, 54, 64
Jewish communities, 50, 58, 66, 76, 86, 87, 89, 90
Josef II, 50
Josephus Flavius, 76
Judah Halevi. *See* Halevi
Judea and Samaria, 73
jury trial, 23, 115
jus regis, 18

Kalonymos, 50, 54
Kehilah, 58
Kermack-McKendrick, 96
Kiryat-Yearim, 42
kwara, 47

La noble leçon, 92, 108, 113, 116
Latin America, 123
law enforcement, 23, 56

Le Pay, 53, 55, 102, 137
Léger, 116
leisure, 17, 75, 85
leveling mechanism, 36
Levinson, 11, 79, 98, 105, 113
Lex Rex, 8, 18, 47, 49, 51, 52, 97, 124, 127, 132
Lexington, 10, 135, 140
London, 69, 71, 78, 79, 81, 91, 98, 99
Lucca, 50
Luther, 108
Lynn, 71n109
Lyon, 61, 68, 69, 107, 113, 140

Madison, 64
Magna Carta, 4, 17, 23, 24, 26, 31, 32
Maimonides, 95, 99
Mainz. *See* Mayence
Malden, 71n109
Marblehead, 71n109
marriage, 42, 105, 130
Massachusetts, 135
matchmaking, 76
Maya, 47, 53
Mayence, 50, 54
Mayflower, 8, 18; compact, 18, 19, 26, 27, 52, 101, 122, 123, 137; gender equality, 135; landing, 25, 27; passengers, 122; slavery, 134
McIlwain, 4, 5, 9, 10, 16, 17, 19–21, 25, 29, 31, 32, 45
Medford, 71n109
mediation, 48, 76
Megiddo, 36, 42, 43
Merneptah, 13
Mesopotamia, 47, 85
Messiah, 50
Metz, 54, 63
Milford, 71
millet, 50
Mohammed II, 50
Moldavian, 51
Moldova, 51
Monarchic Israel, 37, 38
Morpurgo, 50

Morris of Pennsylvania, Gouverneur, 134
mutation, 29, 75, 116, 129–32, 137

neighbor, 28, 51, 52, 95, 98, 116
New England, 26, 64, 80, 134, 135
New Haven, 79, 135
Nicaean. *See* pre-Nicaean
niduy, 76
Nîmes, Count of, 50
nobilitas, 116
nomads, 14, 28, 48, 75, 76
Norfolk, 18
nundinae, 86

obşte, 51, 52, 65, 66, 70, 93, 95, 98, 102
office holders, 6, 59, 60, 63, 65, 135
oligarchies, 6, 17, 48, 49, 75, 89
Olivetan, 61

Paine, 4, 5, 16–18, 52, 56
Palestine: Roman, 63, 65, 71, 101, 102, 127
Paravy, 3, 61, 62, 69, 70, 99, 108, 113, 116, 119, 124
peer pressure, 10, 76, 77, 84, 86, 95
Pharaoh, 13, 14, 131
Pharisees, 30
Philadelphia, 30, 52, 64
Philistines, 14, 39, 42
Philo of Alexandria, 76, 80
pig remains, 36, 37, 41, 43–45
Pilgrims: association with Israelites, 18, 31, 101, 105, 124, 132; attitude toward the king, 52; Calvinists, 64, 101; congregation, 57, 58; covenant, 27, 105, 122, 133; England, 13, 98; exclusivity, 78; John Quincy Adams, 140; landing, 18, 60; Mayflower Compact, 122; minding other people's business, 95; punishments, 77; righteousness, 96; Scriptures, 105; Tocqueville, 60; women's equality, 135

pio, 47
Plymouth, 8, 18, 22, 27, 52, 64, 135, 137, 140
pork avoidance, 36, 39, 41–43, 46
pork prohibition, 39, 41
Portsmouth, 71
poverty, 78
pre-Nicaean, 108
Presbyterian, 18, 25, 58, 59, 66
pre-state, 5, 29, 35, 73
Priestly Torah, 30, 33
Proto-Israel, 101; assemblies, 76; Bible, 79; burial sites, 44; Canaan, 14, 130; congregation, 124; covenant, 5, 8, 15, 19, 27, 28, 29, 31, 35, 84, 101, 121; egalitarian, 36, 73, 75, 76; equality before the law, 48; freedom, 84; Iron Age I, 14; justice, 73, 76; law and faith, 97; law enforcement, 35, 73; Lex Rex, 49; liberties, 31; literacy, 79; monarchy, 29; no constitution, 14; no king, 8, 28, 78; ordinary folks, 6; organizing principle, 122; origins, 28; pastoralists, 28; peer pressure, 76; to Pilgrims, 31; pork consumption, 36, 37, 39, 41, 44; settling down, 14; structure, 26, 29, 132
Provisions of Oxford, 27
PT. *See* Priestly Torah
Purgatory, 61
Puritans, 3, 19, 26, 31, 57, 60, 61, 64, 78, 80, 95, 96, 98, 99, 101, 124, 133, 134
Pyrenees, 3, 50, 51, 55, 70, 71, 95, 102, 135

Rainier, 116
Raymond de La Côte. *See* de La Côte
Red Guard, 84
repentance, 77, 87, 93–96, 100, 102, 107, 110
repentance mechanism, 86, 88, 89, 92, 102, 107, 110
reverse dominance hierarchy, 59

Rhode Island Charter, 52
Roman: administration, 21; aristocracy, 53, 61, 116; Catholic Church, 63, 102, 103, 106, 108; christianization, 92, 119, 132; civilization, 116; constitution, 15, 16, 17, 23; emperors, 31; Empire, 17, 48, 71, 119, 131, 132, 133; law, 4; power of the people, 26; praetor, 21; Republic, 16, 17, 48, 65; Senate, 48; taxation, 31
Romania, 51, 56, 58, 63, 65, 102, 103
Roman *nundinae*. *See nundinae*
Roman Palestine. *See* Palestine: Roman
Rome, 9, 99; *boni homines*, 65; conflict with Waldensians, 61; constitutionalism, 4, 5, 15, 17; democracy, 123; limiting authority, 16; no conflict with *vesiau*, 51
Rousseau, 123
Roxbury, 71
Russia, 84
Russian, 47, 84, 91
Rutherford, 10, 18, 21, 49

Sabbath: assembly government, 76; Basic Sabbath Number, 86, 87, 88, 89, 90; commandment, 75; day of rest, 75, 110; diaspora, 76; essential covenantal institution, 7, 86, 110; evolution, 75; in hierarchic organizations, 110; holy convocation, 30; meetings, 30; peer pressure, 76; Waldensians, 108, 110; work prohibition, 30, 84, 110
Sacconi, 116
sacraments, 105, 106
sacred assembly, 75
Sadducees, 30
Saint-Augustine. *See* Augustine
Salem, 64, 67, 81, 96, 97, 99, 100, 125, 135
Salzman, 53, 71, 116, 119
Scrooby, 13
security clearance, 76

senatorial advices, 17
seven, 85
Shema Israel, 94
Sherman's compromise, 137
Signoria, 48
SIR, 96, 97, 100
SIRS model, 86, 88, 89
slavery, 133, 134
Smith, Adam, 23
sovereignty: state, 135
Soviets, 84
Spain, 50
Springfield, 71
Stahl, 3, 51, 53, 55, 65, 66, 70, 102, 137
supreme law. *See* fundamental law
survival of the fittest, 129, 130
synedrion, 63
Synod of Verona, 103

Thebes, 14
thesis of this work, 8
Thetford, 18
Tocqueville, 26, 32, 33, 60, 67, 97, 100, 119, 121, 124
town, 14, 19, 20, 30, 41, 43, 57, 58, 63, 64, 66, 74, 78, 79, 130, 135
transgression-free, 86, 87, 93

unconstitutional law, 26

Valdès, 61, 62, 68, 89, 90, 95, 107–10, 113

Valentinian, 23
Venetian Republic, 48
Venice, 48
Verona, 103
vesiau, 50–52, 55, 102, 135
vicinal system, 51, 52, 55

Waldensians, 3; apostolic Christianity, 61, 62, 64, 83, 90, 101, 107, 110, 113; and Calvinists, 64, 83, 90; communities, 62, 90, 111; conflict with Rome, 61, 62, 104, 105; covenantal, 103; covenantal practice, 61; discipline, 95; heretics, 63, 103, 104; hierarchy, 103, 116, 121, 124; inquisition, 63, 106, 115, 116; minding other people's business, 95, 98; organization, 61, 62, 111, 124; persecution, 139; Piedmont Easter Massacre, 98; Pope Francis, 112; practices, 62, 90, 105, 106, 108, 109, 110; repentance, 89; research, 127; sect, 107; Valdès, 61, 107, 110
Weber, 17, 28
Wenham, 71
Wethersfield, 135
Windsor, 71, 135
Winslow, 52
Woburn, 71

zekenim, 65

About the Author

Joseph Livni, M.Sc., began a new vocation in socio-physics after a long career in aerospace engineering, examining sociological concepts by applying mathematical models developed and utilized by physicists. In this monograph, the author synthesizes eight published investigations authored or coauthored by him.

www.ingramcontent.com/pod-product-compliance
Lightning Source LLC
Chambersburg PA
CBHW050909300426
44111CB00010B/1440